HERBS FOR TEXAS

UNIVERSITY OF TEXAS PRESS, AUSTIN

HERBS *for* TEXAS

*A study of the landscape, culinary, and medicinal uses
and benefits of the herbs that can be grown in Texas*

HOWARD GARRETT
with **ODENA BRANNAM**

First edition, 2001

Requests for permission to reproduce material from this work should be sent
to Permissions, University of Texas Press, Box 7819, Austin, TX 78713-7819.

∞ The paper used in this book meets the minimum requirements of
ANSI/NISO Z39.48-1992 (R1997) (Permanence of Paper).

LIBRARY OF CONGRESS CATALOGING-IN-PUBLICATION DATA

Garrett, Howard, 1947–
    Herbs for Texas : a study of the landscape, culinary, and medicinal uses and
benefits of the herbs that can be grown in Texas / Howard Garrett with
Odena Brannam.—1st ed.
        p.   cm.
    Includes index.
    ISBN 0-292-78173-3 (cl. : alk. paper) — ISBN 0-292-72830-1 (pbk. :
alk. paper)
    1. Herb gardening—Texas. 2. Cookery (Herbs) 3. Herbs—Therapeutic
use—Texas. I. Brannam, Odena. II. Title.
SB351.H5 G377 2001
635'.7'09764—dc21   00-025817

To Odena Brannam,

who taught me to appreciate

the various uses of

the wonderful plants

we call herbs and who

helped me greatly

with this book.

Contents

Medical Disclaimer

This book does not prescribe medical information. Although it contains a lot of historical and anecdotal information about the use of plants, it doesn't replace professional medical advice. Continue to consult and take the advice of your doctor. Just let the information here suggest additional possibilities. Neither the author nor the University of Texas Press accepts responsibility for the accuracy of the information itself or the consequences from the use or misuse of the information in this book.

Make sure you identify plants properly before using them. Consult your doctor before using medicinal herbs. Remember that any and all plants can cause allergic reactions in some people. You should also avoid eating plants that have been treated with toxic products, such as synthetic fertilizers, fungicides, insecticides, and other poisons. In case of poisoning by plant (or any other source), call 1-800-POISON-1 (1-800-764-7661) or 911.

Preface

Here for Texas gardeners is a wide range of landscape, culinary, and medicinal information about the wonderful plants we call herbs: not only how to select the proper species, but also how to plant, maintain, harvest, and use the herbs. It will suggest new ways to think about and use these plants—for fragrance, cooking, health, and beauty in the landscape. Plants are important to our health. Health and nutrition is what I hope to promote along with an increased appreciation of herbs.

Herbs for Texas is easy to use because of the simple layout and the cross-referencing of common and botanical names.

Herbs are the world's most interesting plants. They make beautiful landscape choices, and their ornamental qualities make them ideal for wreaths, garlands, and potpourris. Some herbs are fragrant bloomers with interesting foliage, and many have decorative seed heads. Herbs are also extremely useful for cooking, controlling pests, healing wounds, and improving the immune systems of pets and people. Some make you more alert, some make you feel better, and some can even help solve serious medical problems.

For example, we've known for some time that cinnamon will at least repel and in some cases kill roaches and ants, but it may help protect against the deadly *E. coli* bacteria, and there is research to back it up. Food microbiologist Daniel Fung at Kansas State University has proven the power of cinnamon and four other common herbs in killing disease organisms. Fung and his team first tested twenty-three different herbs against *E. coli* in the laboratory, then took the five herbs that worked best and used them on store-bought ground beef that had been infected with 100,000 *E. coli* bacteria per gram. One of our favorite herbs, garlic, won the contest by killing the organisms completely, but four others (clove, cinnamon, oregano, and sage) also killed the bacteria to various degrees. Another of Fung's studies combined the herbs with salami and other fermented sausages. Once again the herbs controlled the pathogens on the food.

It has been reported that 20,000 Americans are poisoned by *E. coli* annually and about 250 die. Whether that is accurate or not, this is exciting news about these nutritious herbs. Scientists at Oklahoma State University also discovered that horseradish and mustard can help fight *E. coli* and other food pathogens. These plants are easy to grow here in Texas. Even cinnamon and clove can be grown here if protected in the winter. Simply grow them in pots and move them indoors in cold weather.

For some reason herb gardens have the reputation of being hard to start and grow, difficult to maintain, and messy-looking. Nothing could be further from the truth. Most herbs grow easily in a variety of soils and require minimal attention. Some herbs sometimes seem mysterious, but with careful selection they are very much at home in Texas. They can be grown indoors or out, in containers, in flower beds, and in traditional herb gardens. Exceptions will be covered in the specific entries in the text. For example, plants such as tarragon, valerian, lovage, rosemary, sage, lavender, and parsley need a little special handling.

Annual herbs such as basil and perilla and biennials like parsley are easy to grow from seed and should be used, but many perennials provide beauty and usefulness for years. The perennial herbs that are easiest to grow in Texas include wormwood, southernwood, thyme, comfrey, mint, chives, oregano, lemon balm, and purple coneflower. Bulbs like saffron and garlic and trees like ginkgo, walnut, jujube, and willow are all easy to grow and use. The book covers those in detail for you and also includes for your consideration the lesser-known and harder-to-grow varieties that have benefits worthy of a little mainte-nance trouble. You'll even find plants that you may not consider herbs—such as alfalfa, blackberry, peppers, dandelion, and the rose.

What is a herb? The primary definition given by the dictionary is "a seed-producing annual, biennial, or perennial that does not develop persistent woody tissue but dies down at the end of a growing season." This botanical definition eliminates many plants that are traditionally regarded and used as herbs.

Another traditional definition of a herb is "a herbaceous plant that is used to flavor foods, make teas, provide medicinal properties, and offer up fragrances."

The definition most commonly accepted by herbalists is "a plant or plant part valued for its medicinal, savory, or aromatic qualities." The Herb Society of America puts it this way: "Any plant that may be used for pleasure, fragrance, or physic." To me, herbs include a broad spectrum of plants, trees, shrubs, perennials, annuals, and bulbs that have specific uses other than merely beauty. Simple as that.

Herbs should never be grown without following organic techniques. Anyone who claims to be a herbalist and isn't organic just isn't a herbalist. Organic gardening is much more than merely a method of growing plants. It's a way of life. It's about paying attention to nature. It's about understanding how everything in nature is related. It's about learning from nature and working within nature's perfectly designed system. From the gardening standpoint it is also about using herbs that aren't contaminated with toxic chemicals.

This book was designed for ease of use. I am extremely irritated by books that use the "reference to another entry" approach. If you look up *Monarda*, for example, the index directs you to go to "Horsemint" or "Wild Bergamot." That's a waste of the reader's time and an unnecessary irritation. Why not just put a page number after the word *Monarda*? Good grief! That's what you'll find in this book. If you look in the index or in the body of the book, all the common and all botanical names are listed and cross-referenced. Seems like a simple thing, doesn't it? Hope you appreciate the convenience.

As you'll learn from reading this book and through personal experience, herbs have many attributes, not the least of which is that they are easy to grow, look good, smell interesting, and taste delicious. If you'll let the herbs help you, they will.

Many herbalists have helped me understand the plants we call herbs. Odena Brannam has been the most influential because she has such a good feel for the useful plants and deals with them more from an artistic and practical standpoint than a sterile scientific approach. Of course, the technical aspects of herbs are important, but science would have taken a long time to come up with the fact, for example, that crushed tansy repels fire ants. Odena has taught me to observe and to learn from the plants and to understand that the so-called experts don't necessarily have all the answers. I don't either, but with the help of many others, I'll give you some new ideas to try.

Those who have helped with ideas and details in this book include the following people and companies: Ken Satterwhite, Diane Huff, Blue Moon Gardens, North Haven Gardens, Rohde's Nursery, Redenta's Garden, Green Mama's, Barney Lipscomb, Bob O'Kennon, the Botanical Research Institute of Texas, Madalene Hill, King's Creek Gardens, Misty Hill Farm, the American Botanical Council, and Mary Buchanan. Special thanks go to Dr. Judy Griffin, author of *Mother Nature's Herbal*, and, as always, to my assistant, Tracy Fields. Without Tracy, I would not be able to write my books and columns, do my radio show, and continue my mission of converting the world to organic. Also, special thanks to my wife, Judy, and my daughter, Logan, for keeping my life interesting.

HERBS FOR TEXAS

1 Going Organic

THE TWO BIG LIES

There are two big lies in gardening, horticulture, and agriculture. These lies have been going around since just after World War II. Before that time, gardeners, landscapers, farmers, and ranchers did a pretty good job of using organic techniques—that's all they had. Manure was the primary fertilizer, and sulfur, tobacco, and good bugs were the primary pest controls. Yes, even in those days much of the land ended up being worn out by overproducing. That caused people to move on to fresh, productive land. They were ignorant of the importance of replenishing what crops take away from the soil and what literally vaporizes by tilling and leaving the soil bare. Letting the carbon dioxide escape from land left bare and tilled too often was and still is a common mistake.

That leads us to Big Lie No. 1: *Plants can't tell the difference between organic and artificial fertilizers.*

Well, yes they can. The traditional argument is that plants can only take in fertilizer elements in the basic or ion form. It's a silly notion. These same people will agree that plants take in water, but H_20_2 is a molecule, not an ion. Plants do not take in hydrogen and oxygen in elemental form.

To make the example more dramatic, water a white flowering plant with dye of any color. The color will move easily into the plant and discolor the flower. Is the dye a basic element or ion? Of course not. It's a very large molecule. One more example: herbicides that enter plants and kill by interfering with the normal cellular growth are not ions; they are huge, complex molecules. How do they do that? By disassembling into carbon, hydrogen, and oxygen, then entering the plant and reassembling. It would be a funny idea except that it is often put forward in total seriousness, according to an authority on this subject, Dr. Bargyla Rateaver. She can not only explain how plants absorb chunks of materials, including whole bacteria and other pieces of organic matter, but also demonstrate the process in action using electron microscope photos. (Her books are available by writing her at 9049 Covina Street, San Diego, CA 92126.) She calls the process by which plant roots absorb large molecules "endocytosis." It is not currently taught at any university.

There are other differences as well. Organic fertilizers, whether they are meals, manures, or composted plant material, contain N-P-K (nitrogen, phosphorous, and potassium), trace minerals, enzymes, vitamins, and lots of organic matter. One hundred percent of each bag's ingredients is useful to the soil and plants. Artificial fertilizers are primarily made up of water-soluble mineral salts and phosphorous. They rarely contain very many trace minerals and usually no organic matter. Some of the synthetic fertilizers include sulfur or polymers to slow down the release process—a move in the right direction—but the organic products are decidedly better because they are naturally slow to release and are balanced for proper plant utilization.

There's one more problem. A large percentage of each bag of artificial fertilizer is a mystery. For example, one of the most commonly recommended fertilizers has an analysis of 15-5-10 (the commonly touted 3-1-2 ratio of N-P-K). This particular fertilizer contains 15 percent nitrogen, 5 percent phosphorus, and 10 percent potassium—which adds up to 30 percent. Okay, but what's in that other 70 percent? Beats me, too. That's the problem. Believe it or not, most states, including Texas, do not regulate the inert ingredients in fertilizers and basically anything can be used, even industrial waste and heavy metals. How do you know for sure? Simple: ask the supplier to give you a total analysis (you might notice their knees buckling a little). Although some of the artificial stuff is very clean and uncontaminated, I still don't recommend it. Fertilizers without the energy of carbon are incomplete and detrimental to the soil and to plants.

Then there's Big Lie No. 2: *Toxic chemical pesticides are necessary to control pests and perfectly safe when used according to label directions.*

I spend my life these days explaining this point in detail, but here's the concept in a nutshell. If pesticides worked, this lie might not be so bad. However, with more money spent today on pesticides than ever before, about one-third of all food crops is still lost to pest insects. That's the same percentage as before the pesticides became available. Toxic pesticides kill beneficial insects and beneficial microorganisms. They also damage the frogs, toads, lizards, birds, bats, and other good guys. The irony is that these high-tech pesticides damage the animals that provide powerful natural pest control. Furthermore, healthy soil produces healthy plants that have a natural resistance to insects and diseases. Adapted plants grown in soil full of carbon, rock minerals, living organisms, and available nutrients will not be weakened by stress and will not attract insect pests and diseases.

THE BASIC ORGANIC PROGRAM

The Basic Organic Program is about making good decisions. Before buying any product or deciding to use any procedure, ask the following question. If I use this product or procedure, will it hurt or help the earthworms? Will it stimulate life and health? With every application of high-nitrogen synthetic fertilizers and toxic chemical fertilizers, the soil ends up with less life and less humus, is less productive, and has more insect pests and disease organisms. With every application of organic fertilizers, rock powders, and biological products, the soil gets better and better and better—forever. In the process the pest problems are reduced, production increases, and the economics improve.

What's more, if you spill the organic products on the soil or your dog or yourself, there's nothing to worry about.

Fighting nature and trying to control it is futile. Working with natural laws and systems is the only sane approach. Here's how it works.

PLANTING

Prepare new planting beds by scraping away existing grass and weeds, adding a layer of compost, lava sand, or other volcanic rock material, organic fertilizer, and horticultural cornmeal, and tilling these amendments into the native soil. Excavation and additional ingredients such as concrete sand, topsoil, and pine bark are unnecessary and can even cause problems. More compost is needed for shrubs and flowers than for groundcover. Add Texas greensand to black and white soils, high-calcium lime to acid soils. Loosening the soil to a depth of 12 inches prior to adding the amendments is also helpful. For details, see Chapter 2.

FERTILIZING

Apply an organic fertilizer once or twice a year for most herbs. During the growing season, spray foliage, trunks, limbs, stems, and soil monthly with Garrett Juice (see Appendix), which includes compost tea, seaweed, molasses, and natural apple cider vinegar. Add lava sand or other volcanic material annually at 40–80 pounds per 1,000 square feet. Of course, if your garden already has volcanic soil, you can skip this step. Foliar feeding is not as important in healthy, balanced soils, but it is always an excellent way to provide the plants with trace minerals and practice indirect pest control. The Garrett Juice spray does not harm beneficial insects.

Red rubin basil

Rosemary and cacao shell mulch

Holy basil seedlings

MULCHING

Cover the bare soil around all shrubs, trees, groundcover, perennials, and annuals with 1–3 inches of compost, shredded tree trimmings, or shredded hardwood bark to protect the soil, inhibit weed germination, decrease watering needs, and mediate soil temperature. Shredded native cedar is the best choice, but cacao shell mulch is a close second.

WATERING

The best watering advice is simple: water when the plants need water. Too much or too little can be a problem. It is impossible to give a schedule due to plant varieties, climate, soil types, surface drainage, sun or shade, and other factors. Adjust the watering schedule seasonally to allow for deep, infrequent watering, which will maintain an even moisture level. Start by applying about 1 inch of water per week in the summer and adjust from there. Water needs will vary from site to site. See the specific watering recommendations in the individual herb entries.

WEEDING

First of all, don't worry about weeds so much. A few weeds attract beneficial insects. Hand-pull large noxious weeds and work on soil health for long-term control. Mulch all bare soil in beds. *Do not use synthetic herbicides*, especially pre-emergents, broadleaf treatments, sulfonylurea (SU), herbicides, and soil sterilants. These are unnecessary toxic pollutants. If you really have a problem with weeds, spray broadleaf weeds and grassy weeds with full-strength vinegar plus citrus oil. Use my formula or buy the commercial organic herbicide products.

PRUNING

Cut back or dead-head annuals as the flowers die and start to turn brown. This will encourage an additional flush of blooms on most plants and keep the plants bushy. The only exception is when you want to encourage a plant to produce seed. The seed of fennel, dill, and caraway, for example, are highly desirable and useful. Other plants need to go to maturity to produce seed for next year's crop.

Perennials should basically be cut back in the season opposite their bloom. Others will bloom a second time in the same growing season if cut back when the flowers start to fade. Other plants need to be cut back to keep them from getting floppy or unruly. Pick-prune shrubs and evergreens like rosemary as needed to maintain the desired appearance. Of course, use the clippings as mulch or in the compost. Trees need little pruning if the proper variety has been planted in the appropriate place. Remove dead, diseased, and conflicting limbs. Don't over prune, never make flush cuts, and leave the branch collars intact. Do not paint cuts except on oaks in oak-wilt areas when spring pruning can't be avoided. Remember that tree and shrub pruning is done for your benefit, not the tree's benefit.

MAKING COMPOST

Compost is the very best natural fertilizer and soil amendment. It can be made at home or purchased ready to use. A compost pile can be started any time of the year and can be located in sun or shade, on concrete or on the soil. Good ingredients include leaves, clean hay, grass clippings, tree trimmings, food scraps, bark, sawdust, rice hulls, weeds, nut hulls, and animal manure. In a nutshell, anything once living can and should go into the compost pile—even pet waste, dead animals, and greasy food from the kitchen. Everything that's alive will die and everything that dies will rot and become compost. Mix the ingredients together in a container of wood, hay bales, hog wire, or concrete blocks, or if space allows, pile the material on the ground. I don't use containers—they don't hold enough volume. The ideal mixture is 80 percent vegetative matter and 20 percent animal waste, although any mixture will compost.

Since oxygen is a critical component, the ingredients should be a mix of coarse and fine-textured material to promote air circulation through the pile. Turn the pile as time permits. Turning speeds up the breakdown process but releases nitrogen and other nutrients to the air.

Another critical component is water. A compost pile should have roughly the moisture of a squeezed-out sponge to help the living microorganisms thrive, reproduce, and feed on the raw materials. If green plants and kitchen scraps are used, very little extra water is needed. Compost is ready to use as a soil amendment when the ingredients are no longer identifiable. The color will be dark brown, the texture soft and crumbly, and the fragrance like the forest floor. In this form it is the best soil amendment and should be used liberally in bed preparation in any soil. Rough, unfinished compost can be used as a topdressing mulch around all plantings or it can be tilled into the soil for the future planting season.

MANURE COMPOST TEA

Compost tea (see Appendix) is made by soaking compost in water. Manure compost tea is made best from compost that contains animal manure. Manure compost tea is effective on many pests because of certain naturally occurring microorganisms. Diluted compost tea should be sprayed on fruit trees, perennials and annuals, vegetables, roses, and other plants, especially those that are regularly attacked by insects or fungal pests. It's very effective, for example, on black spot on roses and early blight on tomatoes. Compost tea mixed with natural vinegar, molasses, and seaweed produces Garrett Juice. Add orange oil at no more than 2 ounces per gallon and the mix becomes an effective soil detox product. It also makes an excellent fire ant control.

Ladybug adult and larva

CONTROLLING INSECTS

Controlling pests in the herb garden is a matter of using a little common sense. Spraying toxic chemical pesticides makes no sense in any way at any time. Toxic pesticides kill the helpful insects and microorganisms. True insect control results from healthy soil and healthy plants. For the control of aphids, spider mites, whiteflies, and lacebugs, release ladybugs and green lacewings regularly until natural populations exist. Spray Garrett Juice or garlic-pepper tea (see Appendix) or both. Spray with strong blasts for heavy infestations. For caterpillars and bagworms, release trichogramma wasps and spray *Bacillus thuringiensis* (Bt) as a last resort. This is not my favorite approach because it kills beneficial moths and butterflies. Hand-pick any big worms. For fire ants, drench mounds with the fire ant control formula (see Appendix) or Garrett Juice plus citrus oil and apply beneficial nematodes to the site. Plant lots of different plants and establish biodiversity. Grubworms are generally not a problem in organic gardens; beneficial nematodes and sugar or molasses help, but maintaining soil health is the primary control. For mosquito control, empty standing water or apply *Bacillus thuringiensis* 'Israelensis' (Bti) for larvae in standing water. Citrus oil also works on the larvae. Spray citrus oil or garlic-pepper tea for adults. Lavender, eucalyptus, and citronella sprays repel mosquito adults, and a mixture of vanilla and water is also effective. For slugs, snails, ticks, chinch bugs, roaches, and crickets, spray garlic-pepper tea or dust around the plants being attacked with a mixture of diatomaceous earth, crushed red pepper, and cedar flakes. Citrus oil sprays will also kills these pests. For fleas, apply beneficial nematodes and dust problem areas with natural diatomaceous earth during dry weather.

CONTROLLING DISEASES

For black spot, brown patch, powdery mildew, and other fungal problems, the best control is prevention through soil improvement, avoidance of high-nitrogen fertilizers, and proper watering. Spray Garrett Juice (see Appendix) plus garlic. Add potassium bicarbonate for tough problems. Baking soda will work if you can't find potassium bicarbonate. Treat the soil with horticultural cornmeal—it's the best natural disease fighter of all. Alfalfa meal and mixes containing alfalfa are also good disease fighters.

You can have a herb garden no matter how small your space because many of the herb species can be planted in pots, window boxes, or tiny garden beds. Trees obviously need more space than the smaller plants, but even some types of trees can be grown in pots.

Use 2-inch or 4-inch transplant pots for annuals and perennials and set them out in well-prepared soil. Prepare beds by tilling or forking the following amendments into the existing soil to a depth of 6 to 8 inches. The quantities are based on 1,000 square feet.

80 pounds lava sand
50 pounds of corn or corn/bran product
40 pounds Texas greensand
   (replace with high-calcium lime in acid soils)
5 pounds dry molasses
3–5 inches quality finished compost
1 inch earthworm castings (optional)

Some gardeners like to loosen the soil to a depth of 12 inches prior to adding the amendments. The cooler parts of the year are the best times to install new plants, but herbs can be planted year round in most of Texas.

When planting during the heat of summer, it is critical to soak the root balls of transplants in water before installing them. Add a tablespoon of seaweed or Garrett Juice per gallon of water and let the plants sit in the water until thoroughly soaked, then plant in moist beds. The root ball should be sopping wet and dripping before it goes into the moist soil. Don't work in beds that are sloppy wet, but never plant transplants in dry beds and never plant dry root balls. If you do, expect sick plants and lots of transplant shock. After planting, the beds should be mulched with at least 1 or 2 inches of organic mulch such as compost or shredded tree trimmings. Herbs that are sensitive to wet soil—such as rosemary, lavender, and sage—should be mulched only lightly.

Fertilize twice a year, at the most, with gentle organic fertilizer such as earthworm castings, alfalfa meal, cornmeal, or other natural fertilizers. The manufactured blends such as Garden-Ville Soil Food, Alliance Milling, Maestro-Gro, GreenSense, Sustane, Bradfield, and Bioform Dry are recommended if not overused. Herbs tend to have better flavor if kept slightly on the hungry side. After the first year, one dry fertilizer application a year may suffice if regular foliar feeding is done. Adding additional rock minerals annually should continue for several years.

You will enjoy all the various uses of herbs, so plant as many as you can afford. Here are some good easy-to-grow choices for a start. Wormwood is a good moth repellent, and the juice from comfrey, used topically, stops the itch and sting of insect bites and poison ivy. Mint has a wonderful fragrance, and many herbs are used in food and herb teas. Good choices include rosemary, lemongrass, oregano, and anise hyssop. The vitamins, minerals, and medicinal properties of these beautiful plants are substantial. Herb gardens are worth planting if for no other reason than having a source for herb teas. Try some herb tea every day. Pick fresh leaves, crush them, and put in the tea pot. Pour hot water over the leaves and let steep for at least three minutes—that's all there is to it. See Chapter 3 for more details.

Even if you only have a small space, a herb garden can be productive and one of the most enjoyable gardens. A planting area as small as 6 feet by 12 feet can make an effective herb garden. Herbs can also be planted in pots and brought indoors during periods of bad weather. Herbs such as basil, lemon verbena, savory, mint, peppers, oregano, parsley, chives, and bay make good choices for pots.

Here are some plant selection guidelines.

Marigolds and pineapple sage

HERBS FOR SMALL AREAS

Background—lavender, rosemary, comfrey, mullein, wormwood

Middle—lemon balm, sweet marigold, perilla, purple coneflower, calendula, salad burnet, sage, garlic, winter savory, garlic chives, coriander, sorrel, basil

Front—creeping thyme, Greek or native oregano, violets, onion chives, purslane, gotu kola

HERBS FOR LARGE AREAS

Background—elderberry, hoja santa, ginkgo, roselle

Middle—wormwood, rosemary, southernwood, lemon balm, sweet marigold, perilla, purple coneflower, calendula, salad burnet, sage, garlic, winter savory, garlic chives, cilantro, sorrel

Front—creeping thyme, Greek or native oregano, violets, basil, onion chives, purslane, gotu kola, peppermint, spearmint

Several of the herbs mentioned above have a rather serious fault: they spread and can become pests. They include elderberry, hoja santa, comfrey, lemon balm, and mint; garlic, garlic chives, and perilla will spread badly if allowed to go to seed. If these plants are left out of the inventory, you will still have an effective herb garden. Another option is to put them together in a separate area where invasive spreading won't be a problem. They can also be planted in pots plunged into the soil.

One more note to new gardeners. Herb gardening should always be organic gardening. Why spray poisons on plants that children are encouraged to touch, smell, and eat or that you may use to treat wounds? Furthermore, herbs are easy to grow without poisonous chemicals. And like most plants, they are more fun to grow with organic techniques. Beauty, delicious taste, and good health—what could be better?

It's not only possible but easy to create a landscape in which every plant has a use other than looking pretty. Although some of the plants included in this chapter are food crops, they can all be considered herbs because they have practical as well as aesthetic uses.

SHADE TREES

GINKGO

This distinctive shade tree will grow well in all soils except solid white rock. The leaves can be harvested right off the tree for use in teas to help your memory and other mental functions. It's a good conversation tree, too, because it was growing on Earth at the time of the dinosaurs. This living fossil grows well under an organic program.

JUJUBE

Before planting it, make sure you want this unusual fruit tree. It spreads by suckers and seed and produces a brown date-like fruit in the late summer and fall that tastes somewhat like dried apples. It is also an important medicinal herb.

LINDEN

Underused but becoming more popular. The flowers of both the European imports like little leaf linden and the native Carolina basswood have wonderfully fragrant flowers in the summer. The flowers are used in teas, and bees make a delicious honey from their nectar. Linden flowers are also used in cosmetics.

MULBERRY

The fruitless mulberry is a big weed and shouldn't be planted. Some people say that's a bad attitude, that all trees are useful in the right place. Well, they're wrong. There is no proper place for the fruitless mulberry. It's a weedy junk tree developed through hybridization. It has no native habitat. It doesn't even make good firewood. On the other hand, the fruiting mulberry, which is messy, does have a place in the edible landscape. Its fruit is delicious. A smaller, white-fruited form is less messy and produces even more delicious fruit than the common red-fruit form. Either tree planted away from decks, walks, and drives is a good landscape choice. The fruit is high in A, C, B, B_2, and linoleic acid. It is beneficial for anemic and constipated individuals as well as insomniacs.

PECAN

Yes, it's a beautiful shade tree as well as a wonderful source of food. The native nuts are smaller and have thicker shells, but the quality of the meat and oil is superior to that of the hybrids. Other small-nut varieties include Caddo and Kanza. The experts at Texas A&M University now agree and have revised their recommendations accordingly. It's about time.

PERSIMMON

Diospyros virginiana is a large shade tree that produces edible fruit in the late fall; it is usually sour until after the first frost. The common persimmon has dark, heavily fissured bark and lovely yellow-orange fall color. It's better food for wildlife than for people. The Texas persimmon, *Diospyros texana*, is much smaller with smaller but similar fall-maturing fruit. Several oriental persimmons are also useful choices.

WALNUT

Not as well adapted as the pecan but a source of terrific nuts, even though they're hard to shell. The little walnut, *Juglans microcarpa*, is a better choice for a shade tree. You can see a great specimen of this tree at the Texas A&M Research Station on Coit Road in Dallas.

ORNAMENTAL TREES

FRUIT TREES

Most of the common fruit trees make good ornamental landscape trees. The easiest to grow and maintain are figs and pears, the most difficult peaches and nectarines. None of the apple, peach, pear, apricot, nectarine, or fig trees is native to Texas, so they all require more care than our native trees. The fruit, of course, is edible, but the flower petals are too (although figs don't have flowers).

MEXICAN PLUM

One of my favorites of all ornamental trees. It has beautiful foliage in the summer and fall, fragrant and edible flowers in the spring, and small purple plums in the fall for making jams and jellies. They're not great for eating all by themselves, however.

REDBUD

Both the white- and purple-flowering forms are delightful to see in the early spring, and their flowers are delicious to eat, either in salads or as a garnish.

WITCH HAZEL

A small, interesting tree that produces edible seed; the leaves make an excellent ingredient in herb tea, and the flowers add fragrance to the garden. *Hamamelis virginiana* is excellent for the skin when taken as a tea. It is also used as an astringent, an anti-inflammatory, and a gargle for sore throats and tonsillitis.

SHRUBS

AGARITA

One of our few evergreen native shrubs. The yellow spring flowers attract beneficial insects, and the red berries that mature in May and June can be made into jellies and jams and a delicious wine. Be careful when harvesting—the spiny leaves can eat you up.

ALTHEA

A tall deciduous shrub that has edible flowers, like many of the other plants in the mallow family. Eat the petals only. It's best to plant althea in full or morning sun along with evergreens because it looks pretty bare and ugly in the winter.

BAY

Some call it sweet bay. It's a small evergreen tree that can be grown in pots or in the ground. Freeze damage is usually not a problem, especially if maintained organically. The exception is the far northern part of the state. The leaves repel moths when placed in the house and are used in cooking and in teas. Don't eat the leaves. They are indigestible and can cut the intestinal tissues.

GERMANDER

This is a shrub-like herb that should be used more. It's an evergreen with dark green foliage and rose-pink flowers in the summer. It can be clipped into a border or low hedge. The foliage, which can be cut year round and used with cut flowers indoors, reputedly helps purify the air.

POMEGRANATE

A colorful shrub for summer color and a source of fruit if you buy the right plant. Many people are frustrated when their pomegranate doesn't set fruit. Guess what? Some are only ornamental and will never have fruit. One of the fruiting varieties that can be found in this market is called 'Wonderful'.

TURK'S CAP

A large-growing and very durable perennial for sun or shade. Flowers and fruit make good herb tea ingredients. The pulp of the fruit, when cooked down, makes a good jelly or syrup. The plant also attracts hummingbirds.

VINES

BEANS AND PEAS

These plants produce great food, obviously, but the flowers are also edible. On the other hand, don't eat the flowers of the sweet pea—they're poisonous.

GOURDS

These fast-growing vines produce large fruit that, when mature and dried, have many uses—from birdhouses and dippers to musical instruments.

GRAPE

Grape vines produce delicious fruit for eating and making wine, the vines are beautiful on fences and arbors, and the leaves are edible in dishes such as stuffed grape leaves, a traditional Lebanese dish. The vines can be cooked into a tea for use as a diuretic. They are also used to make wreaths.

LUFFA

A beautiful vine that produces the loofah gourd used for scrubbing the skin and cleaning dishes. In addition, the flower buds, shoots, leaves, and fruits are edible. Even the seeds produce an edible oil.

MALABAR SPINACH

Not a true spinach but a good substitute that grows easily in the heat of summer. It has beautiful red stems and shiny green leaves. Be sure you like this plant before you plant it, though, because it sprouts easily from seed, which are prolific. It also makes a colorful summer groundcover.

PASSION FLOWER

This dramatic flowering vine has several uses. The fruit has a fragrant pulp that can be eaten or made into drinks and ice cream. Native Americans used the entire plant in teas to treat irritated eyes. The leaves are also used in teas as an antidepressant and a remedy for insomnia, anxiety, rapid heartbeat, and high blood pressure. Watch where you plant passion flower—it spreads aggressively.

GROUNDCOVERS

CLOVER

Common white clover is too often the target of toxic herbicides, but it is an excellent groundcover and turf builder. It stays green year round; has white flowers in spring, summer, and fall; and, as a legume, fixes nitrogen and improves the soil. The dried flowers are used in herb teas. According to Dr. Judy Griffin's *Mother Nature's Herbal*, clover is a blood coagulant and relieves spasmodic coughing.

CREEPING THYME

A perennial herb that makes a fantastic groundcover, especially when used around stepping stones and beside walks. When stepped on, its fragrance is delightful. The flowers and foliage are used for flavoring food and in teas as an antiseptic.

GOTU KOLA

An annual shade-loving groundcover that looks a lot like gill ivy. Odena recommends it for use in teas to aid circulation to the brain and mental functions. As a tea, it is beneficial topically for skin lesions, says Dr. Griffin.

MINT

Several of the mints make effective groundcovers, but they all spread far and wide so be careful where you plant them. It's best to plant them in dedicated beds. Peppermint is an excellent digestive aid, pain reliever, and caffeine substitute. Spearmint is cooling and reduces fever.

OREGANO

Another evergreen herb that makes a good groundcover. The foliage has a wonderful flavor for cooking and the pretty flowers are edible.

Regular and variegated garden sage and thyme

Greek oregano is cold-tolerant and should be used more as a landscape groundcover. It can be used topically to reduce swelling and pain. As a tea, it stimulates digestion.

VIOLETS

Another perennial groundcover that is commonly treated as a weed and sprayed with toxic herbicides. Eat the young foliage in salads and use the foliage and flowers in teas. The flowers are beneficial for coughs and as a children's tonic.

PERENNIALS

ANISE HYSSOP

This beautiful perennial has edible flowers that attract bees, and the foliage makes a delicious tea. It grows well in sun or part shade and can be planted in pots.

BLACKBERRIES

A good hedgerow plant that provides habitat for wildlife and a source of edible berries. The foliage is also a tasty ingredient in herb tea, which can be used to reduce diarrhea. Cuttings can be used on top of mulch to keep dogs and cats away from plantings. Blackberries can be grown almost anywhere in Texas. Raspberries can be grown in areas with acid, sandy soils.

CHIVES

Both onion and garlic chives produce edible foliage and flowers and make attractive additions to the landscape, especially the perennial garden.

DAYLILIES

The flowers of the daylily have been called "gourmet flowers" because the edible petals are so delicious. The flowers can also be dried and stored for use later in soups. Asians eat unopened buds in soups and teas to help reduce anxiety. The leaves of daffodils and narcissus look similar to those of the daylily, so don't mix them up. Daffodils and other narcissus are poisonous.

GARLIC

Garlic is well known for its edible greens and cloves. This very important food and medicinal herb also makes a good-looking landscape perennial. The flower heads can be cut, hung upside down, and dried for use in indoor arrangements.

HIBISCUS

All types of hibiscus (annuals and perennials) provide edible flowers. Use the petals only, not the reproductive parts, in salads, on sandwiches, and for garnish. Hibiscus flowers also make beautiful, colorful teas.

HORSEMINT

This is one of the monardas that is probably too strong to ingest, but it makes an excellent insect repellent. The fresh or dried flowers, when crushed and rubbed on pants and socks, repel fleas, ticks, and chiggers.

JERUSALEM ARTICHOKE

Sunchoke is a big, tall-growing sunflower. The roots are delicious, full of food value, and used much the same way as potatoes. The flower petals are also edible. Be careful where you plant—it is aggressive and can spread to become a pest. It's a good potato substitute for those with hypoglycemia and diabetes.

LAVENDER

An extract of this beautiful herb repels mosquitoes effectively. The flowers are edible, and the foliage can be used in teas. A great low-water landscape plant—excellent drainage is a must.

PEPPERS

Peppers are edible, of course, but they have medicinal importance: they improve the cardiovascular system. Peppers—in garlic-pepper tea and pepper spray, for example—are also used as insecticides and repellents. Ground hot pepper helps repel animal pests, slugs, snails, and pill bugs.

PURPLE CONEFLOWER

All parts of the plant are used for teas. The roots and seed have the greatest concentration of the immune-building properties for which echinacea is famous. When you feel a cold or the flu coming on, take some capsules or drink some tea—you'll be amazed. And purple coneflower is not only a native wildflower but one of the most beautiful perennials for Texas gardens.

ROSEMARY

The leaves and flowers of rosemary are used to flavor foods and to make herb teas. This evergreen will survive most winters in all but the extreme northern regions of Texas. It can be grown in pots or in the ground as a beautiful and fragrant landscape plant.

ROSES

The rose is the most misused of all edible plants. The petals are delicious in salads and useful in teas, and the fruits or hips can be used to make teas that provide an excellent source of natural vitamin C. Unfortunately many rose growers follow the advice of organiphobes and spray regularly with systemic insecticides, fungicides, and other poisons that turn roses into toxic plants not fit for consumption.

SALVIA

The sages provide edible flowers and foliage for teas. The beautiful red-flowering pineapple sage is one of the best. Pineapple sage tea is most effective as a cold-water infusion. Leaves and flowers can lose their flavor when heated.

SWEET MARIGOLD

The more common name for this plant is Mexican mint marigold, which is a dopey name since the plant is unrelated to mint. Sweet marigold is a very powerful flavoring for food and tea, but it should be used only as a fresh herb. It loses much of its flavor when dried.

ANNUALS

These are the best annuals to include in the landscape plan. But be sure to check and abide by the rules on eating plants (see "Important Rules for Eating Flowers" later in this chapter).

BEGONIAS

Beautiful, easy-to-grow annuals for sun or shade. If you want to give your family or dinner guests a pleasant surprise, serve them sherbet topped with flowers of begonia. The flowers of all begonia plants have a crisp, fresh taste.

DIANTHUS

The perennial and annual forms of dianthus have flowers that are both edible as well as beautiful. Remove the bitter off-white base and use the flowers in fruit dishes, teas, soups, sauces, liqueurs, and wines.

GINGER

The roots of ginger are used for food, seasoning, and tea. Ginger promotes blood circulation, alleviates respiratory problems, and helps prevent motion sickness. The flowers of ginger are eaten raw or cooked. You can plant your own. Buy ginger roots from the grocery store, cut up into thumb-size pieces, coat with fireplace ashes, allow to dry in a cool place, and plant in pots in organic potting soil or in beds. You'll have to keep the pots indoors during the winter and set out the plants in the spring.

HIBISCUS

The flowers of both annual and perennial hibiscus are delicious used with or instead of lettuce on sandwiches or in salads or as a garnish. Be sure to use only the petals of the larger flowers. The reproductive parts can be bitter or even toxic.

Texas star hibiscus

JOHNNY-JUMP-UPS

The flowers of Johnny-jump-ups and pansies, members of the violet family, are edible. Toss them in salads or use for garnish. The small Johnny-jump-up flowers can be frozen in ice cubes for special additions to drinks.

NASTURTIUMS

This good-looking annual is easy to grow from seed, and every part of the plant is edible and delicious—flowers, stems, foliage, and roots. The buds are maybe the best with their nutty flavor. Use the plant in salads and teas or just graze on it in the garden.

PANSIES

Pansy flowers are edible. Toss them in salads or use for teas or garnish. Harvesting the flowers makes for better overall flower production.

PEANUTS

An easy-to-grow food plant that makes a decorative potted plant. Plant the raw peanuts in healthy, organic potting soil or loose, well-drained beds for a summer crop.

PURSLANE

Don't spray this herb with toxic herbicides as many gardeners do. Both the improved cultivars and the wild "weed" are delicious, either cooked or raw in salads. Purslane is very high in iron and vitamin C.

SUNFLOWER

The seed of the sunflower is nutritious, of course, but the flowers are also edible. The stem end of the flowers can be bitter and should be removed. Jerusalem artichoke rootlet can be eaten raw or cooked like potatoes. The fall-blooming perennial, Maximilian sunflower, also has edible seed and roots. Harvest the roots anytime after flowering through late winter.

A QUICK REFERENCE LIST OF EDIBLE AND MEDICINAL LANDSCAPING PLANTS

SHADE TREES
Ginkgo—tea from leaves
Jujube—fruit
Linden—tea from flowers
Mulberry—fruit
Pecan—nuts
Persimmon—fruit
Walnut—nuts

ORNAMENTAL TREES
Apple—fruit and flower petals
Apricot—fruit and flower petals
Citrus—fruit

Crabapple—fruit and flower petals
Fig—fruit and flower petals
Mexican plum—fruit
Peach—fruit and flower petals
Pear—fruit and flower petals
Persimmon—fruit
Plum—fruit and flower petals
Redbud—flowers
Rusty blackhaw viburnum—berries
Witch hazel—tea from leaves

SHRUBS
Agarita—fruit for wine
Althea—flowers
Bay—tea and food seasoning from leaves
Germander—freshens air indoors
Pomegranate—fruit
Turk's cap—flowers and fruit for tea

VINES
Beans and peas—pods and seed
Gourds—dippers and birdhouses
Grapes—food (fruit and leaves)
Luffa—flowers, shoots, and fruits; sponges from the dried fruit
Malabar spinach—foliage
Passion flower—fruit, tea from leaves

GROUNDCOVERS
Clover—tea from leaves and flowers
Creeping thyme—teas and food flavoring
Gotu kola—tea from leaves
Mints—food and teas from flowers and leaves
Oregano—teas and food flavoring
Violets—foliage, tea from flowers and leaves

PERENNIALS
Anise hyssop—flowers, tea from leaves
Blackberries—berries, tea from leaves
Chives—foliage and flowers
Daylilies—flowers
Garlic—flowers, greens, and cloves
Hibiscus—flowers
Hoja santa—leaves for flavoring foods
Horsemint—insect repellent
Jerusalem artichoke—roots

Lavender—teas and insect repellent
Monarda—flowers, teas from leaves
Peppers—fruit, tea from fruit
Purple coneflower—teas from leaves, roots, and seed
Rosemary—food and tea from leaves and flowers
Roses—teas from petals and hips
Salvia—flowers, teas from leaves
Sweet marigold—food, flavoring, and tea from leaves and flowers
Tansy—chopped and crushed foliage repels ants
Turk's cap—teas from flowers and fruit

ANNUALS
Begonias—flowers
Dianthus—flowers
Ginger—food, seasoning, and tea from roots
Hibiscus—flowers
Johnny-jump-ups—flowers
Nasturtium—leaves
Pansies—flowers
Peanuts—nuts
Purslane—leaves
Sunflower—seeds and flower petals

EDIBLE FLOWERS

Flowers have been eaten throughout the world for centuries. Roses and orange flowers are commonly used in Middle Eastern and Persian foods; lilies are used in China; cherry blossoms and chrysanthemums are used in Japan; lavender is a favorite in England and France; and the Mediterranean countries enjoy saffron in their food. Of course, not all flowers are edible—some are poisonous either naturally or from toxic chemical pesticides. Eat only those flowers that have been grown organically. Flowers from florists, nurseries, and traditional garden centers should not be eaten. If your garden center is organic, eat away.

Edible flowers can be used to enhance food at breakfast, lunch, and dinner. They can also be used in teas. Here are some of the best choices for plants with edible flowers: aloe vera, althea, apple, arugula, basil, bee balm, begonia, borage, broccoli, calendula, chicory, chives (onion and garlic), clover, coriander, dandelion, dill, elderberry, English daisy, fennel, hyssop, lavender, lemon, lilac, mint, mum (base of petal is bitter), mustard, okra, orange, oregano, pea (except for sweet peas), pineapple sage, radish, redbud, rosemary, scented geranium, society garlic, sweet woodruff, squash blossoms, thyme, violet, winter savory, and yucca (petals only).

Dianthus

Hibiscus

Marigold

Violets

Borage

Monarda

Johnny-jump-ups

Begonia

Rosemary

Purslane

Roses

Pansies

Daylilies

Nasturtium

French hollyhock

Redbud

IMPORTANT RULES FOR EATING FLOWERS

1. Not all flowers are edible. Some are poisonous. Learn the difference.
2. Eat flowers only when you are positive they are edible and nontoxic.
3. Eat only flowers that have been grown organically.
4. Do not eat flowers from florists, nurseries, or garden centers unless you know they've been grown organically.
5. Do not eat flowers if you have hay fever, asthma, or allergies.
6. Do not eat flowers growing along the side of the road.
7. Remove pistils and stamens from flowers before eating. Eat only the petals of the larger flowers.
8. Introduce flowers into your diet the way you would new foods to a baby—one at a time in small quantities.

Note: Pregnant women should avoid all strong herbs. No one should ingest any plant in excess at any time. None of these plants should be eaten unless they have been properly identified and grown organically.

Redbud

HARVESTING

Harvest a few fresh leaves or flowers whenever you need some, but remember that the best time of day is early to mid-morning after the dew has dried and before the sun has sapped some of the plant's volatile oils. This is not as important in the fall as in the heat of summer. The best flavor from leafy herbs usually comes just before flowering—just as the plants start to form buds and always before they are in full bloom. After flowering, some herbs will have a stronger and sometimes bitter taste. Roots and bark should be gathered in the fall.

Frequent heavy pruning is actually good for many herbs, but don't cut plants back more than about 50 percent. Harvest edible flowers either in the bud stage or in full flower to suit your taste. Collect herb seeds when they have turned from green to ripe brown but before they fall from the plant. Strip large leaves from the stems. Small ones like those of thyme can remain attached to the stems. Use a sharp knife or shears rather than hurriedly snapping the herbs off by hand, as I often do. You do damage to the cuttings and the mother plant with this sloppy approach. Cut the entire stem from the plants rather than plucking the foliage and leaving bare stems.

FREEZING

A good way to preserve many of the herbs is to freeze the fresh foliage and flowers. Toss the flowers and leaves into a plastic bag. This is an effective technique for basil, lemon verbena, lemongrass, borage, lemon balm, mints, and perilla. Edible flowers of all kinds and fine-textured herb foliage can be frozen in ice cubes to make tasty and beautiful additions to drinks.

DRYING

Some herbs are better dried. Rinse them lightly, then hang in bunches upside down and allow to dry in a cool, well-ventilated space. Screens and drying racks can also be used. When dried, store in glass containers. Seeds from coriander, dill, fennel, parsley, and others can be dried by hanging the seed heads upside down in paper bags. When dry, shake the bag to release the seeds, then store them in airtight containers or freeze. Label all the containers carefully.

Herbs can also be dried in the oven, microwave, or electric dryers. Always use very low heat to avoid injuring the herbs. Some gardeners even leave them in the car to dry. That works well in the cooler parts of the year, but it's best to crack the windows in the summer. In the oven put herbs on stainless steel cookie sheets and leave the door partly open. In a gas oven the pilot light is usually enough heat. The leaves are done when they feel dry and crispy. In the microwave, sandwich the herbs between two sheets of paper towels and cook for 30-second periods until dry and crispy. If you smell burning, you've gone too far. If possible, avoid using the microwave.

STORAGE

Rinse the fresh leaves lightly and discard discolored or damaged leaves. Some herbs such as basil, coriander, epazote, oregano, parsley, pineapple sage, and sweet marigold can be stored as cuttings in water for days. The herbs look pretty and will often root in the water. Change the water daily and remove the lower leaves that touch the water. Coriander and parsley can be stored even longer in water if the cuttings are covered by plastic in the refrigerator. To store herbs longer, put them in tightly sealed glass or plastic containers in the refrigerator. Glass is always the best choice. Use this method for herbs such as dill, fennel, mint, marjoram, oregano, parsley, rosemary, sage, tarragon, and thyme. Resealable plastic bags will also work. In order to prevent mold, make sure the leaves are dry. I often freeze herb cuttings in plastic bags or containers. This method works well for ginkgo leaves, basil, oregano, thyme, lemongrass, and lemon verbena. Leaves can be left whole or chopped. You can also puree them with water and pour into ice cube trays. The cubes can be tossed into dishes while cooking or into cold drinks.

PREPARATION

Use a sharp knife or, even better, sharp kitchen scissors to avoid bruising the delicate herbs when preparing them for cooking and teas.

USE

Most leafy herbs should be added to chili, soup, stew, and other slowly cooked dishes the last ten or fifteen minutes of cooking time. This preserves the flavor and the health-giving vitamins. Winter savory, rosemary, thyme, bay, and lemongrass are exceptions and should be cooked longer. Most herbs that are used in making teas should simply be covered with boiling water and left to steep for three to five minutes. Some herbalists say that the flavor of thyme and lemongrass tea is better if the herbs are exposed to boiling water for a few minutes before the steeping period begins, but this reduces the power of the herbs. For cold foods such as spreads, butters, pasta, salads, tabboulleh, and cold drinks, the herbs should be added hours or even days before serving.

Lemon verbena, sweet
marigold, oregano, lemon
balm, lemongrass, chili pequin,
begonia flowers, and rosemary.

5 *Making Herb Teas*

Since I get so many questions on herb teas, I thought the subject needed an entire chapter. I start the nine o'clock hour of my Sunday radio show every week with a special feature called "In Howard's Garden." I talk about what to plant, what and how to fertilize, what to prune, and other topics—all timely recommendations. During this monologue I explain the herb tea I have made that day and brought with me to sip during the show. Herb tea is one of the best by-products of organic gardening. My favorite herbs for tea include lemon verbena, peppermint (especially chocolate peppermint), thyme, anise hyssop, basil, ginkgo, lemongrass, oregano, spearmint, and chamomile. The flowers of linden, hibiscus, begonia, sambac jasmine, and Turk's cap can also be used. I also like to make tea with young witch hazel leaves along with blackberries and blackberry leaves.

To prepare herb teas, simply pick fresh leaves or appropriate flowers from herbs, put them in a teapot, and pour in hot water after bringing it to a boil. I use a glass kettle to boil the filtered water and a ceramic teapot. Letting the boiling water cool down slightly before pouring it in the teapot is a good idea because boiling the leaves destroys many of the healthy vitamins. Let the brew steep from 3 to 10 minutes, depending on your taste. If steeped too long, tannic acid in the leaves will build up and make the tea bitter. A single herb or a mix of various plants can be used. I often use chocolate peppermint and lemongrass as a base and add various other herbs to create different tastes. A good lemony tea, for example, can be made from equal amounts of lemongrass, lemon verbena, and lemon balm. Try all the wonderful culinary herbs in your teas and let me know which are your favorites.

Natural teas taste great all by themselves, but lemon juice or honey can be added if you prefer. By the way, it's really important to use clean, filtered water. Chlorine and other contaminants can ruin the taste and quality of any good drink, to say nothing of your health. Real tea can also be added to the herbs. Japanese green tea is my favorite. It tastes great and reportedly helps prevent degenerative diseases. It does contain some caffeine, though.

Leftover tea has other uses. Pour it on the plants as a liquid fertilizer after it has cooled or put it into your foliar spray solution. Or drink it cold over ice the next day (toss a couple of fresh leaves into your iced drink for additional flavor). The extra tea can also be frozen into ice cubes to be added to other drinks later.

The rose is a greatly underused herb. Roses can be used to make good-tasting teas and health drinks. Tea made from rose petals is believed to fortify the heart and brain and to alleviate female problems, stomach disorders, and other ailments. Hips, which are the colorful fruits that follow the flowers, are particularly high in vitamins A, B, E, and especially C. To make a wonderful tea from roses, use the flower petals before they unfold or the hips after they mature to a red color in the fall. Opened flower petals taste good, but they won't have as many vitamins and minerals. Use 1 teaspoon of dried petals or 2 teaspoons of fresh petals for each cup of boiling water. Add a little honey and enjoy hot or cold. The *Rugosa* roses have large hips and are the richest in vitamin C. Obviously you should never make tea from roses that have been sprayed with systemic, toxic poisons. If you are still using unnecessary chemical contaminants like Dursban, diazinon, Orthene, Orthonex, Funginex, Sevin, kelthane, or any other toxic pesticide—stop! The synthetics are dangerous and a waste of money. If you don't know how to avoid these chemicals, try my Organic Rose Program (see Appendix). It works well.

Here are the best herbs for teas and the part of the plant to be gathered when making a tea.

Agrimony—flowers, leaves, and stems
Alfalfa—leaves and seeds
Angelica—leaves, seeds, and roots
Anise hyssop—leaves, flowers, and seed
Basil—leaves
Bay—leaves
Blackberry—leaves, flowers, and fruit
Borage—leaves and flowers
Burdock—root and seed
Calendula—flowers
Caraway—seed
Catnip—leaves
Chamomile—flowers
Chicory—root
Chrysanthemum—flowers
Citrus—leaves and flowers
Clover—leaves and flowers
Coriander—leaves, flowers, and seed
Dandelion—leaves and roots
Dill—leaves
Echinacea—roots, flowers, leaves, and seed
Elecampane—root
Fennel—leaves and seed
Fenugreek—leaves and seed

Feverfew—leaves and flowers
Garlic—cloves and leaves
Ginger—roots
Ginkgo—leaves
Ginseng—roots
Goldenrod—young leaves and flowers
Gotu kola—leaves, stems, and roots
Hibiscus—flowers
Hollyhock—flowers (petals only)
Horehound—leaves
Hyssop—leaves, stems, and flowers
Lavender—flowers and leaves
Lemon balm—leaves
Lemon verbena—leaves
Licorice—root
Linden—flowers
Lovage—roots
Marjoram—leaves and flowers
Marsh mallow—roots and leaves
Mint—leaves and flowers
Monarda—leaves and flowers
Mugwort—leaves and flowers
Mullein—leaves and flowers
Oregano—leaves and flowers
Parsley—leaves and flowers
Pepper—fruit
Raspberry—leaves, flowers, and fruit
Rose—petals and hips
Rosemary—leaves and flowers
Sage—leaves
Salad burnet—leaves
Sambac jasmine—flowers
Savory—leaves
Saw palmetto—berries
Scented geranium—leaves
Strawberry—leaves
Thyme—leaves
Violet—leaves and flowers
Yarrow—flowers

Certain herb teas are also excellent as foliar sprays (see Appendix).
They not only feed the plants through the foliage but also repel insect
pests and disease organisms. An herbal foliar spray is an excellent tool
for use in the herb garden.

6 The Herbs

Achillea millefolium—see **YARROW**
Agastache foeniculum—see **ANISE HYSSOP**
Agrimonia eupatoria—see **AGRIMONY**

AGRIMONY

Agrimonia eupatoria
ag-rah-MOAN-ee-ah you-pa-TORE-ee-ah

COMMON NAMES	AGRIMONY, STICKWORT, LIVERWORT, CHURCH STEEPLES.
FAMILY	Rosaceae (Rose).
TYPE	Herbaceous perennial.
LOCATION	Sun or light shade. A location with morning sun and afternoon shade is best. By the way, this type of location is best for a large percentage of both ornamental and useful plants here in the heat of Texas.
PLANTING	Plant seed, divisions, cuttings, or transplants from spring through fall. The best program is to start the seed indoors in the winter and set out the young plants in the spring after the last freeze.
HEIGHT	1 to 4 feet.
SPREAD	12 to 15 inches.
FINAL SPACING	12 to 15 inches.
BLOOM/FRUIT	Yellow flower spires that have a honey scent. The seed will stick to your clothes.
GROWTH HABITS/CULTURE	Agrimony is an easy-to-grow perennial with long yellow flower spires. This vigorous plant is especially good for cooler climates. It has dark green leaves, blooms more or less all summer, and is a little weedy-looking. It grows in any well-drained soil and needs at least a half day of sun. It's not a long-lasting perennial but self-seeds.
PROBLEMS	Kind of ugly!
HARVEST/STORAGE	Harvest the entire top growth of the plant when in flower. Roots and bark should be gathered in the fall, fruit and seeds when mature.
CULINARY USES	Apricot-like flavoring for food.
MEDICINAL USES	Agrimony is used to treat throat diseases, skin problems, and liver disorders. It is also used to make a yellow dye. Traditionally agrimony was used for eye problems, kidney stones, and digestive problems. The aerial portions of the plant contain vitamins B and K.
LANDSCAPE USES	Use in the perennial garden—sort of back in the back. It's not a good-looking plant.
INSIGHT	Agrimony is related to our wild cocklebur. It is a native of the British Isles, where it used in teas and wines.

ALFALFA

Medicago sativa
med-ee-CA-go sa-TEE-va

COMMON NAMES	ALFALFA, LUCERNE, PURPLE MEDICK, BUFFALO HERB.
FAMILY	Fabaceae (Legume).
TYPE	Perennial legume.
LOCATION	Full sun.
PLANTING	Plant seed at 20–30 pounds per acre or 1–2 pounds per 1,000 square feet from late summer to early fall.
HEIGHT	To 30 inches.
SPREAD	12 to 18 inches.
FINAL SPACING	6 to 10 inches apart.
BLOOM/FRUIT	Purple flowers in spring and early summer followed by spiraling seed pods.
GROWTH HABITS/CULTURE	Alfalfa is a deep-rooted legume with trifoliate (three leaflets) leaves. It is a cool-season broadleaf perennial.
PROBLEMS	Cotton root rot is a major concern. Blister beetles, leafhoppers, and aphids are sometimes pests. Use the Basic Organic Program, apply beneficial organism products, and spray with Garrett Juice plus garlic.
HARVEST/STORAGE	The leaves and sprouts should be eaten fresh. Seed should be harvested when mature and stored in glass.
CULINARY USES	Leaves and sprouted seed are used in salads, on sandwiches, and in health drinks. Leaves and seed are used in teas.
MEDICINAL USES	Alfalfa leaves are a commercial source of chlorophyll and have been used to reduce blood thinning on easy bleeders. They contain vitamin K and should not be used by those on blood thinners. Alfalfa is often taken to relieve arthritis and other pains and is reported to stimulate appetite and aid the treatment of alcohol and drug addiction.
LANDSCAPE USES	Winter groundcover for large areas. It is also an excellent nursery plant for beneficial insects.

Alfalfa

OTHER USES	Alfalfa is fed to horses, cattle, and other livestock. It is said to increase lactation in nursing mothers. It is an excellent green manure crop, and the seeds yield a yellow dye. There is some evidence that alfalfa may trigger lupus in sensitive individuals.
INSIGHT	Alfalfa can be grown in containers or even flats for the production of alfalfa sprouts. For the best germination and establishment of the nitrogen-fixing nodules, treat seed with the proper rhizobia bacteria when planting. Alfalfa is extremely deep-rooted and is rich in trace minerals.

Allium cepa—see **ONION**
Allium sativum—see **GARLIC**
Allium schoenoprasum—see **CHIVES**
Allium tuberosum—see **CHIVES**

ALLSPICE

Pimenta dioica
pa-MINT-ta dee-oh-EE-ka

COMMON NAMES	ALLSPICE.
FAMILY	Myrtaceae (Myrtle).
TYPE	Tropical tree.
LOCATION	Hot, dry sites in full sun.
PLANTING	Seed in the spring.
HEIGHT	Up to 30 feet.
SPREAD	15–20 feet.
FINAL SPACING	One is enough.
BLOOM/FRUIT	Small greenish-white flowers followed by dark brown to black berries that look like peppercorns.
GROWTH HABITS/CULTURE	Small, tropical, evergreen tree native to South America and the West Indies. It has aromatic bark, leaves, berries, and bunches of flowers and glossy foliage.
PROBLEMS	It will freeze in all parts of Texas except the southern tip of the state.
HARVEST/STORAGE	Berries are gathered when mature but still green and then dried for use. Allspice is the dried ripe fruit.
CULINARY USES	Allspice is used to flavor food, especially to sweeten dishes with its peppery taste. Leaves can be used in teas.
MEDICINAL USES	A warming medicine, given as a tea for chills and flatulence.
LANDSCAPE USES	Greenhouse or container plant.
OTHER USES	Berries are eaten as a breath sweetener. Leaves and berries are used to make oil for cosmetics.
INSIGHT	Seeds are now available from specialty seed companies. Dried allspice seed sold in grocery stores has probably been heat-treated and will not be viable. In Texas the plant can be grown only in pots, in the extreme southern part of the state, and in greenhouses.

Allspice

Allspice

ALOE VERA

Aloe vera or *Aloe barbadensis*
al-low VER-a, al-low bar-ba-DEN-sis

COMMON NAMES	ALOE VERA, ALOE.
FAMILY	Liliaceae (Lily).
TYPE	Tender perennial.
LOCATION	Full sun.
PLANTING	Spring to fall by divisions or transplants.
HEIGHT	Up to 35 inches.
SPREAD	24 inches.
FINAL SPACING	Use individually or in clusters.
BLOOM/FRUIT	Golden-orange tubular flowers on spikes that usually bloom in the fall.
GROWTH HABITS/CULTURE	Aloe grows upright with thick, succulent leaves in a rosette. The flower stems range in size from very short to over 20 feet tall. Aloe is easy to grow in containers or in beds. It usually won't survive freezing winter temperatures anywhere but the southern Rio Grande Valley. It likes healthy soil and excellent drainage.
PROBLEMS	Can sunburn in full sun if quickly moved from indoors or a shady place. Roots can rot if overwatered. Bacterial diseases are a threat in wet soil.
HARVEST/STORAGE	Cut lower leaves off and use the gel and juice directly. Cut leaves will last for several days in cool temperatures; however, the fresh gel quickly loses its potency and effectiveness when exposed to air.
CULINARY USES	The flowers are edible. Pick and eat before they open fully.
MEDICINAL USES	Aloe has been used as a healing herb since the dawn of time. The sticky gel is applied topically to skin abrasions, sunburn, insect bites, poison ivy rashes, and burns. It is taken internally for constipation, stomach problems, mouth ulcers, and a poor immune system. Experi-

ments show that aloe protects the skin from ultraviolet rays and may help in the treatment of cataracts and skin cancer. It is included in many beauty creams, lotions, and health drinks. Some African tribes rub aloe on their skin to remove the human scent before they stalk their prey.

LANDSCAPE USES Good ornamental container plant.

OTHER USES Body-care products. Check out the range of Manapol products at www.aloevera.com.

INSIGHT Aloe speeds the regeneration of cells in plants and animals. Even if you aren't a gardener, keep an aloe plant in your kitchen to use on burns and cuts. To apply, simply cut a leaf off the plant and squeeze the gel onto the wound. For more serious burns or cuts, you can slit open the leaf lengthwise and apply it as a poultice.

Aloysia triphylla—see **LEMON VERBENA**
Althea officinalis—see **MARSH MALLOW**
AMERICAN WORMSEED—see **EPAZOTE**
Amorpha fruiticosa—see **FALSE INDIGO**
Anethum graveolens—see **DILL**

Aloe vera

Giant aloe vera

Angelica

ANGELICA

Angelica archangelica
an-GEL-ee-kah arc-an-GEL-ee-kah

COMMON NAMES	ANGELICA, EUROPEAN ANGELICA, GARDEN ANGELICA.
FAMILY	Apiaceae (Umbelliferae) (Carrot or Parsley).
TYPE	Biennial.
LOCATION	Shade.
PLANTING	Spring through fall by seeds and division. Seeds must be planted immediately after maturing.
HEIGHT	Up to 6 feet.
SPREAD	24 inches.
FINAL SPACING	24 inches.
BLOOM/FRUIT	Clusters of small greenish white to yellowish flowers, oblong fruit.
GROWTH HABITS/CULTURE	Angelica is a big plant. It is a taprooted, three-year biennial with large umbels of greenish white flowers. After the third year, it seeds and dies. It has bright green compound leaves 2 to 3 feet long. Once established, it reseeds easily. All parts of the plants are fragrant. It likes good soil and shade and is easy to grow in healthy soil once established. Needs plenty of water.
PROBLEMS	Angelica is hard to establish in much of Texas because it does not like summer heat.
HARVEST/STORAGE	Harvest stems in May or June, leaves before flowering, roots in autumn and seeds after maturing.
CULINARY USES	Stems of leaves are used as a sugar extender. Crystallized stems are used for cake decoration. Young shoots can be used in salads. The second-year stems can be cooked and used like celery.
MEDICINAL USES	All parts of the plants are used in tonics and teas to aid digestion, reduce flatulence, and increase perspiration.
LANDSCAPE USES	Plant as a background foliage plant in shade gardens.

OTHER USES	Angelica is used to flavor gin, vermouth, and perfumes. Seeds are used to flavor Chartreuse liqueur.
INSIGHT	The juice of the plant should never come into contact with the eyes. Dried roots keep for years.

ANISE

Pimpinella anisum
PIMP-ah-nell-ah ah-NEE-sum

COMMON NAMES	ANISE, ANISEED.
FAMILY	Apiaceae (Umbelliferae) (Carrot or Parsley).
TYPE	Annual.
LOCATION	Full sun.
PLANTING	Anise is best when started in very early spring in pots and then set out in the garden, although it can be planted in fall. Sow seed directly in the garden in early spring or fall.
HEIGHT	18 to 24 inches.
SPREAD	12 inches.
FINAL SPACING	2 to 4 inches.
BLOOM/FRUIT	Anise needs a spot protected from strong winds because the thin stems are fragile. It produces umbels of tiny white flowers followed by seeds containing the oil of commerce.
GROWTH HABITS/CULTURE	White flowers resemble those of a large Queen Anne's Lace. It is a cool-weather plant that will bolt in hot weather, but it is easy to grow from seed. Looks like a very large and coarse carrot. The leaves are

Anise

rounded and toothed when young but become feathery with age, much like coriander.

PROBLEMS	None serious.
HARVEST/STORAGE	Gather the seeds when they begin to turn brown and store in glass containers.
CULINARY USES	Anise has a licorice-like flavor, and the leaves are good in salad. It is also used to flavor liqueurs. Grown primarily for the seeds, which are used in cooking and baking breads, cakes, and pastries.
MEDICINAL USES	Anise has been used traditionally to make other medicines taste better. It is said to promote estrogen production, aid digestion, quell nausea, and ease colic. It is also used in the treatment of colds, fevers, asthma, and bronchitis. Make a tea from the seeds.
LANDSCAPE USES	None.
OTHER USES	Anise oil is said to be effective on bait as a fish attractant. The oil is used in toothpastes, mouthwashes, and perfumes. The flowers attract beneficial insects to the garden.
INSIGHT	Like most herbs, anise needs rich, well-drained soil. When taken in large amounts, it can be toxic, so use it carefully.

ANISE FERN—see **CICELY**

ANISE HYSSOP

Agastache foeniculum
ah-guh-STAH-she fee-NIK-yew-lum

COMMON NAMES	ANISE HYSSOP.
FAMILY	Lamiaceae (Labiatae) (Mint).
TYPE	Herbaceous perennial.
LOCATION	Sun or part shade.
PLANTING	Plant seed, cuttings, and transplants from spring through fall.
HEIGHT	24 to 36 inches.
SPREAD	12 to 18 inches.
FINAL SPACING	18 to 24 inches.
BLOOM/FRUIT	Purple, rose, or mauve flower spikes in summer.
GROWTH HABITS/CULTURE	Anise hyssop is an easy-to-grow, upright plant with triangular, anise-scented leaves. Grows to 3 feet with nectar-loaded flower spikes; self-sows readily. Plant it in a location that gets morning sun and use normal bed preparation techniques. Cut the plant back severely when it gets tall and floppy. It responds quickly.
PROBLEMS	None serious.
HARVEST/STORAGE	Pick and dry the flowers as they bloom. Harvest leaves anytime and use fresh or store dry. Flowers can also be used fresh or dried, although the fresh ones are better.
CULINARY USES	Leaves and flowers are excellent for tea. The flowers are good in salads.
MEDICINAL USES	Anise hyssop is an aromatic digestant and can be taken as a tea for

Anise hyssop

Arugula

respiratory problems such as coughs. Sip a cup of tea with a meal to help prevent gas and bloating.

LANDSCAPE USES   Nice-looking flowering plant for the landscape, especially the perennial garden.

OTHER USES   Anise hyssop is a very fragrant plant; it attracts bees and produces excellent honey. It is also good for potpourri and arrangements.

INSIGHT   An easy-care herb with many uses and a sweet fragrance. It should be a part of all tea and fragrance gardens.

ANISE MARIGOLD—see **SWEET MARIGOLD**
Anthriscus cerefolium—see **CHERVIL**
Apium graveolens—see **CELERY**
Arctium lappa—see **BURDOCK**
Armoracia rusticana—see **HORSERADISH**
Artemisia abrotanum—see **SOUTHERNWOOD**
Artemisia absinthium—see **WORMWOOD**
Artemisia annua—see **SWEET ANNIE**
Artemisia dracunculus—see **TARRAGON**
Artemisia vulgaris—see **MUGWORT**

ARUGULA

Eruca vesicaria (subspecies: *sativa*)
e-RUE-ka ves-ee-CAR-ee-ah

COMMON NAMES	ARUGULA, ROQUETTE, CORN SALAD, ROCKET SALAD.
FAMILY	Brassicaceae (Cruciferae) (Mustard).
TYPE	Annual.
LOCATION	Full sun to part shade.
PLANTING	Plant in early spring and then again in late summer for the fall garden. You can do a successive planting of seeds from early September through April.
HEIGHT	Foliage to 8 inches, flowering stems to 3 feet.
SPREAD	18 inches.
FINAL SPACING	Thin to 12 inches apart.
BLOOM/FRUIT	Small, creamy yellow, four-petaled blossoms flecked with brown on tall stalks.
GROWTH HABITS/CULTURE	Arugula has a rosette growth habit. It bolts in hot weather with tall stalks. Needs moist, well-drained soil in full sun or at least morning sun. Reseeds readily.
PROBLEMS	Bolts quickly in warm weather. Harlequin bugs, flat red insects with distinctive black markings, are especially destructive in warm weather. Pick the bugs off or pull up infested plants. Caterpillars may also cause damage. Flea beetles leave numerous tiny holes on leaves. Control the insect pests with citrus products or neem. Releasing trichogramma wasps early in the spring will usually control the caterpillars.
HARVEST/STORAGE	Harvest often to keep the leaves tender and the plants full.
CULINARY USES	Arugula supposedly stimulates the taste buds so you can appreciate other flavors. It is a green salad ingredient in Italian cuisine having a peppery and nutty taste—some say a bitter taste. It's really bitter after it has flowered.
MEDICINAL USES	Arugula is a digestive aid, contains lots of vitamins, and is used as a diuretic.
LANDSCAPE USES	None—in fact, it's a pretty ratty-looking plant.
INSIGHT	Any bitter plant is a digestive aid. They should be used medicinally for only short periods of time—1 to 3 weeks.

Asclepias tuberosa—see **BUTTERFLY WEED**
ASHE JUNIPER—see **JUNIPER**
Atriplex hortensis—see **ORACH**

BALM—see **LEMON BALM**

BASIL

Ocimum basilicum
OH-see-mum ba-SEE-li-kum

COMMON NAMES	BASIL, SWEET BASIL, COMMON BASIL, ST. JOSEPHWORT.
FAMILY	Lamiaceae (Labiatae) (Mint).
TYPE	Annual.
LOCATION	Full sun or morning sun with afternoon shade.
PLANTING	Plant seed or transplants in spring after the last frost. Grows well from seed when soil and air temperatures are warm. Root stem cuttings in organic potting soil.
HEIGHT	2 to 3 feet.
SPREAD	18 inches.
FINAL SPACING	12 to 18 inches.
BLOOM/FRUIT	Small white or purple flowers in summer. It's best to keep them cut off; they are edible and good in teas.
GROWTH HABITS/CULTURE	This highly aromatic herb has square stems and soft leaves; it is easy to grow and reseeds easily. The leaves range in color from dark purple to pale green, serrated or smooth, glossy or crinkly. The flowers range from white to purple. Add unfinished compost or native cedar tree trimmings as a mulch in mid-summer to keep the purple color.

Green and purple holy basil

Purple ruffle basil

African blue basil

Garrett Juice foliar spray will also help. Pinch out flowers and growing tips to encourage a bushy shape. Use flowers in potpourri or teas. Dark opal basil is used in cooking and in potpourris; it has a heavy perfume and grows to 18 inches. Holy basil is good in potpourris.

PROBLEMS Caterpillars cause some damage—treat with *Bacillus thuringiensis* as a last resort. The fire ant control formula or garlic-pepper tea is usually all that's needed. Basil is very susceptible to frost.

HARVEST/STORAGE Make sure leaves are thoroughly dry before storage or use. Moisture promotes the growth of molds, encouraging early spoilage. If you must wash the basil leaves before mixing in oil, blot them completely dry with paper towels. Basil freezes beautifully and keeps its lovely green color, too, but it's best to use fresh.

CULINARY USES Salads, vegetables, vinegars, oils, butter for seasoning, and fragrance. Probably the most popular culinary herb.

MEDICINAL USES Basil is generally used for stomach ailments. It is good for gas and digestive problems. It has been used to kill internal parasites and to treat ringworm, insect bites, and acne. It is a sedative and antibacterial. Use it in teas and eat it fresh.

LANDSCAPE USES Summer groundcover or border plant.

OTHER USES Grows well in containers. It has been used as a mosquito repellent.

INSIGHT Avoid using during pregnancy. According to Dr. Judy Griffin, dried basil becomes carcinogenic quickly due to its high concentration of volatile oils. Use within six months or freeze the fresh leaves. The proper pronunciation rhymes with "dazzle."

BASSWOOD—see **LINDEN**

BASTARD SAFFRON—see **SAFFLOWER**

BAY

Laurus nobilis
LAR-us NO-bi-lis

COMMON NAMES	BAY, SWEET BAY, TRUE LAUREL, ROMAN LAUREL, DAPHNE.
FAMILY	Lauraceae (Laurel).
TYPE	Tender evergreen shrub or small tree.
LOCATION	Sun or partial shade.
PLANTING	Year round from containers. Take stem cuttings in late winter.
HEIGHT	50 feet in warmer climates, usually under 8 feet in the northern half of the state.
SPREAD	5 to 20 feet.
FINAL SPACING	5 to 10 feet.
BLOOM/FRUIT	Small creamy flowers in late spring, followed by shiny black berries on mature trees.
GROWTH HABITS/CULTURE	Slow-growing herb that will eventually develop into a small tree or large shrub. It needs some protection against harsh winter winds in the northern half of Texas. Easy to grow in almost any situation, but it prefers healthy, well-drained soil. Mostly grown as a dwarfed, aromatic foliage plant.
PROBLEMS	Few other than freeze damage in severe winters.

Sweet basil

Bay

HARVEST/STORAGE	Collect the evergreen leaves year round and use fresh or store the dried leaves in glass containers. Collect the fruit when mature.
CULINARY USES	Flavoring for many foods and teas. Do not eat the leaves—they can cut into intestinal tissue.
MEDICINAL USES	Oil of bay is used for skin diseases and bruises. Tea is used to treat sprains and aching joints. It is said to be mildly narcotic, a digestive aid, and an appetite stimulant.
LANDSCAPE USES	Centerpiece, patio plant, or container plant.
OTHER USES	Bay is used for potpourri, wreaths, and in stored grains to repel weevils and other insects. Leaves can also be put in cabinets to repel insect pests. Fruit oil is used in making soap.
INSIGHT	Golden bay is said to be hardier than sweet bay. It is used in the same way. Personally, I like the green form better. Native laurels, such as Texas mountain laurel, are toxic and only ornamental.

BEE BALM

Monarda didyma

mo-NAR-da DID-ih-ma

COMMON NAMES	BEE BALM, BERGAMOT, SCARLET MONARDA, BLUE BALM.
FAMILY	Lamiaceae (Labiatae) (Mint).
TYPE	Perennial.
LOCATION	Full sun.
PLANTING	Plant seed, transplants, and stolons from spring through fall.
HEIGHT	2 to 3 feet.
SPREAD	18 to 36 inches.
FINAL SPACING	12 inches.
BLOOM/FRUIT	Shaggy heads of scarlet or pink flowers above red bracts in the late summer.

Wild bergamot

Spotted bee balm

Bee balm

GROWTH HABITS/CULTURE	Spreading to 3 feet, *Monarda fistulosa* is the feathery purple wild bergamot, *Monarda alba* is white. *Monarda citriodora* is horsemint (see entry). *Monarda punctata* is white spotted bee balm.
PROBLEMS	None serious.
HARVEST/STORAGE	Gather leaves in the spring before the plant blooms; dry and store for tea. Cut the flowers for making dried arrangements and potpourri or for using in teas.
CULINARY USES	The leaves and flowers make great teas. Young leaves and flowers are used to flavor drinks, salads, and stuffings.
MEDICINAL USES	Teas for colds, fevers, and respiratory problems. Use much like the mints.
LANDSCAPE USES	Perennial garden.
OTHER USES	An excellent bee-attracting plant.
INSIGHT	It is reported that nothing browses any of the monardas—not even deer.

BEEFSTEAK PLANT—see **PERILLA**

BEGONIA

Begonia semperflorens
beh-GON-ee-ah sim-per-FLOR-enz

COMMON NAMES	BEGONIA, WAX BEGONIA.
FAMILY	Begoniaceae (Begonia).
TYPE	Annual bedding plant.
LOCATION	Partial shade to full sun.
PLANTING	Start seed indoors in the winter. Install transplants or cuttings in the spring after the last frost. It's best to plant well-rooted 4-inch transplants.
HEIGHT	6 to 15 inches.
SPREAD	12 to 18 inches.
FINAL SPACING	9 to 12 inches.
BLOOM/FRUIT	Red, pink, or white summer flowers that bloom throughout the summer. The flowers are edible.
GROWTH HABITS/CULTURE	Easy to grow and versatile. Waxy leaves and red, pink, or white summer flowers. Under an organic program, begonias will sometimes perennialize. Begonias do best in healthy, loose, organic soil. Plant the red-leaf varieties in sun to partial shade, the green-leaf varieties in partial shade to shade. Leggy plants can be cut back in summer for additional blooming. Use the Basic Organic Program and spray often with Garrett Juice.
PROBLEMS	Foliage and flowers burn when the tender varieties are placed in sunny areas. Treat slugs and cutworms with natural diatomaceous earth, hot pepper, and cedar flakes dusted under plants.
HARVEST/STORAGE	Edible flowers can be picked and eaten or used in teas at any time, with one exception. Most bedding plants are commercially grown

Begonia

using toxic pesticides and synthetic fertilizers. Unless the plants have been grown and maintained in an organic program, they will not be safe to eat.

CULINARY USES   The flowers are delicious on sherbet and other desserts, especially cold ones. They can also be used in salads and teas.

MEDICINAL USES   None.

LANDSCAPE USES   Annual bedding plant with edible flowers.

INSIGHT   The flowers of all begonias are edible.

BERGAMOT—see **BEE BALM**
BLACK WALNUT—see **WALNUT, BLACK**

BLACKBERRY

Rubus spp.
ROO-bus

COMMON NAMES   BLACKBERRY.

FAMILY   Rosaceae (Rose).

TYPE   Perennial with edible flowers and fruit.

LOCATION   Full sun.

PLANTING   Plant root cuttings in late winter at a depth of 2 inches in clay soils and 4 inches in sandy soil. Use finger-sized cuttings about 6 to 8 inches long. Store in plastic bags at 45 degrees if necessary before planting.

HEIGHT   3 to 5 feet.

SPREAD   Far and wide if you don't control the plants.

Blackberries

FINAL SPACING	24 to 36 inches apart in rows or 8 to 15 feet apart in hills. Use three plants per hill and space the hills 8 feet apart.
BLOOM/FRUIT	Small white flowers in the spring.
GROWTH HABITS/CULTURE	Easy to grow in almost any soil in full sun. Does best in healthy soil. Two-year-old canes bloom and produce fruit, then die after the fruit has matured. Prune the old canes out after harvesting because they will never produce again. Keep the plants cut to form a 3-foot-high hedge. Do not prune during the winter because the buds are formed in September.
PROBLEMS	Double blossom (rosette), anthracnose, redneck cane borer, and a few other minor problems. These are rare in an organic program. The worst problem with blackberries is their tendency to spread aggressively.
HARVEST/STORAGE	Harvest the berries as they ripen and turn dark purple. Eat right away or store in the refrigerator at 32–40 degrees for no longer than about two weeks.
CULINARY USES	Edible fruit, and the leaves are a good ingredient in tea.
MEDICINAL USES	Blackberry tea is a long-used remedy for diarrhea. It is also reported to help relieve intestinal problems. According to *Mother Nature's Herbal* by Dr. Judy Griffin, blackberry and raspberry teas are beneficial as a sedative and antispasmodic. The leaves and berries are rich in vitamin C and bioflavonoids.
LANDSCAPE USES	Not very useful in the urban landscape.

INSIGHT   Don't allow suckers at the base of plants to spread.

OTHER USES   It can be an important plant for border and fence planting and for hedgerows in vegetable gardens and agricultural fields. It is an excellent plant for creating biodiversity by giving protection to many forms of wildlife.

BLUE DANDELION—see **CHICORY**

BORAGE

Borago officinalis
bo-RA-go oh-FIS-ih-NAH-lis

COMMON NAMES   BORAGE, BURRAGE, BUGLOSS, BURAGE, STARFLOWER.

FAMILY   Boraginaceae (Forget-Me-Not or Borage).

TYPE   Annual.

LOCATION   Sun to partial shade.

PLANTING   Plant in spring after the last frost and again in early and mid-summer. Sow in the fall for flowering in late spring. Very easy to grow by seed, will reseed easily.

HEIGHT   18 to 24 inches.

SPREAD   12 to 24 inches.

FINAL SPACING   18 inches.

BLOOM/FRUIT   Flowers are bright bluish purple, five-petaled, and star-shaped with cones of black anthers.

GROWTH HABITS/CULTURE   Borage loves dry soil and full sun but can tolerate some shade. Fast-growing, fuzzy leaves, beautiful small bluish purple flowers. Leaves are 6 to 8 inches long. Stems, leaves, and flower buds are covered with silvery hairs. The plant has a long fleshy taproot and does not transplant easily. Gets floppy if not staked or cut back frequently.

PROBLEMS   Grasshoppers occasionally. Chlorosis in poor soil. Treat soil with compost, lava sand, and Texas greensand. Leaves do not freeze or dry well.

Borage

HARVEST/STORAGE	Collect the leaves when young and tender, the flowers while in bloom, and the seeds after they have matured. Leaves can be dried or frozen, flowers can be frozen, and seed can be stored dry in glass. Fresh leaves should be used whenever possible because they lose color and flavor when dried.
CULINARY USES	Cucumber flavor. Good in vinegars and cooling teas. Flowers can be used as a garnish or candied or frozen into ice cubes to add an interesting touch to punches and other iced drinks. Float flowers in drinks and teas. Leaves can be boiled and eaten. Also useful in soups. Leaves are high in mineral salts such as calcium and potassium. Young leaves and flowers can be used in salads. Seeds can be crushed and used to make tea.
MEDICINAL USES	Tea from the leaves is used to dispel melancholy and as a sedative and diuretic. Soothes bronchitis, pleurisy, and rheumatism. Reduces fevers, dry coughs, and dry-skin rashes. Borage seeds reportedly stimulate lactation in nursing mothers, aid weight loss, slow the aging process, reverse hair loss, and reduce depression. Seeds yield omega 3 essential fatty acids, which can reduce certain inflammatory conditions leading to heart disease. Borage has very high levels of gamma linolenic acid (GLA) which is effective against cancer.
LANDSCAPE USES	Good-looking decorative annual.
OTHER USES	Excellent plant for attracting bees.
INSIGHT	Borage has high mucilage content. Leaves should be eaten only in moderation. Sepals of the flowers are not edible.

Borago officinalis—see **BORAGE**

BOUNCING BET

Saponaria officinalis
sap-oh-NAR-ee-ah oh-fis-ih-NAH-lis

COMMON NAMES	BOUNCING BET, SOAPWORT, SOAP ROOT, LATHERWORT, CROW SOAP, WILD SWEET WILLIAM, FULLER'S HERB.
FAMILY	Caryophyllaceae (Pink or Carnation).
TYPE	Perennial.
LOCATION	Full sun or partial shade.
PLANTING	Plant seed in fall, root divisions in spring.
HEIGHT	1 to 2 feet.
SPREAD	2 to 3 feet
FINAL SPACING	12 to 18 inches.
BLOOM/FRUIT	Fragrant double pink and white phloxlike flowers from late spring until early fall. Blooms throughout summer.
GROWTH HABITS/CULTURE	Clumping, sun-loving plant with pale pink flowers that bloom from spring until fall. Very easy to grow in any well-drained soil; can tolerate moist soil.
PROBLEMS	Few if any.

Bouncing bet

HARVEST/STORAGE	Pick and dry flowers for potpourri anytime.
CULINARY USES	Flowers can be added to salads and to beer to produce a head.
MEDICINAL USES	Use in the wash water as a water softener to treat skin diseases.
LANDSCAPE USES	Good for the perennial garden.
OTHER USES	Cleaning materials are made from the roots, stems, and bark. Also used as a water softener. Good-looking landscape plant for shady areas. Used to clean old lace, tapestries, and other old fabrics. Beer maidens have historically used bouncing bet to clean the mugs.
INSIGHT	Easy to grow. A sturdy Texas native that loves being neglected.

Brassica spp.—see **MUSTARD**

BURDOCK

Arctium lappa
ARC-tee-um LAP-ah

COMMON NAMES	BURDOCK, BEGGAR'S BUTTONS, BURR SEED, COCKLE BUT-TONS, COCKLEBUR, GREAT BURR, THORNY BURR.
FAMILY	Asteraceae (Compositae) (Sunflower or Daisy).
TYPE	Biennial.
LOCATION	Ditches, waterways, meadows.
PLANTING	Plant seed or transplants in the spring after the last frost.
HEIGHT	6 to 8 feet.
SPREAD	3 feet.
FINAL SPACING	3 to 4 feet.
BLOOM/FRUIT	Purple flower heads with spiky bracts; resembles thistle.
GROWTH HABITS/CULTURE	Large, sprawling, invasive biennial with very large leaves. Needs lots of space.
PROBLEMS	Extremely coarse plant.

Burdock

HARVEST/STORAGE	Roots and seed in the fall.
CULINARY USES	Young leaves are used in salads and soups. Young roots and stems are eaten boiled.
MEDICINAL USES	Drink as a tea to act as a blood purifier, diuretic, and tonic. Burdock is important as a medicinal plant for treating rheumatism, gout, respiratory problems, skin irritations, cystitis, stomach problems, and kidney stones. Seeds are used in tea to treat skin problems. Pregnant women should avoid burdock.
LANDSCAPE USES	Wherever you need a big coarse plant.
OTHER USES	None.
INSIGHT	Not a plant for ordinary gardens and small spaces. Normally considered a weed.

BURNET, SALAD—see SALAD BURNET

BUTTERFLY WEED

Asclepias tuberosa
az-KLEP-ee-us too-ber-OH-sah

COMMON NAMES	BUTTERFLY WEED, PLEURISY ROOT, CANADA ROOT.
FAMILY	Asclepiadaceae (Milkweed).
TYPE	Herbaceous perennial.
LOCATION	Full sun.
PLANTING	Plant seed or transplants in the spring. Seed can be started indoors in the winter.

FRONT O
Coupts

HEIGHT	1 to 2 feet.
SPREAD	2 to 3 feet.
FINAL SPACING	12 to 18 inches.
BLOOM/FRUIT	Orangey yellow flowers. Attractive long thin seed pods. Silk connected to the seeds. Takes two seasons to bloom from seed.
GROWTH HABITS/CULTURE	Strong stems with narrow leaves. Tall and sprawling, with a long taproot. It attracts butterflies, especially monarchs, thus its name. It is a hardy member of the milkweed family. The flowers are rich in nectar and also attractive to bees. Not particular about soil but needs excellent drainage. Slow-growing and not good in pots. Does not transplant easily.
PROBLEMS	Too much water, aphids. Difficult to transplant.
HARVEST/STORAGE	Dig roots and store in glass container.
CULINARY USES	None.
MEDICINAL USES	Butterfly weed is sometimes called pleurisy root because its root has been widely used as a treatment for pleurisy. Tea made from the root is said to be a remedy for bronchitis, pneumonia, and dysentery.
LANDSCAPE USES	Showy ornamental perennial.
OTHER USES	The silk connected to the seeds is used as a pillow stuffing.
INSIGHT	Can be poisonous in large doses. All milkweeds are potentially dangerous.

Butterfly weed

CALENDULA

Calendula officinalis
ka-LEN-dew-la oh-fis-ih-NAH-lis

COMMON NAMES	POT MARIGOLD, POT HERB, CALENDULA.
FAMILY	Asteraceae (Compositae) (Sunflower or Daisy).
TYPE	Annual.
LOCATION	Full sun.
PLANTING	Transplant container plants in the fall or early spring in the northern part of the state.
HEIGHT	12 to 15 inches.
SPREAD	12 to 15 inches.
FINAL SPACING	12 inches.
BLOOM/FRUIT	Yellow to orange mum-like flowers.
GROWTH HABITS/CULTURE	Leafy, sprawling annual that likes cool weather. Easy to grow in any well-drained soil. A cool-weather plant that grows over the winter.
PROBLEMS	Hot weather.
HARVEST/STORAGE	Harvest flowers when in full bloom.

Calendula

CULINARY USES	The young hairy leaves can be used in salads and soups. Flowers can be used in rice and fish dishes.
MEDICINAL USES	Use a tea from the flowers to reduce fever, promote healing of burns, relieve ulcer problems, ease menstrual cramps, and treat skin diseases. Taken internally, calendula stimulates the liver and is said to reduce alcoholics' cravings. Flower petals provide a yellow dye and soothing eyewash. Flower petals are used in homeopathy.
LANDSCAPE USES	Beautiful cool-season annual. Good container plant.
OTHER USES	Dry flowers are used in potpourri.
INSIGHT	One of those plants that should be used more in organic herb gardens.

Capsicum spp.—see **PEPPER**

CARAWAY

Carum carvi
KA-rum CAR-vee

COMMON NAMES	CARAWAY.
FAMILY	Apiaceae (Umbelliferae) (Carrot or Parsley).
TYPE	Biennial.
LOCATION	Full sun.
PLANTING	Plant seed directly in the garden from late summer through fall, transplants in the early spring.
HEIGHT	18 to 30 inches.
SPREAD	8 inches.
FINAL SPACING	12 inches.
BLOOM/FRUIT	Umbels of small white flowers. Seed are brown and ribbed.
GROWTH HABITS/CULTURE	A hardy biennial with a pleasing informal look. Finely cut thread-like leaves and creamy white flowers in umbels. Plants die after the seeds ripen in mid-summer. Does not transplant well but is easy to grow in any well-drained soil. Its culture is similar to dill.
PROBLEMS	Few if any.
HARVEST/STORAGE	Harvest the seed just before they start to drop—as they start to turn brown.
CULINARY USES	Mild flavor—between dill and parsley. Used in teas, breads, cookies, candy, cakes, meat dishes, vegetables, soups, salads, and liqueurs. Parsnip-like roots are edible. Dip a piece of apple in the seeds. Use leaves in salads. Use the seeds to flavor pork, sauerkraut, cheese, pickles, and cabbage.
MEDICINAL USES	Eat the seeds as an appetite suppressant, to mask the taste of medicines, and to sweeten the breath. Also serves as a digestive aid.
LANDSCAPE USES	Flowers attract beneficial insects, including honeybees.
OTHER USES	To make caraway tea, crush 2 tablespoons seed in a mortar and pestle and put in a teapot of boiling water, steep for 7–10 minutes. Sweeten with honey.
INSIGHT	Start seed in the fall in order to harvest seed in the spring.

Caraway

Cardamom

CARDAMOM

Elettaria cardamomum
el-eh-TAR-ree-ah kar-da-MO-mum

COMMON NAMES	CARDAMOM.
FAMILY	Zingiberaceae (Ginger).
TYPE	Perennial.
LOCATION	Full sun to dappled shade.
PLANTING	Plant transplants in spring or anytime in protected pots.
HEIGHT	3 to 5 feet or taller.
SPREAD	3 to 5 feet.
FINAL SPACING	24 to 30 inches.
BLOOM/FRUIT	Aromatic green fruits follow dramatic violet-striped white flowers.
GROWTH HABITS/CULTURE	Easy to grow, spreads by rhizomes. Resembles ginger, with beautiful yellow, pink, and lavender flowers. Likes moist, well-drained soil.
PROBLEMS	Freezes out easily.
HARVEST/STORAGE	Harvest seed when mature.
CULINARY USES	Seeds are used to flavor coffee, breads, and cakes.
MEDICINAL USES	Seeds are eaten to stimulate circulation, aid digestion, relieve gas, and sweeten the breath. Tea from the rhizome is used to relieve fatigue and fever. Reported to help with common colds, fevers, and bronchitis.

LANDSCAPE USES The foliage provides interesting contrast. Won't survive the winters in most of Texas. Can be dramatic in the perennial garden.

OTHER USES Excellent houseplant when given plenty of light.

INSIGHT Likes plenty of water but requires little care. A support is often needed to prevent wind damage unless it is planted in a protected place. Doesn't flower or set seed every year.

CARDOON

Cynara cardunculus
sigh-NAH-ra car-doon-KEW-lus

COMMON NAMES CARDOON.

FAMILY Asteraceae (Compositae) (Sunflower or Daisy).

TYPE Tender herbaceous perennial.

LOCATION Full sun.

Cardoon

PLANTING	Sow seed two weeks before the average last frost or start the seed indoors and transplant outdoors after there is no chance of a freeze.
HEIGHT	6 to 8 feet.
SPREAD	4 to 5 feet.
FINAL SPACING	3 to 4 feet.
BLOOM/FRUIT	Cardoon forms dramatic purple flowers that resemble thistle.
GROWTH HABITS/CULTURE	Large, dramatic plant that should normally be treated as an annual. It has huge gray-green, deeply cut, fuzzy leaves. It likes deep, moist soil during the growing season but will rot in wet soil in the winter. Needs about the same conditions as celery.
PROBLEMS	Can't stand wet feet. Grows very large, not suitable for small herb gardens.
HARVEST/STORAGE	Harvest the leaf stalks as needed and use fresh.
CULINARY USES	Chop the leaf stalks into small pieces and add to soups and stews. The pieces can also be pureed for dips or steamed for salads.
MEDICINAL USES	Leaves, roots, and flowers have been used historically to detoxify the liver, gallbladder, and blood. The leaves contain cynarin, which is the medicinally potent part of the plant.
LANDSCAPE USES	Cardoon makes a dramatic or decorative specimen or a backdrop plant for larger herb gardens.
OTHER USES	Some herbalists say that cardoon can be used to make a yellow dye.
INSIGHT	Mice like the seed, so be careful with the propagation location. Some gardeners like to wrap the young plants with cardboard or other material to blanch the stems. Blanching doesn't make much sense to me. It does make the stalks tenderer, but it removes chlorophyll, vitamins, and minerals. Cardoon is a very close relative of the edible globe artichoke.

Carthamus tinctorius—see **SAFFLOWER**
Carum carvi—see **CARAWAY**

CATNIP

Nepeta cataria
NAY-peh-tah ka-TAH-ree-ah

COMMON NAMES	CATNIP.
FAMILY	Lamiaceae (Labiatae) (Mint).
TYPE	Perennial.
LOCATION	Full sun to dappled shade.
PLANTING	Seeds, transplants, and divisions can be planted year round, but the best time is early spring.
HEIGHT	18 to 24 inches.
SPREAD	36 to 48 inches.
FINAL SPACING	12 to 18 inches.
BLOOM/FRUIT	Mauve to white flowers in summer. Keep flowers cut off to keep tiny seed from spreading or use them as cut flowers in the house.

Catnip

Catmint

GROWTH HABITS/CULTURE	Catnip has gray-green foliage and bushy growth. Catmint is a woodier and more compact plant with tiny gray leaves. Catnip has a hot peppery flavor. Keep it cut back and don't allow it to flower. Both are easy to grow.
PROBLEMS	Cats go nutty for it.
HARVEST/STORAGE	Harvest and dry foliage before it flowers. The best time is August and September.
CULINARY USES	Good sleep-inducing or social tea.
MEDICINAL USES	Traditional baby tea for colic. Will also reduce fever. A sedative tea that is soothing to the nerves.
LANDSCAPE USES	Tall, gray-leafed groundcover.
OTHER USES	Toys for cats. A tea of catnip or the dried and crushed powder is somewhat effective at repelling roaches and other pests. Research at Iowa State University has shown that catnip can be used to repel insects more effectively than toxic chemicals.
INSIGHT	Stick it in the ground and forget it. Catnip is one of the easiest of all the herbs to grow. *Nepeta mussinii* is catmint. Cats are not as attracted to it as they are to catnip.

CAT THYME

Teucrium marum
TOO-kree-um MAH-rum

COMMON NAMES	CAT THYME.
FAMILY	Labiatae.
TYPE	Tender perennial.
LOCATION	Full sun.
PLANTING	Start cuttings in spring or fall. Install transplants year round.
HEIGHT	Up to 24 inches.
SPREAD	12 inches.
FINAL SPACING	18 inches.
BLOOM/FRUIT	Small purple-pink flowers in summer.

GROWTH HABITS/CULTURE	Small hardy shrub with small gray-green leaves. Very pungent.
PROBLEMS	Few if any.
HARVEST/STORAGE	Dry and store leaves and root bark for medicinal use.
CULINARY USES	None.
MEDICINAL USES	Cat thyme is used as a stimulant and astringent as well as for nervous complaints and weight control. Steep in wine or take as a tea.
LANDSCAPE USES	Attractive as an accent plant or a small hedge. Cats love it.
OTHER USES	Toys for cats.
INSIGHT	Long-term use (over three weeks) could damage the liver. A good container plant.

Cat thyme

CEDAR—see **JUNIPER**

CELERIAC

Apium graveolens var. *rapaceum*
A-pee-um gra-vay-OH-lenz var. ra-PAH-kee-um

COMMON NAMES	CELERIAC.
FAMILY	Apiaceae (Umbelliferae) (Carrot or Parsley).
TYPE	Biennial.
PLANTING	Plant from seed in the fall.
HEIGHT	12 inches.
SPREAD	6 to 8 inches.
FINAL SPACING	6 inches.
BLOOM/FRUIT	Should not be allowed to flower.
GROWTH HABITS/CULTURE	Needs rich soil, excellent drainage, and early fall planting. Makes a knob above ground with leaf cluster and flower stem above.
PROBLEMS	Doesn't like the Texas heat.
HARVEST/STORAGE	Harvest and use fresh.
CULINARY USES	Use knobs in salads, soups, and other dishes. Very good in salads. Makes a good snack. Use leaves as you would celery. Its root is also edible.
MEDICINAL USES	Celeriac functions as a sedative and diuretic when eaten.
LANDSCAPE USES	None.
OTHER USES	Seeds mixed with salt make a celery salt. Always use sea salt.
INSIGHT	In most areas of the South, celeriac should be planted in late summer or early fall, whether started from seed or seedlings. The celery-flavored leaves are a great addition to the soup pot and salad bowl. It will taste bitter if conditions are too hot and the soil lacks trace minerals. Celeriac is easier to grow than celery.

CELERY

Apium graveolens var. *dulce*

A-pee-um gra-vay-OH-lenz var. dul-KEE

COMMON NAMES	CELERY, SMALLAGE, WILD CELERY.
FAMILY	Apiaceae (Umbelliferae) (Carrot or Parsley).
TYPE	Biennial.
LOCATION	Sun or part shade; grows best in shade.
PLANTING	Can be planted from seed in early spring, but the best time for planting is fourteen to sixteen weeks before the average first frost for the fall garden. Transplants work well for the home gardener.
HEIGHT	12 to 15 inches.
SPREAD	6 to 8 inches.
FINAL SPACING	8 inches.
BLOOM/FRUIT	The white flowers shouldn't be allowed to form.
GROWTH HABITS/CULTURE	Cool-weather plant. Relatively easy to grow in the cool weather of the spring and fall. Will freeze during harsh winters. Prevent moisture stress on young plants. Improve the soil with lots of compost, lava sand, and Texas greensand.
PROBLEMS	Hot weather, calcium deficiency, and boron deficiency. Not that easy to grow.
HARVEST/STORAGE	Collect seeds in the fall when ripe. Collect the leaves and stalks anytime, allow to dry and store in glass containers.
CULINARY USES	Use in salads, soups, tuna dishes, and with other foods. Blends well with other herbs.
MEDICINAL USES	Eat often to help arthritis and rheumatism. Celery is a diuretic, sedative, digestive aid, and stimulant that contains iron, magnesium, vitamin C, and carotene.
LANDSCAPE USES	None.
OTHER USES	Used in facial masks to help keep the skin supple.
INSIGHT	Celeriac (*Apium graveolens* var. *rapaceum*) is the knob-rooted variety and is sometimes sold as celery root.

Centella asiatica—see **GOTU KOLA**

Chamaemelum nobile—see **CHAMOMILE**

CHAMOMILE

Chamaemelum nobile

ka-mee-MAY-lum NO-bill

COMMON NAMES	CHAMOMILE, ROMAN CHAMOMILE, GROUND APPLE, WHIG PLANT.
FAMILY	Asteraceae (Compositae) (Sunflower or Daisy).
TYPE	Usually considered an annual, although it can perennialize.
LOCATION	Full sun to dappled shade.
PLANTING	Plant from seed in the late winter or use transplants in the early spring. It will take some frost but not a lot.

Chamomile

HEIGHT	18 inches.
SPREAD	36 inches.
FINAL SPACING	12 inches.
BLOOM/FRUIT	White flowers with a yellow, cone-shaped center.
GROWTH HABITS/CULTURE	Delicate fern-like foliage and small white daisy-like flowers. Easy to grow in any well-drained soil.
PROBLEMS	Caterpillars and slugs. Spray the worms with a citrus-based product or Bt product as a last resort. To control the slugs, sprinkle a mix of natural diatomaceous earth, hot pepper, and cedar flakes under problem plants.
HARVEST/STORAGE	Cut the flowers when in full bloom, dry and store in a cool place. The fresh flowers are more potent and make a delicious tea during the growing season.
CULINARY USES	Social tea and children's tea.
MEDICINAL USES	Sleep-inducing tea. The flowers are primarily used, but leaves can also be used. Chamomile has been used to treat gout, indigestion, headache, and colic. Dried flowers in a tea will help relieve indigestion, nausea, nightmares, and insomnia. It can increase appetite, help smokers stop smoking, and benefit the kidneys and spleen. Chamomile tea has also been used to treat menstrual problems, asthma, diarrhea, gallstones, toothache, and ear infections. Pregnant women should limit their intake and avoid totally if they have a history of miscarriage.

LANDSCAPE USES Perennial flowers. Sometimes used as a low mass planting. Attracts beneficial insects.

OTHER USES Shampoos of this herb have been used to highlight blonde hair. In the garden it reportedly helps revive nearby ailing plants. According to *Mother Nature's Herbal*, it keeps mint from spreading.

INSIGHT Avoid excessive use of chamomile. Persons allergic to ragweed, asters, or mums should avoid chamomile.

CHAPARRAL—see **CREOSOTE BUSH**

CHAYA

Cnidoscolus chayamansa
NY-DOS-co-lus chi-ah-MAN-sah

COMMON NAMES CHAYA, SPINACH TREE, TREE SPINACH.

FAMILY Euphorbiaceae (Spurge).

TYPE Tropical.

LOCATION Sun.

PLANTING Plant from cuttings or transplants in the spring.

HEIGHT 7 to 15 feet.

SPREAD 3 to 5 feet.

FINAL SPACING Don't need but one.

BLOOM/FRUIT Clusters of white flowers about 3 inches in diameter. Blooms intermittently throughout summer. No fruit or seed.

GROWTH HABITS/CULTURE Native to southern Mexico and Central America. Upright fast growth. Likes rich fertile soil and ample moisture. Can be grown in containers. Dark green leathery leaves are lobed like castor bean leaves but are smaller. Best location is one with morning sun or full sun. Low fertilizer requirements.

Chaya

PROBLEMS | Will sometimes freeze outdoors in Texas winters. Leaves can be toxic until cooked. Rodents like it because of the high protein. No serious insect or disease pests. Even cooked it can be toxic.

HARVEST/STORAGE | Pick leaves fresh in the summer and cook.

CULINARY USES | Cook as spinach and use in quiche or soups. Contains up to 33 percent protein. The typical Mayan dish called *tzotobilchay* or Brazo de Reina is prepared with cornmeal, chaya, chopped boiled eggs, pumpkin seeds, and spices.

MEDICINAL USES | Chaya is nutritious—high in protein, carbohydrates, beta-carotene, calcium, iron, phosphorus, and vitamins A, B, C, and others. It also contains essential amino acids and has more good stuff than spinach or alfalfa. It helps to harden fingernails and is used in a general body tonic. It has been used to combat blindness in children and to treat obesity, high cholesterol, diabetes, arthritis, kidney stones, and poor circulation.

LANDSCAPE USES | Makes an attractive summer foliage plant. It is considered a tropical plant but has perennialized fairly well here in Texas.

INSIGHT | The native people of the Yucatan Peninsula and Central America have eaten chaya for thousands of years. Several U.S. herbalists consider it dangerous to eat.

Chenopodium album—see **LAMB'S-QUARTER**
Chenopodium ambrosioides—see **EPAZOTE**

CHERVIL

Anthriscus cerefolium
an-THRIS-kus kay-ree-FOE-lee-um

COMMON NAMES | CHERVIL, GOURMET PARSLEY.

FAMILY | Apiaceae (Umbelliferae) (Carrot or Parsley).

TYPE | Annual.

LOCATION | Partial shade is best.

PLANTING | Plant transplants or seed in the fall.

HEIGHT | Up to 2 feet.

SPREAD | 6 inches.

FINAL SPACING | 6 to 12 inches.

BLOOM/FRUIT | Umbels of tiny white flowers in early summer.

GROWTH HABITS/CULTURE | Leafy annual herb that readily self-seeds. Branched hollow stems and bright green, finely textured leaves that look like Italian parsley. Likes cool weather and partial shade; can tolerate some frost. Will bolt during the first warm days of spring. Keep well watered to prevent premature seeding.

PROBLEMS | None serious.

HARVEST/STORAGE | Harvest anytime. Best to use fresh from the garden.

CULINARY USES | Use like parsley in salads, soups, sauces, and garnishes. Flavor has a hint of licorice.

Chervil

Chicory

MEDICINAL USES	Eat or use as a tea to help purify the body. Chervil is a mild digestive, helps circulation, and can soothe painful joints. The leaves contain vitamin C, carotene, iron, and magnesium. Chervil is also said to reduce phlegm, alleviate liver problems, and improve the skin.
LANDSCAPE USES	Too short-lived for large areas.
INSIGHT	Blends well with other herbs.

CHICORY

Cichorium intybus
ki-KO-ree-um IN-tew-bus

COMMON NAMES	CHICORY, BLUE DANDELION.
FAMILY	Asteraceae (Compositae) (Sunflower or Daisy).
TYPE	Perennial.
LOCATION	Full sun.
PLANTING	From seed in early spring or from transplants later. Can also be planted in the fall in the southern half of the state.
HEIGHT	To 3 feet.
SPREAD	18 to 24 inches.
FINAL SPACING	18 inches.
BLOOM/FRUIT	Lots of small, light blue flowers with fluted petals. Blooms in summer.
GROWTH HABITS/CULTURE	Easy to grow, has a deep taproot. Related to sunflowers and grows like endive. Each bloom lasts only till noon. Tolerates drought, likes cool weather. Start seed early. Does well in alkaline soils.
PROBLEMS	Few if any. Earwigs are sometimes a problem, but they can be controlled with citrus-based sprays. Other pests can be controlled with regular foliar feeding and healthy soil.
HARVEST/STORAGE	Use the leaves fresh. Split the root to dry.

CULINARY USES
: The root is steamed as a vegetable or roasted and mixed with coffee to counteract its stimulant effect or substituted for coffee altogether. Use the leaves in salads and the flowers to garnish salads. Buds, which are eaten pickled, have a peppery flavor. Popular as a coffee substitute in Louisiana.

MEDICINAL USES
: Digestive tonic, mildly diuretic. Good for skin problems.

LANDSCAPE USES
: Easy-to-grow summer flowers.

OTHER USES
: Leaves are a bitter Passover herb and yield a blue dye. Research from the USDA-ARS Appalachian Farming Systems Research Center has found that chicory works as a biological sponge to soak up excess nitrogen and other nutrients from the soil.

INSIGHT
: All bitter herbs are good for digestion. Radicchio is the red-leafed chicory.

CHINESE PARSLEY—see **CORIANDER**

CHIVES

Allium schoenoprasum—**ONION CHIVES**
AL-lee-um skoyn-o-PRAH-sum
Allium tuberosum—**GARLIC CHIVES**
AL-lee-um tew-bah-ROE-sum

COMMON NAMES
: ONION CHIVES, CHIVES, GARLIC CHIVES.

FAMILY
: Liliaceae (Lily).

TYPE
: Hardy perennial.

LOCATION
: Full sun to partial shade.

PLANTING
: Seed can be started indoors anytime. Plant seed or divisions in the fall and early spring, transplants in the spring.

HEIGHT
: 12 to 18 inches.

SPREAD
: 6 to 12 inches.

FINAL SPACING
: 6 to 12 inches.

Garlic chives

Onion chives

BLOOM/FRUIT	Onion chives have pink or purple flowers in spring or early summer. Garlic chives have white flowers and bloom in late summer.
GROWTH HABITS/CULTURE	Garlic chives have flat leaves, onion chives have hollow round leaves. Clumps should last four to five years before dividing.
PROBLEMS	None serious. Wet soil can cause root disease. Occasional slug and snail damage. If you let chives go to seed, they will spread everywhere.
HARVEST/STORAGE	Cut and use fresh or dry for soup mixtures. Harvest by pinching off at the base to prevent unsightly brown stubs. Cut chives just before use to preserve the vitamins, aroma, and flavor. Prepare using kitchen shears rather than mortar and pestle or knives. Cooking chives will destroy the herb's Vitamin C and digestive properties. Drying causes a loss of flavor.
CULINARY USES	Seasoning for butters, salads, soups, and other foods. Leaves used for vinegars and breads. Cut the flowers off when growing the plant for culinary use. Especially good on baked potatoes and in scrambled eggs. Flowers can be added to salads and make a beautiful salad vinegar that is rosy red.
MEDICINAL USES	Chives have mild diuretic and antibacterial properties. They also have laxative and digestive powers. The high vitamin C content is good for colds and respiratory problems. Foliage and flowers are also high in vitamin A, folic acid (a B vitamin), and potassium. Chives are said to help alleviate stomach problems and protect against heart disease and stroke. Recent research has shown that chives can stimulate the digestion of fat and may help control cholesterol.
LANDSCAPE USES	Good border or window box plant. Easy to grow in small pots and other containers. Both onion and garlic chives are good-looking landscape plants.
OTHER USES	Dried flowers can be used for wreaths and dried arrangements.
INSIGHT	For the best flavor and food value, add fresh-cut chives to food just before serving. Society garlic (*Talbaghia violacea*) is a similar herb with lilac flowers. All are extremely easy to grow.

Society garlic

Chrysanthemum balsamita—see **COSTMARY**
Chrysanthemum cinerariifolium—see **PYRETHRUM**
Chrysanthemum parthenium—see **FEVERFEW**

CICELY

Myrrhis odorata
MI-ris o-do-RAH-ta

COMMON NAMES	SWEET CICELY, MYRRH, CICELY, SWEET CHERVIL, ANISE FERN, SWEET FERN, BRITISH MYRRH.
FAMILY	Apiaceae (Umbelliferae) (Carrot or Parsley).
TYPE	Perennial.
LOCATION	Shade.
PLANTING	Plant seed or divisions in spring or fall. Precooled seeds germinate in about half the time. Seeds planted in the fall make seedlings in the spring.
HEIGHT	3 feet.
SPREAD	18 inches.
FINAL SPACING	12 to 18 inches.
BLOOM/FRUIT	Creamy white umbels in spring and early summer.
GROWTH HABITS/CULTURE	Cicely grows upright and has a licorice or anise fragrance, spicy green seeds, and pungent roots. The fern-like, anise-scented foliage looks good in shade or partially shaded locations. It is one of the first plants to produce new growth in the spring, and it holds its foliage until mid-winter.
PROBLEMS	It's a little too hot for this herb in Texas. It has a tendency to fall over and sprawl.
HARVEST/STORAGE	Harvest in spring before flowering. Do not save seeds for more than one year.
CULINARY USES	Use like parsley or chervil in salads and other dishes. Use as a sugar substitute for diabetics. Leaves are cooked with acid fruits to reduce their tartness. Chop and add to omelettes, soups, and fruit salads. Roots are used in salads or pickled or cooked. The anise-scented leaves and the green seeds are eaten raw. Ripe seeds are used for flavoring but usually not eaten.
MEDICINAL USES	Mild antiseptic, tonic, and digestive. Also used to treat anemia in the elderly. Drink tea or eat in salads.
LANDSCAPE USES	None.
OTHER USES	Cut-flower arrangements and potpourri.

Cichorium intybus—see **CHICORY**
CILANTRO—see **CORIANDER**

CITRUS

Citrus spp.

SIT-rus

COMMON NAMES	CITRUS.
FAMILY	Rutaceae (Citrus or Rue).
TYPE	Tropical evergreen trees: orange, grapefruit, lemon, lime, tangerine, kumquat.
LOCATION	Full sun.
PLANTING	Seed or stem cuttings can be planted anytime as long as they are protected from freezing weather. Best to plant in warm soil and warm weather in the spring but can be grown in pots.
HEIGHT	Varies greatly.
SPREAD	Varies greatly.
FINAL SPACING	Varies greatly.
BLOOM/FRUIT	Fragrant white flowers in spring followed by summer fruit.
GROWTH HABITS/CULTURE	Citrus trees like healthy, well-drained, slightly acidic soil. Plant all citrus high, with the graft union well above the soil line. Citrus needs

Citrus

Thai lime

little or no pruning; in fact, pruning is detrimental to fruit production. If citrus is left outdoors in the northern part of the state, a greenhouse-like structure with heat must be provided. In most of the state, it's best to grow citrus in containers. Protect in the winter, move plants outside into the sun when the temperature is over 30 degrees. Citrus matures in four to five years.

PROBLEMS   To prevent soil and root diseases, treat the soil with cornmeal and follow the Basic Organic Program. Use citrus pulp for root knot nematodes.

HARVEST/STORAGE   Fruit ripens in late summer. Use while fresh. Store in a cool place if necessary. Freeze peelings for later use in teas. Stems should be cut, not pulled. Eating the fruit fresh from the tree is, of course, best. The flowers that form in the summer can be harvested and eaten anytime. Fruit can be stored on the tree. After ripe and removed from the tree, store above 50 degrees. Will keep two to six weeks.

CULINARY USES   Peelings of citrus are used to flavor food and drinks and to provide Vitamin C. Citrus flowers, especially those of orange and lemon trees, are edible and make good teas, as are grated peelings. Make sure the fruit is organically grown because the pesticides collect in the flowers and rind. Add the leaves of grapefruit, lemon, lime, kumquat, or orange to rice, soups, or stews. Seeds of various citrus will grow into decorative plants for leaf harvest. Quality of fruit will be a mystery.

MEDICINAL USES   Orange peel is used as a diuretic and digestive aid. I use organically grown oranges and other citrus peelings in my herb teas.

LANDSCAPE USES   Tropical evergreen trees. Grow on the south side of the house so plastic can be pulled down from the eave to make a greenhouse-type shelter in winter; move potted plants into a greenhouse or grow in a greenhouse year round. In general, citrus grown in Texas will bear fruit only on the spring bloom. Satsuma is the one most often recommended citrus trees for pots, but it still needs protection in the winter. Chang Sa, a tangerine, is hardier and has a much better flavor. It will also come true from seed and grows well on its own root system. *Citrus hystrix*, commonly called kaffir lime, thai lime, or lime leaf, has very interesting double leaves and a lemony taste and makes an excellent ingredient for herb tea.

OTHER USES   Fruit and fruit juice. Essential oils from the peelings are used in cosmetic and perfumes. Seed oils are used in soaps.

CLOVER

Trifolium spp.
Trifolium pratense—**RED CLOVER**
tri-FO-lee-um pray-TENSE
Trifolium repens—**DUTCH WHITE CLOVER**
tri-FO-lee-um REP-enz

COMMON NAMES   CLOVER.

FAMILY   Fabaceae (Leguminosae) (Legume).

Young white clover seedlings

Mature dwarf white clover

TYPE	Perennial groundcover legume.
LOCATION	Full sun to fairly heavy shade.
PLANTING	Clover is easily grown from seed planted in the fall.
HEIGHT	6 to 24 inches.
SPREAD	Creeper.
FINAL SPACING	1 pound of seed per 1,000 square feet or 30 to 40 pounds per acre.
BLOOM/FRUIT	Red clover has red flowers in the spring, Dwarf white clover white flowers in the spring and early summer. Both are fragrant and attract beneficial insects.
GROWTH HABITS/CULTURE	White clover is easy to grow in any soil, the red clover prefers a sandier soil. Clovers have creeping stems and three-part, dark green leaves. Roots form at the joints of the stems. Clover is a deeply rooted short-lived perennial that needs to be reseeded from time to time.
PROBLEMS	Usually considered a weed but should be encouraged.
HARVEST/STORAGE	Harvest the flowers when in full bloom; use fresh or dry and store in glass containers for later use.
CULINARY USES	Clover flowers are used to make teas. They blend well with other herbs.
MEDICINAL USES	According to Dr. Judy Griffin's *Mother Nature's Herbal*, clover is a blood coagulant and relieves spasmodic coughing. The tea is said to stimulate the liver and gallbladder. According to Lesley Bremness in *Herbs*, red clover is used as an anti-inflammatory cleansing treatment for skin problems and arthritis. There is some indication that clover in teas can be used to treat various cancers.
LANDSCAPE USES	Clover, especially white clover, makes a good groundcover, attracts pollinator insects, and is the source of high-quality sweet honey.
OTHER USES	Finding four-leafed clovers!
INSIGHT	Clover is one of the plants that has been demonized by the organiphobes. They recommend spraying it all with broadleaf herbicides that contaminate the environment and waste a beautiful and valuable plant.

Coleus amboinicus—see **CUBAN OREGANO**

COMFREY

Symphytum officinale
sim-FI-tum oh-fish-ih-NAL-lee

COMMON NAMES	COMFREY, KNITBONE, ASS EAR, HEALING HERB, BLACK ROOT.
FAMILY	Boraginaceae (Forget-Me-Not or Borage).
TYPE	Perennial.
LOCATION	Partial shade to full sun.
PLANTING	Year-round planting of transplants or root divisions.
HEIGHT	24 to 36 inches.
SPREAD	36 to 48 inches or more.
FINAL SPACING	24 to 36 inches.
BLOOM/FRUIT	Bell-shaped flowers in several colors.
GROWTH HABITS/CULTURE	Deep-rooted, tough, spreading perennial. Large bristly leaves 8 to 18 inches long with light blue, pink, or red bell-like flowers in spring and summer. Needs ample water but that's about it. Comfrey is very easy to grow. It will do better in healthy soil and grows best in locations with morning sun and afternoon shade.
PROBLEMS	Can be invasive. Roots are tenacious and, once established, difficult to dig up. Small pieces will generate new plants.
HARVEST/STORAGE	Cut and use leaves and stems anytime. Concentrated tea for animal skin problems should be kept refrigerated.
CULINARY USES	Should not be taken internally.
MEDICINAL USES	Topical treatment of rashes, scrapes, and especially insect bites and stings. High in calcium, phosphorus, potassium, and trace minerals. Poultices made with the juice from leaves and stems are used to remove warts and other growths and to treat poison ivy. Comfrey can be used as a rinse for skin problems on pets. Infused oil is used to treat arthritis, skin wounds, and diseases such as psoriasis.

Comfrey

Comfrey

LANDSCAPE USES   Handsome specimen perennial.

OTHER USES   Good-looking coarse-textured perennial for the landscape. Old leaves are excellent for the compost pile. Infused oil is said to make a good antiwrinkle cosmetic.

INSIGHT   USP (U.S. Pharmacopeia) advisory panelists have determined that the internal use of comfrey—a botanical, or plant-based, dietary supplement—can be harmful. Reports of liver damage in humans and animals after the use of comfrey, and the lack of adequate scientific evidence in medical and scientific literature that supports the safe use of comfrey, have prompted USP to issue a negative monograph discouraging its use. USP emphasizes the dangers of the use of comfrey by children, pregnant or nursing women, and people with liver disease. Medical literature indicates that these people may be especially susceptible to comfrey's toxic effects. USP also advises that comfrey should not be taken with any other medication or when a serious medical condition is present. The use of topical comfrey on broken skin also should be avoided because of the possibility of systemic absorption. (According to Dr. Judy Griffin, this risk is minimal because comfrey is very healing to wounds due to its allantoin content.) Studies have reported the development of cancerous liver tumors and liver damage in animals after ingesting or being injected with various amounts of comfrey. There are also reports of liver damage in humans after oral comfrey long- and short-term use (a few weeks to several months) in various amounts and forms (leaves, roots, and pills). A leaflet about comfrey is available from USP's Web site at www.usp.org/ddd/mgraphs/botanica. The full comfrey monograph, containing tables outlining the principal constituents of comfrey, along with references, is available from USP's Document Disclosure Department. In short, comfrey is a very powerful and important herb that shouldn't be overused or misused.

COMMON BASIL—see **BASIL**
COMMON GARDEN SAGE—see **SAGE**

CORIANDER

Coriandrum sativum
ko-ree-AN-drum sa-TEE-vum

COMMON NAMES	CORIANDER, CHINESE PARSLEY, CILANTRO.
FAMILY	Apiaceae (Umbelliferae) (Carrot or Parsley).
TYPE	Annual.
LOCATION	Full sun or morning sun with afternoon shade.
PLANTING	Sow seeds in the fall, thin seedlings to 12 inches apart. Halloween is the best time to plant for most gardeners. The taproot makes transplanting difficult once the plant is established.
HEIGHT	18 to 24 inches.
SPREAD	18 to 24 inches.
FINAL SPACING	12 to 15 inches.
BLOOM/FRUIT	Umbels of small white flowers in late spring or early summer.
GROWTH HABITS/CULTURE	The entire plant is pungently aromatic. Original leaves are flat and wide, resembling Italian parsley; they become feathery as white or

Coriander—cilantro

Costmary

mauve flowers appear with umbrella-shaped clusters of round seeds. Very easy to grow from seed in any well-drained soil. Likes lots of compost and other organic amendments.

PROBLEMS	Weevils may attack dried seeds. Store with bay leaves.
HARVEST/STORAGE	Cut and use the foliage anytime. Collect the seed when they mature and turn brown.
CULINARY USES	Seed is delicious raw. Use the fresh foliage in salads and with various meat dishes. Roots can be used to flavor curries.
MEDICINAL USES	Tea is taken to help avoid flatulence, ointment is used for arthritis and in massage oils. Coriander is also good for preventing or relieving indigestion. The seed is the most powerful part of the plant.
LANDSCAPE USES	Very little because it gets ratty-looking.
OTHER USES	Coriander can serve as a meat preservative.
INSIGHT	Attracts beneficial insects and deters harmful ones with its strong odor. Hard to transplant. Cilantro is the Spanish word for this herb.

Coriandrum sativum—see **CORIANDER**

COSTMARY

Chrysanthemum balsamita
kris-ANTH-ee-mum bal-sa-MEE-tah

COMMON NAMES	COSTMARY, ALECOST, BIBLE LEAF, SWEET MAUDELINE.
FAMILY	Asteraceae (Compositae) (Sunflower or Daisy).
TYPE	Hardy perennial.
LOCATION	Sun to part shade.
PLANTING	Plant seed or root divisions in early spring.
HEIGHT	18 to 24 inches.
SPREAD	24 inches.
FINAL SPACING	12 to 18 inches.
BLOOM/FRUIT	Small pale yellow flowers.
GROWTH HABITS/CULTURE	Oval, scalloped, silvery green leaves and small yellow flowers. Leafy herb forming upright clumps. Leaves and flowers are mint-scented. The plant becomes leggy if allowed to develop flowers. Plant on the east side of the house to get the morning sun and afternoon shade.
PROBLEMS	Center of the plant sometimes dies out. Cornmeal in the soil around the plant will help with this fungus problem.
HARVEST/STORAGE	Dry the leaves and store in a dry place in glass containers.
CULINARY USES	Leaves are good in scrambled eggs. Has been used to make ale. Leaves give a tang to salads, soups, and wild game. Tender young leaves are best for cooking and making teas.
MEDICINAL USES	Taken as a tea, it acts as an astringent and antiseptic, relieves dysentery, and helps with liver and gallbladder problems. It is reported to relieve colds, phlegm, upset stomachs, and cramps.
LANDSCAPE USES	Good foliage plant for the perennial garden.

OTHER USES   Aromatic leaves are sometimes used as bookmarks and in potpourri. Also used to make herb pillows but reportedly causes weird dreams.

INSIGHT   An interesting plant that should be grown more widely. Also sold as *Balsamita major*.

CREEPING THYME—see THYME

CREOSOTE BUSH

Larrea tridentata
LA-ree-ah tri-den-TAH-dah

COMMON NAMES   CREOSOTE BUSH, CHAPARRAL, GREASEWOOD.

FAMILY   Zygophyllaceae (Caltrop).

TYPE   Evergreen bush.

LOCATION   Full sun.

PLANTING   Plant seed after drilling a hole or filing a notch in the hard seed coating. Germination can also be improved by hulling the seeds or soaking them in water or sanding them with sandpaper. Plant some seeds in the fall and more in the spring. I'm not sure which works better.

HEIGHT   3 to 10 feet.

SPREAD   8 to 10 feet.

FINAL SPACING   3 to 5 feet.

BLOOM/FRUIT   Twisted gray stems with small, strongly scented, resinous leaves. Beautiful yellow dime-size flowers cover the plant in the spring followed by pea-size white fruit.

GROWTH HABITS/CULTURE   Creosote bush has a distinctive fragrance after a rain. It is a bushy plant with small, olive green leaves and an open appearance. Needs loose, well-drained soil. Extremely drought-tolerant.

PROBLEMS   Galls on water-stressed plants. Pest control is rarely needed. Consid-

Creosote bush

ered unsafe by some experts. Liver damage resulting from the consumption of tablets has been reported.

HARVEST/STORAGE	Harvest twigs and leaves, dry and store in a cool place.
CULINARY USES	None.
MEDICINAL USES	According to Odena, creosote bush is considered an anti-cancer plant; a tea is made from the leaves. It has also been used as an antioxidant and antiseptic as well as a remedy for skin diseases, warts, and bronchial and respiratory conditions. It also helps with weight reduction. As a mouthwash, it has been shown to prevent tooth decay.
LANDSCAPE USES	Good ornamental plant that has a strong fragrance after a rain.
INSIGHT	Hard to propagate from cuttings and extremely difficult to transplant. Nothing will grow under it. A creosote bush in the Mojave Desert is said to be the oldest living plant in the world. The tea tastes terrible. The FDA considers chaparral unsafe for human consumption, and the herb has no proven medical value according to *The Honest Herbal* by Varro E. Tyler. The same book says that the lifespan of mosquitoes lengthened from 29 to 45 days when they were fed NDGA, an acid compound found in chaparral. This plant is also listed in some books as *L. divaricata* and *L. mexicana*.

CRESS—see **PEPPERGRASS**
Crocus sativus—see **SAFFRON**

CUBAN OREGANO

Coleus amboinicus
KO-lee-us am-BOYNE-ah-cuss

COMMON NAMES	CUBAN OREGANO.
FAMILY	Lamiaceae (Labiatae) (Mint).
TYPE	Tender perennial.
LOCATION	Sun to part shade.
PLANTING	Plant stem cuttings or transplants in the spring.
HEIGHT	1½ to 3 feet.
SPREAD	18 inches.
FINAL SPACING	12 inches.
BLOOM/FRUIT	Pale purple flowers.
GROWTH HABITS/CULTURE	Plants and seeds are not easy to locate, but they are easy to grow. This plant will not winter outdoors in most of Texas since it cannot tolerate any frost. Grow it in partial shade and well-drained soil and keep it moist.
PROBLEMS	Few except freeze damage.
HARVEST/STORAGE	Use fresh.
CULINARY USES	Cuban oregano is used in many dishes in the West Indies, Dominican Republic, and Cuba. It has the taste of a cross between regular oregano and camphor.

Cuban oregano

MEDICINAL USES	None that we know of.
LANDSCAPE USES	Colorful annual bedding plant, especially in borders.
OTHER USES	Does well in pots and hanging baskets.
INSIGHT	This aromatic, fleshy-leaf tender coleus has the fragrance of camphor. Its green and white leaves do not sport any of the red and yellow coloring normally associated with coleuses.

CUMIN

Cuminum cyminum
KOO-mah-num sy-MIN-um

COMMON NAMES	CUMIN.
FAMILY	Apiaceae (Umbelliferae) (Carrot or Parsley).
TYPE	Annual.
LOCATION	Full sun.
PLANTING	Plant seed or transplants in the spring. Seed can be started in the winter indoors and set out after the last frost.
HEIGHT	12 inches.
SPREAD	6 to 8 inches.
FINAL SPACING	4 to 6 inches.
BLOOM/FRUIT	Small heads of tiny pink or white flowers followed by small tan aromatic seed with tiny bristles.

GROWTH HABITS/CULTURE	Low-growing annual that's easy to grow from seed. Grass-like leaves that often look droopy. Hot, dry summers produce the best seeds. Grows best in well-prepared and well-drained soils. Use lots of compost and granite sand.
PROBLEMS	Rain can ruin the seed harvest. Plants usually need protection from winds.
HARVEST/STORAGE	Harvest seeds as they mature and store in a dry place in glass containers.
CULINARY USES	Cumin is primarily grown for its seed. Use to season chili, meats, breads, and vegetable dishes. The herb is common in Mexican cuisine, and the stems are used to flavor Vietnamese and Cajun dishes.
MEDICINAL USES	According to Lesley Bremness in *Herbs*, the oil is used for massages to reduce cellulite. The crushed seeds aid digestion and relieve flatulence, colic, and diarrhea. Take as a tea.
LANDSCAPE USES	None.
OTHER USES	Cumin is included in some veterinary medicines.
INSIGHT	Cumin is one of the herbs mentioned in the Bible.

Curcuma domestica—see **TURMERIC**

CURRY

Helichrysum italicum
hay-li-KRIS-um eye-TAL-ee-cum

COMMON NAMES	CURRY, CURRY PLANT.
FAMILY	Asteraceae (Compositae) (Sunflower or Daisy).
TYPE	Perennial or subshrub.
LOCATION	Full sun.
PLANTING	Transplants, cuttings, and seeds can be planted in the spring or fall.

Curry plant

HEIGHT	Up to 20 inches.
SPREAD	20 inches.
FINAL SPACING	12 to 18 inches.
BLOOM/FRUIT	Clusters of small yellow flowers in summer followed by shiny round white fruits.
GROWTH HABITS/CULTURE	Perennial or subshrub with very fragrant silver-gray foliage. Smells like the food spice curry (*Murraye koenigii*) but has little culinary value. Plant in well-drained soils and provide moderate amounts of water and fertilizer.
PROBLEMS	Curry plant must have excellent drainage.
HARVEST/STORAGE	Harvest foliage anytime. Cut and use the flowers for potpourri just after the flowers open.
CULINARY USES	Limited use. Leaves are sometimes used to give a curry flavor to soups, casseroles, and other dishes but if not removed before eating they can cause stomachache. This plant is not used to make curry blends.
MEDICINAL USES	Essential oil can be used therapeutically to treat acne, psoriasis, sunburn, and inflamed skin.
LANDSCAPE USES	The gray foliage is attractive and fragrant in the ornamental garden.
OTHER USES	Potpourri and cut foliage.
INSIGHT	Good plant for containers.

Cymbopogon citratus—see **LEMONGRASS**

D-E-F

DALMATION DAISY—see **PYRETHRUM**

DANDELION

Taraxacum officinale
ta-RAX-ih-cum oh-fis-ih-NALE

COMMON NAMES	DANDELION, BLOWBALL, CANKERWORT, LION'S TOOTH.
FAMILY	Asteraceae (Compositae) (Sunflower or Daisy).
TYPE	Perennial.
LOCATION	Sun or partial shade.
PLANTING	Seeds are spread by the wind. Transplants should be made in the fall.
HEIGHT	6 to 18 inches.
SPREAD	6 to 8 inches.
FINAL SPACING	Normally no need to plant. If the hybrids are desired, space about 12 inches apart.
BLOOM/FRUIT	Yellow flowers followed by a myriad of seeds.
GROWTH HABITS/CULTURE	Weed-like. Will grow in any soil but prefers low fertility.
PROBLEMS	Considered a weed. Seed heads grow fast and can look unsightly in lawns.
HARVEST/STORAGE	Harvest the root anytime and dry. Cut and use the young leaves fresh in salads. Use mature flowers to make wine or cookies.
CULINARY USES	Dandelion greens are excellent in salads. Young leaves are rich in vitamins and minerals and can be cooked like spinach. Dandelion

Dandelions

Dandelions

wines and fritters can be made from the flowers. Roots can be used to make a tea as well as a drink that serves as a coffee substitute. Buds can be pickled and also used as a coffee substitute.

MEDICINAL USES Dandelion offers many medicinal benefits. It can help detoxify the blood, prevent or expel kidney stones, and aid the gallbladder and liver. It is a diuretic, tonic, digestive, and laxative; it is loaded with trace minerals, especially potassium, which is present in the leaves. In fact, the dandelion has the most balanced mineral pattern of the herbs.

LANDSCAPE USES Wildflower.

INSIGHT The ubiquitous dandelion should be one of the gardener's most used plants. If you have to remove them, spray with straight vinegar with orange oil or pop them out with a hand weeder. See the Appendix for an organic herbicide formula.

DEVIL ROOT—see **HORSERADISH**

DILL

Anethum graveolens
a-NAY-thum gra-vay-OH-lenz

COMMON NAMES DILL, DILLY.

FAMILY Apiaceae (Umbelliferae) (Carrot or Parsley).

TYPE Annual.

LOCATION Full sun, protected from strong winds.

PLANTING Plant seed in the early spring and every two weeks thereafter to have a continuous succession of plants. Set out transplants in the spring. Seed can also be sown in the fall for an additional crop.

HEIGHT 24 to 36 inches.

SPREAD 12 to 24 inches.

FINAL SPACING 12 inches.

BLOOM/FRUIT Yellow, umbrella-shaped flower heads produce small oval-shaped seeds, which are delicious.

GROWTH HABITS/CULTURE Upright growth, hollow stalk. Foliage is aromatic, feathery and fern-like plumes, bluish-green when young, then dark green. Dill is easy to grow in healthy soil.

PROBLEMS Caterpillars of the swallowtail butterfly cause damage, but who cares? The butterflies are worth a little damage, so share. Strong winds can blow tall plants over.

HARVEST/STORAGE Cut and gather the leaves to use fresh—dill doesn't save well. As the seeds turn brown, cut off the tops of plant and hang upside down in a paper bag to catch the seed.

CULINARY USES The herb gives dill pickles their distinctive taste. Dill foliage and seeds are excellent for salads, breads, baked potatoes, soups, and butters. For vinegar use dill seed, fresh or dried. Use fresh leaves in green beans and with fish. The fresh immature green seed heads produce the best flavor. Also a good condiment for refried beans or any bean dish as

Dill

Dill seed

well as fish, greens, salads, and spinach. Add dill seed or leaves to tuna salad or tartar sauce. Try adding some to salmon croquettes. It is something special. Experiment on your own: rub it into a pork roast, add a pinch to steamed carrots and canned green beans and other dishes.

MEDICINAL USES   Tea made from the seed or leaves promotes sleep and reduces nervousness. The seed aids digestion.

LANDSCAPE USES   Attractive in the ornamental garden when closely clumped. The flowers attract beneficial insects, and the foliage can be used in cut-flower arrangements.

INSIGHT   "Dill" is from the Norse word *dulla*, which means "sleep" or "lull."

DITTANY OF CRETE

Origanum dictamnus
o-ree-GAH-num dik-TAM-nus

COMMON NAMES   DITTANY OF CRETE.

FAMILY   Lamiaceae (Labiatae) (Mint).

TYPE   Half-hardy perennial.

LOCATION   Full sun to light shade.

PLANTING   Cuttings, seed, and transplants can be planted in the spring or fall.

HEIGHT   24 inches.

SPREAD   15 inches.

FINAL SPACING   15 inches.

BLOOM/FRUIT   Small pinkish purple flowers extend from cone-like heads that hang downward.

GROWTH HABITS/CULTURE   Dittany of Crete is a low-growing, spreading plant with slender, arching stems to 12 inches long, woolly-white to gray rounded leaves, and small pinkish purple flowers in summer. Camphor-scented. Needs

Dittany of Crete

excellent drainage and protection in the winter. Best to grow in containers so they can be moved inside during cold weather.

PROBLEMS Overwatering—does not like wet or humid conditions.

CULINARY USES Tea from the flower heads. Leaves are used like those of other oreganos.

MEDICINAL USES For insect bites and stings, use the juice from foliage and apply directly to the skin.

LANDSCAPE USES Excellent for potted plants and hanging baskets. Also good in rock gardens.

INSIGHT Will freeze easily in the northern part of the state.

DUTCH WHITE CLOVER—see **CLOVER**

EASTERN RED CEDAR—see **JUNIPER**

ECHINACEA

Echinacea spp.

ek-ih-NAY-see-ah

COMMON NAMES ECHINACEA, PURPLE CONEFLOWER, BLACK SAMPSON.

FAMILY Asteraceae (Compositae) (Sunflower or Daisy).

TYPE Perennial herb.

LOCATION Sun to partial shade.

PLANTING Plant year round from transplants. Seed and root divisions are best planted in the fall and late winter. Seed can be sown all summer and through fall.

HEIGHT 2 to 3 feet.

SPREAD 2 to 4 feet.

FINAL SPACING 1 to 2 feet.

BLOOM/FRUIT Dark pink to lavender flowers with yellow centers. There is also a white-flowering variety.

GROWTH HABITS/CULTURE Brightly flowered perennial that blooms on long stems from early to mid-summer. Carefree, drought-tolerant, and easy to grow in most Texas soils.

PROBLEMS Does not like to be overwatered.

HARVEST/STORAGE Dig, dry, and store the roots (rhizomes) in the fall and winter. Collect and store the seed in glass containers when they have dried on the plant in the summer and fall.

CULINARY USES None.

MEDICINAL USES Roots that are three years old or older are the primary medicinal part of the plant, but all parts provide medicinal benefits. Purple coneflower is an antibiotic that fights infections and is good for the lymph and immune systems. It's also a blood purifier. Odena recommends eating the seed two or three times a day; however, Dr. Judy Griffin says the seed are toxic and can cause hallucinations. User beware.

LANDSCAPE USES Beautiful perennial herb for the border or perennial garden.

Purple coneflower

OTHER USES	Good cut flower.
INSIGHT	*Echinacea purpurea* and *Echinacea angustifolia* both have the same beneficial properties as the white cultivars.

EDIBLE SAGE—see **SAGE**

ELDERBERRY

Sambucus canadensis
sam-BEW-cus can-ah-DEN-sis

COMMON NAMES	ELDERBERRY, ELDER, MOTHER ELDER.
FAMILY	Caprifoliaceae (Honeysuckle).
TYPE	Perennial shrub or small tree.
LOCATION	Full sun to light shade.
PLANTING	Install transplants year round. Make cuttings from summer through fall or very early spring before bud break.
HEIGHT	10 to 12 feet.
SPREAD	8 to 10 feet.
FINAL SPACING	6 to 8 feet.
BLOOM/FRUIT	White flowers in the spring, followed by purple-black berries. The flowers are known as elderblow.
GROWTH HABITS/CULTURE	Grows easily to 12 feet. Grows like a weed, especially in moist soils; grows wild in many parts of Texas in a variety of soils.
PROBLEMS	Spreads and can take over.
HARVEST/STORAGE	Use flowers fresh or dried. Use berries fresh. You'll have to move fast or the birds will beat you to them.
CULINARY USES	The flower heads will produce a dark musky wine that is said to be good for whatever ails you; the berries can also be used for wines as well as jellies and pies. Coat the flowers in batter and deep-fry to make excellent fritters. The berries are delicious.

Elderberry

Purple coneflower—close up

MEDICINAL USES	Elderberry has been used to treat eye and skin diseases, epilepsy, fevers, and kidney ailments. Make a tea from the flowers and berries to treat sore throats, colds, allergies, arthritis, and other ailments. The roots, bark, leaves, and stems have been used for centuries in traditional herbal medicine.
LANDSCAPE USES	Dramatic plant for moist, shady locations.
OTHER USES	Attracts birds. Good landscape plant. Whistles for children can be made from the stems.
INSIGHT	Plant and stay out of the way. Elderberry has been called the medicine-chest plant.

ELECAMPANE

Inula helenium

IN-ew-la he-LEN-ee-um

COMMON NAMES	ELECAMPANE, HORSEHEAL, HORSE-ELDER, ELFDOCK.
FAMILY	Asteraceae (Compositae) (Sunflower or Daisy).
TYPE	Perennial.
LOCATION	Full sun to partial shade. Morning sun and afternoon shade is the best location.
PLANTING	Start seed in the early spring, set out transplants after the last frost. Container plants can be set out in spring or fall. Division by offshoots in the fall.
HEIGHT	3 to 8 feet.
SPREAD	3 to 5 feet.
FINAL SPACING	24 inches.
BLOOM/FRUIT	Yellow aster- or sunflower-like flowers in summer followed by small sunflower-like seed.
GROWTH HABITS/CULTURE	Grows wild in some parts of Texas. Grows very tall on a strong central stem. Looks like an annual sunflower. Needs average bed preparation

Elecampane

Elecampane

and maintenance—nothing fancy. Has very large leaves that are bristly on top and soft underneath.

PROBLEMS   Some chewing insects will eat holes in the foliage. In shady locations, be careful to avoid overwatering.

HARVEST/STORAGE   Harvest and dry the root in the fall of the second year's growth.

CULINARY USES   The root is eaten both dried and cooked. It is creamy and aromatic. Use very small portions because it is bitter.

MEDICINAL USES   The rootstock has a wide range of medicinal properties. It can be used as a remedy for coughs, poor digestion, bronchitis, urinary tract inflammation, menstrual discomfort, and intestinal parasites. Also used in veterinary medicines. It is an expectorant as well as an antifungal and antibacterial agent. Some herbalists recommend drinking up to 3 cups a day of a tea made by adding one teaspoon of the herb to boiling water and simmering for 20 minutes.

LANDSCAPE USES   Looks good as a background plant in the perennial garden.

INSIGHT   Has a long history of use. According to Lesley Bremness in *Herbs*, Helen of Troy was gathering elecampane when she was abducted, starting the Trojan War.

Elettaria cardamomum—see **CARDAMOM**

EPAZOTE

Chenopodium ambrosioides
chin-no-PO-dee-um am-BROS-ee-oid-eez

COMMON NAMES   EPAZOTE, EPASOTE, JERUSALEM OAK, AMERICAN WORMSEED.

FAMILY   Chenopodiaceae (Goosefoot or Pigweed).

TYPE   Short-lived perennial or annual.

LOCATION   Full sun to part shade. Likes morning sun and afternoon shade best.

PLANTING   Easily started from seed in the spring or fall. Set out transplants anytime.

HEIGHT   To 6 feet.

SPREAD   3 feet.

FINAL SPACING   One plant is enough. It spreads readily by reseeding.

BLOOM/FRUIT   Summer flowers are small greenish balls.

GROWTH HABITS/CULTURE   Looks and grows like a weed. Has pungent, spear-shaped, deeply toothed leaves. Needs no fertilizer and very little water. Once established, it will come back from seed forever except in thick mulch.

PROBLEMS   Can spread and take over.

HARVEST/STORAGE   Use the leaves fresh anytime. Harvest the seed when mature. Dry both leaves and seed and keep in a cool place.

CULINARY USES   Leaves are used to flavor Mexican food and to marinate meats and flavor a wide range of dishes. Lucinda Hutson's *The Herb Garden Cookbook* contains wonderful recipes using this herb.

MEDICINAL USES   Add 2 teaspoons of leaves to the bean pot prior to the last 10 minutes

Epazote

of cooking to take gas out of the beans. Seeds are used as a vermifuge for pinworm and other internal parasites in humans and animals. All parts of the plant are toxic and should be used only by qualified practitioners.

LANDSCAPE USES   Too weedy looking for most ornamental gardens.

OTHER USES   I make a tea for spraying minor insect pests by soaking leaves in water. Can be mixed with other liquid sprays, such as Garrett Juice.

Equisetum—see **HORSETAIL REED**
Eruca vesicara—see **ARUGULA**

EVENING PRIMROSE

Oenothera biennis
ee-NOTH-er-ah bee-EN-is

COMMON NAMES	EVENING PRIMROSE, BUTTERCUP, FEVER PLANT, SUNDROP.
FAMILY	Onagraceae (Evening Primrose).
TYPE	Hardy biennial.
LOCATION	Full sun.
PLANTING	Plant from seed in the fall.
HEIGHT	18 to 24 inches.
SPREAD	18 to 24 inches.
FINAL SPACING	18 inches.
BLOOM/FRUIT	Large yellow flowers on upright stems.
GROWTH HABITS/CULTURE	Rosettes of long pointed leaves in the first year. Erect stems and yellow flowers in the second year. Taller than the common pink evening primrose that covers many of the roadsides of Texas. Looks weedy when not in bloom. It will grow in most soils and is very undemanding.
PROBLEMS	Looks weedy.
HARVEST/STORAGE	Cut and dry the foliage while the plant is in bloom.

False indigo

Evening primrose

CULINARY USES	Leaves, stem, and roots can be boiled as food.
MEDICINAL USES	Cold expressed oils of the seeds have an important medicinal use as an omega 6 essential fatty acid. The herb is taken for weight reduction and to help control mental problems. It is reported to prevent heart disease and stroke. It has also been used to treat Parkinson's disease and alcoholism, lower blood pressure, ease menstrual problems, and restore red blood cells. Take as a tea, capsules, or tincture. The oil comes in capsules only. You'll know if it's good by the price.
LANDSCAPE USES	Wildflower for larger areas.

FALSE INDIGO

Amorpha fruiticosa
ah-MOR-fah froo-teh-COH-sah

COMMON NAMES	FALSE INDIGO, INDIGO BUSH, RIVER LOCUST.
FAMILY	Fabaceae (Leguminosae) (Legume).
TYPE	Deciduous.
LOCATION	Full sun to part shade.
PLANTING	Can be started year round from seed, softwood or hardwood cuttings, or transplants.
HEIGHT	10 feet.
SPREAD	10 to 12 feet.
FINAL SPACING	7 to 12 feet.
BLOOM/FRUIT	Purple 6- to 8-inch spikes in late spring.
GROWTH HABITS/CULTURE	Grows well in almost any soil, even wet and poorly drained soils, but adapts well to normal garden soils. Usually has many stems growing from the ground but can be trimmed into a small tree.
PROBLEMS	Few if any serious ones because it contains natural chemicals that repel insects. Caterpillars will sometimes attack it, but they can be easily removed by hand.

HARVEST/STORAGE	Harvest leaves in the summer, dry and store. Harvest seed when mature and store dry.
CULINARY USES	None.
LANDSCAPE USES	Specimen plant, good in wet soils or for erosion control. 'Dark Lance' is a good-looking cultivar.
OTHER USES	Extracts from the leaves and seeds can be used to control aphids, grain moths, cotton bollworms, and other pests. Crush one part leaves with 25 parts water, filter, and spray on food and ornamental crops. It is harmless to beneficial insects and animals. It also helps repel pests when interplanted with other food crops.
INSIGHT	The herb known as wild false indigo, *Baptisia australis*, is a dye plant and under research as an immune system booster.

FALSE SAFFRON—see **SAFFLOWER**

FENNEL

Foeniculum vulgare
fee-NIK-ew-lum vul-GAR-ree

COMMON NAMES	FENNEL, SWEET FENNEL, WILD ANISE.
FAMILY	Apiaceae (Umbelliferae) (Carrot or Parsley).
TYPE	Annual or very tender perennial.
LOCATION	Full sun to part shade.
PLANTING	Transplants or seed in spring or fall.
HEIGHT	3 to 6 feet.
SPREAD	24 inches.
FINAL SPACING	18 to 24 inches.
BLOOM/FRUIT	Yellow umbels of flowers followed by aromatic seeds.
GROWTH HABITS/CULTURE	Looks like bright green or bronze dill, with finely cut feathery foliage, hollow stems, a subtle anise or licorice scent, golden seed heads or umbels; but grows taller than dill. Sweet fennel has green foliage. Bronze fennel (*F. vulgare* var. *purpureum*) has copper-tinged to purplish foliage. Easy to grow in healthy soil.
PROBLEMS	Swallowtail butterflies—but just plant enough fennel for them and you. If there are too many caterpillars on your plants, pick some of them off. Let the kids see the metamorphosis of the striped caterpillars as they change into the pupal cases and then emerge as gorgeous swallowtail butterflies.
HARVEST/STORAGE	Harvest mature seeds and store in a dry glass container. Collect and use the leaves before the plant flowers.
CULINARY USES	Fennel is used in liqueurs, chicken broth, and salads. Excellent for flavoring fish. Stalks are edible when young. Use the fresh foliage in salads and the dry seeds in breads. Fennel has a licorice-like flavor.
MEDICINAL USES	The seeds are used to suppress the appetite, relieve gas, and reduce the craving for alcohol. Eat or make tea from the crushed seed. Chewing

Fennel

Fennel

the seed sweetens the breath. Fennel is also reported to soothe digestive problems and comfort babies suffering from colic.

LANDSCAPE USES A good decorative landscape plant. Bronze fennel is the most attractive for landscape use.

OTHER USES Attracts bees and butterflies.

INSIGHT Fennel is one of the easiest herbs to grow. *Foeniculum vulgare* var. *azoricum* is Florence fennel, commonly grown as a vegetable. It has a milder flavor and is used primarily for its fleshy stems. Because of its possible estrogenic effects, fennel should be avoided during pregnancy. Fennel volatile oil is toxic and should not be used at all.

FENUGREEK

Trigonella foenum-graecum
trig-ah-NELL-ah FEE-num GRI-cum

COMMON NAMES FENUGREEK.

FAMILY Fabaceae (Leguminosae) (Legume).

TYPE Annual.

LOCATION Full sun to dappled shade.

PLANTING Start from seed or transplants in the spring or fall.

HEIGHT	18 to 24 inches.
SPREAD	12 to 18 inches.
FINAL SPACING	6 to 8 inches.
BLOOM/FRUIT	Small fragrant yellow-white summer flowers and aromatic seeds in a 16-seed legume pod.
GROWTH HABITS/CULTURE	Fenugreek, with its triple leaflets, looks a little like clover. Its growth is open and not that attractive, but it does well in most soils, needs minimal care, and is easy to grow.
PROBLEMS	None serious, except rodents love it.
HARVEST/STORAGE	Gather seeds as they turn brown, the leaves when green.
CULINARY USES	Imitation maple syrup is made from the seed. Use seeds or sprouted seeds in salads. Fenugreek is an ingredient in curry powder, and the seeds are also used to flavor curries and chutneys.
MEDICINAL USES	Seeds in chicken broth or teas make a good tonic. Fenugreek contains steroids used in sex hormone preparation. Seeds can be chewed to stimulate digestion, relieve fevers, and control the craving for nicotine.
OTHER USES	Seeds are used in embalming oils, in potpourri, to make a yellow dye, and in a veterinary medicine.
INSIGHT	Fenugreek is worth growing. Sprout seed indoors on moist paper towels or in a moist sprouting jar. They germinate in about six days.

Fenugreek

Feverfew

FEVERFEW

Chrysanthemum parthenium
kris-ANTH-ee-mum par-THIN-ee-um

COMMON NAMES	FEVERFEW, FEATHERFEW, MIDSUMMER DAISY.
FAMILY	Asteraceae (Compositae) (Sunflower or Daisy).
TYPE	Annual or short-lived perennial.
LOCATION	Full sun to partial shade. Morning sun and afternoon shade is the ideal location.
PLANTING	Transplants can be set out anytime other than winter. Start seed in late winter indoors; take cuttings anytime during the growing season.
HEIGHT	9 to 24 inches.
SPREAD	12 inches.
FINAL SPACING	12 inches.
BLOOM/FRUIT	White flowers with yellow centers from summer into fall.
GROWTH HABITS/CULTURE	Erect, compact growth. White and yellow forms available. Soft, light green, serrated leaves. Easy to grow in any well-drained soil. Will self-sow easily. Feverfew needs moist soil for best results.
PROBLEMS	Can scorch in full sun. Likes morning sun and afternoon shade best.
HARVEST/STORAGE	Cut, dry, and store leaves and flowers in glass containers. Harvest the leaves before the flowers form. Pick the flowers just before they open and hang upside down to dry.
CULINARY USES	None.
MEDICINAL USES	Tea from the flowers alleviates migraine headaches and muscular tension. A tea from the leaves may also be used for migraines as well as menstrual problems. It should be avoided if skin photosensitivity occurs.
LANDSCAPE USES	Good in the perennial garden and in containers.
OTHER USES	Dry flowers for potpourri, dried arrangements, or wreaths.
INSIGHT	Also sold as *Tanacetum parthenium*. May be listed in catalogs as *Matricaria eximia*. Feverfew should be avoided by pregnant and lactating women. It is said that bees dislike the smell of feverfew.

FLANNEL LEAF—see **MULLEIN**
FLORIDA CRANBERRY—see **ROSELLE**
Foeniculum vulgare—see **FENNEL**
FRENCH SORREL—see **SORREL**
FRENCH TARRAGON—see **TARRAGON**

Gallium odoratum—see **SWEET WOODRUFF**
GARDEN SAGE—see **SAGE**
GARDEN SORREL—see **SORREL**

GARLIC

Allium sativum
AL-lee-um sa-TEA-vum

COMMON NAMES	GARLIC, POOR MAN'S TREACLE, CLOVE GARLIC.
FAMILY	Liliaceae (Amaryllidaceae) (Lily).
TYPE	Perennial bulb.
LOCATION	Sun or dappled shade.
PLANTING	Cloves or transplants can be set out in the fall or spring.
HEIGHT	Up to 4 feet.
SPREAD	6 inches.
FINAL SPACING	4 to 6 inches.
BLOOM/FRUIT	Some garlic has twisting and serpentine flower heads that are very decorative. Others have straight flower shoots, and some have no flowers at all. For larger bulbs, cut off the flowering stems as they emerge from the foliage.
GROWTH HABITS/CULTURE	Flat, strap-like, gray-green leaves, underground bulbs with many cloves. Cool weather is important for garlic. To grow a successful crop of garlic, start with well-prepared soil full of compost, rock powder,

Garlic bulbs

Harvested garlic

Serpenthead garlic

and organic fertilizer. Purchase big healthy bulbs (organically grown, if possible) and break them apart into cloves. Each clove should be planted 3 to 4 inches apart about 1 inch deep in clay soils, 2 inches deep in sandy soils. It's best to place the pointed end up, although garlic seems to grow fine if the cloves are sideways. After planting the cloves, cover the planting area with about 2 inches of mulch. Here is a good place to use your partially completed compost. The new garlic bulbs will start to grow right away and you will see green shoots before freezing weather begins. A little frost burn to the foliage tips is normal. During hard freezes the plants can be covered with hay or floating row cover for protection, but that's usually unnecessary.

PROBLEMS Few if any except occasional slug nibbles. Overwatering can rot the bulbs.

HARVEST/STORAGE For larger bulbs, cut the flower stalk off as soon as it starts to emerge. Or let the stalk grow and cut the flower off before it opens. Then hang it upside down to dry and use as dry arrangement material. The third method is to allow the seed heads to mature and open. Collect the small bulblets before they scatter or you'll have garlic everywhere. When the tips of the leaves first begin to turn yellow in early summer, the bulbs are ready for harvest. Don't wait until the entire top is brown; energy and food value is used up as the foliage deteriorates. Dig the garlic out gently with a turning fork. You can cut the tops off or tie or braid them and hang in the garage or a partially shaded place to dry. Store in a cool dry area. Use your garlic freely but save some of the larger bulbs for the next year's planting.

CULINARY USES Garlic leaves and cloves are great for eating and for seasoning vegetables, meats, sauces, gravies, soups, and just about anything else. Try the young leaves in scrambled eggs and garlic powder on most any meat dish. Fresh garlic is even better. If you're worried about garlic breath, chew on a few fresh leaves of parsley or sweet basil. The high chlorophyll content of these herbs will neutralize the garlic smell. Of course, if everyone eats garlic, no one will notice the smell.

MEDICINAL USES Garlic is taken for the prevention and treatment of colds and bronchitis. It is also said to help in treating lead poisoning, normalizing blood pressure, killing bacteria (it's a natural antibiotic), and detoxifying blood. Garlic is said to increase endurance, ease earaches, remove skin blemishes, and, of course, ward off vampires!

LANDSCAPE USES A beautiful ornamental plant or a nice addition to mass plantings or interspersed in the perennial or rose garden.

OTHER USES Deters many insect pests. Garlic oil, when poured or sprayed into standing water, stagnant ponds, and other wet breeding spots, will control mosquito larvae quite well. Spraying the air with garlic tea works as well as toxic chemicals in getting rid of flying adult mosquitoes. For years, organic gardeners have interplanted garlic among ornamental landscape plants as well as food crops to ward off various pests. Tomatoes seldom have spider mite problems when garlic is planted nearby. On the other hand, garlic is reported to slow the growth of beans and peas. Garlic tea sprayed on plant foliage prior to heavy insect infestations works as a powerful repellent to most problem insects and many diseases. Gardeners who pour garlic tea on fire ant mounds claim excellent results. When hot pepper oil is added to the garlic, it becomes a mild but effective broad-spectrum insecticide. Garlic also has significant fungicidal powers. It will aid in the control of anthracnose, powdery mildew, downy mildew, rust, tomato blight, brown rot on stone fruit, and other disease problems. Even scientists like Charles L. Wilson with the U.S. Department of Agriculture report that members of the garlic and pepper families have effective fungicidal components (see Appendix for recipes).

INSIGHT   Garlic is one of the world's most health-giving foods, an important medicinal herb, a key ingredient in homemade insect spray, and a good-looking landscape plant. Garlic should be a staple of every garden. The cloves are great for seasoning all kinds of foods or for roasting and eating whole. Young garlic greens are prized by cooks and chefs for use as a chive-like garnish for numerous dishes, including garlic pesto. Besides tasting good, there is scientific evidence confirming the health benefits of garlic. Garlic can grow botulisms when stored in oil too long, so use garlic oil soon after making it. Garlic is too "hot" for those with gastrointestinal problems. Giant garlic, or elephant garlic, *Allium scorodoprasum*, has a milder flavor than true garlic and produces a fist-size bulb. It is actually a leek. Its culture is the same.

GARLIC CHIVES—see **CHIVES**
GERANIUM, SCENTED—see **SCENTED GERANIUM**

GERMANDER

Teucrium spp.
TOO-kree-um

COMMON NAMES	GERMANDER, WALL GERMANDER.
FAMILY	Lamiaceae (Labiatae) (Mint).
TYPE	Perennial evergreen.
LOCATION	Full sun.
PLANTING	Use cuttings and transplants anytime during the growing season.
HEIGHT	2 feet.
SPREAD	6 to 12 inches.
FINAL SPACING	6 to 12 inches.
BLOOM/FRUIT	Whorls of purple-pink flowers in summer.

Germander

GROWTH HABITS/CULTURE	Small evergreen shrub with faintly aromatic leaves. It may also be clipped into a border or low perennial hedge. Easy to grow, no particular cultural requirements. Propagate by seeds, cuttings, or divisions. Likes to be sheared. Other species of *Teucrium* include the following: *Teucrium fruticans* is called tutti-frutti and is a perennial growing to 3½ to 4 feet tall. *Teucrium lucidum* is a beautiful gray-leaf variety. *Teucrium canadense* has rose blossoms and a creeping growth habit. *Teucrium arum*, called cat thyme, is a small, aromatic, gray-leaf plant best grown in containers. Dwarf germanders are also available. *Teucrium chamaedrys* is common germander with rose-pink summer flowers.
PROBLEMS	None.
HARVEST/STORAGE	Cut green foliage anytime to use with cut flowers indoors.
CULINARY USES	None.
MEDICINAL USES	Formerly used as a treatment for gout, now used almost exclusively as a landscape plant. The aerial parts of the plant are said to be digestive, diuretic, and antiseptic.
LANDSCAPE USES	Dark green attractive hedge or border. Fragrant foliage.
OTHER USES	Used in knot gardens. Excellent cut foliage for use in interior arrangements.
INSIGHT	This easy-to-grow evergreen should be used more in the landscape.

GINGER

Zingiber officinale
ZING-gi-ber oh-fis-ih-NAH-lee

COMMON NAMES	GINGER.
FAMILY	Zingiberaceae (Ginger).
TYPE	Tender perennial.
LOCATION	Partial shade.
PLANTING	Plant the rhizomes in the spring after the last frost. Plants can be started indoors in the winter by cutting up pieces of the rhizomes, letting them dry, dusting with fireplace ashes, and planting very shallowly in pots. Part of each cutting should still be visible after planting. Keep warm, apply bottom heat, and transplant outdoors in the spring when the weather has warmed.
HEIGHT	To 6 feet.
SPREAD	12 to 24 inches.
FINAL SPACING	12 to 18 inches.
BLOOM/FRUIT	Fragrant yellow-purple flowers in late summer or early fall.
GROWTH HABITS/CULTURE	Upright, jointed stems similar to bamboo. Easy to grow in healthy soil in warm weather. All gingers are heavy feeders; besides a soil rich with humus, they need regular fertilizing with a balanced organic fertilizer and regular watering. Some ornamental gingers will tolerate temperatures in the low twenties without serious damage. If grown in containers, they need plenty of light. Cut back ornamental gingers in the late

Ginger

Ginger

fall and allow them to rest through the winter. Mature plants may be dug up and divided.

PROBLEMS Subject to wind damage if not protected. Freezes easily.

HARVEST/STORAGE Dig up roots in the late summer or fall (before the temperature drops below 50 degrees) and store in a cool place.

CULINARY USES For making teas and flavoring many foods, including vegetables, meats, and desserts. The roots of all gingers are edible. Use young leaves as wrappers to bake other foods. The flowers of ginger can be eaten raw or cooked and are sometimes used to make gingerbread and gingersnaps.

MEDICINAL USES Ginger has been taken to promote circulation of the blood, expel gas, and treat respiratory problems, voice problems, nausea, and motion sickness. It's also a strong antioxidant. Some people chew a small piece every day, but ginger is too hot for those who suffer gastrointestinal problems or who are easy bleeders. Ginger tea is especially warming and good for circulation.

LANDSCAPE USES Excellent container and greenhouse plant.

INSIGHT The rhizomes or roots are called hands. Ginger does not freeze well; it becomes stringy and tough.

GINKGO

Ginkgo biloba
GINK-oh bye-LOBE-ah

COMMON NAMES GINKGO, MAIDENHAIR TREE.

FAMILY Ginkgoaceae (Ginkgo).

TYPE Deciduous tree.

LOCATION Full sun.

PLANTING   Container-grown transplants can be installed year round. Seed, layers, cuttings, and graphs can be started anytime during the growing season.

HEIGHT   60 feet or more in deep soils.

SPREAD   30 feet.

FINAL SPACING   20 to 40 feet.

BLOOM/FRUIT   Puny, waxy flowers, awful-smelling fruit on mature trees. It is the female trees that produce the fleshy fruit with an edible kernel if a male tree is close by. Most nurseries claim to have only male trees, but there is no sure way to tell since the fruit doesn't start developing until the tree is several years old.

GROWTH HABITS/CULTURE   The leaves can have two lobes and the cleft can be deep, but the leaf characteristics seem to vary from tree to tree. The short-lived fall color is bright yellow. The ginkgo tree is slow-growing as a seedling and gangly when young. It grows faster as it ages. Some trees in China and Japan have been known to live 600 years. They can grow in a variety of soils and have some drought resistance, although they prefer deep, moist soil. Ginkgo is uniquely open-branching and notoriously slow-growing except in organic, healthy soil, where annual growth can be as much as 2 feet.

Ginkgo

Ginkgo

PROBLEMS	Very few, although the foliage will burn in shallow or white-rock soils.
HARVEST/STORAGE	Pick leaves while green, dry and store in glass containers. Leaves are best used in tea when they are fresh-picked from the tree. Store in glass containers if possible.
CULINARY USES	None.
MEDICINAL USES	Ginkgo is the longevity herb. It helps the memory and is used as a treatment for bronchitis, cerebral and vascular problems, and hearing problems. It is said to improve brain efficiency and cellular energy. Take capsules or use fresh green leaves in tea, although it takes lots of leaves and tea to obtain a medicinal effect.
LANDSCAPE USES	Beautiful shade and fall-color tree. Can be kept dwarfed for large containers or even bonzaied. It is one of the most distinctive trees available.
INSIGHT	Ginkgo is said to be the sole survivor of a primitive order of plants that apparently lived up to 200 years ago. This is the tree that taught me how important the organic program really is. Most ginkgos under a synthetic fertilizer program only grow only about 1 to 2 inches a year. My ginkgo, planted in 1985 when my daughter Logan was born, has grown from a sapling 1½ inches in diameter to a 15-inch-caliper, 40-foot-high shade tree in 2000. Since the ginkgo is an ancient tree, the soil's organic material and strong biological activity are critical.

GINSENG

Panax quinquefolius
PAN-ax quin-que-FOLE-ee-us

COMMON NAMES	GINSENG.
FAMILY	Araliaceae (Ginseng).
TYPE	Perennial.
LOCATION	Full shade.
PLANTING	Plant roots in spring or fall. For best results, roots should be dug in the fall and planted in the spring.
HEIGHT	10 to 20 inches.
SPREAD	8 to 12 inches.
FINAL SPACING	12 inches.
BLOOM/FRUIT	After maturation (three years), small yellow-green flowers, then berries.
GROWTH HABITS/CULTURE	Likes cool, shady spots. Ginseng is a small plant with a long root and compound leaves of five leaflets with toothed edges. Summer-borne flowers are greenish yellow, followed by small red berries. Big fleshy roots can grow to a 2-foot depth. Needs deep, well-drained, acid soil.
PROBLEMS	Heat, some damage from chewing insects. Needs plenty of moisture and shade. Slow-growing. Seed germination takes 18–24 months.
HARVEST/STORAGE	Don't harvest for at least three years. The fifth or sixth year is best. Dig the roots in the fall.
CULINARY USES	None.

Ginseng. Photograph by Norman Flaigg and the Lady Bird Johnson Wildflower Center.

MEDICINAL USES   General tonic. Used as a tonic and to treat a wide range of ailments, including nausea, vomiting, and irregular menstrual flow. Ginseng is also reputed to be an aphrodisiac and energy-booster. Siberian ginseng is reported to be the most powerful as a sexual stimulant. American ginseng is excellent for endurance, vitality, and relief from depression. According to Dr. Judy Griffin, the ginseng grown in Texas lacks good medicinal qualities. To prevent loss of medicinal power, ginseng tea should not be stored more than a day.

LANDSCAPE USES   None.

OTHER USES   Makes a fairly good container plant.

INSIGHT   Ginseng gets its name from the Chinese word *schinseng*, meaning "man-shaped." Ginseng can have the same effect on sleep as caffeine.

Glycyrrhiza glabra—see **LICORICE**

GOLDENROD

Solidago virgaurea
sal-eh-DAY-go vir-GAR-re-ah

COMMON NAMES   GOLDENROD, AARON'S ROD, WOUNDWORT.

FAMILY   Asteraceae (Compositae) (Sunflower or Daisy).

TYPE   Perennial.

Goldenrod

LOCATION	Sun to partial shade.
PLANTING	Transplants in the spring, seeds or root divisions in the fall.
HEIGHT	2 to 7 feet.
SPREAD	Wide-spreading.
FINAL SPACING	One or two is enough.
BLOOM/FRUIT	Striking yellow pyramids of flowers on tall stalks in the late summer and fall.
GROWTH HABITS/CULTURE	Upright perennial with beautiful fall color. Very easy to grow in any soil. Treat as a wildflower.
PROBLEMS	Very aggressive, sometimes gets out of control. Remove the faded flowers to prevent spreading.
HARVEST/STORAGE	Harvest the flowers just after they form. Use the leaves in tea when they are young and fresh. Both can be dried and stored in glass containers.
CULINARY USES	None.
MEDICINAL USES	Leaves and flowers are expectorant, anti-inflammatory, diuretic, and mildly sedative. Goldenrod is also used to treat kidney and bladder problems, coughs, fevers, sore throat, and asthma. It can be taken as a tea.
INSIGHT	Goldenrod pollen has the undeserved reputation of causing hay fever. Some people are allergic to the plant, but the pollen is too heavy to cause common allergies. Goldenrod is in my perennial garden and should be in more gardens. Ragweed pollen is responsible for the allergy problem that is so notorious. Dwarf goldenrod only grows 24 to 36 inches high. Fireworks is a dwarf that doesn't spread so badly by suckers, as do the larger plants. All goldenrod species are useful, but *Solidago odora* is the most fragrant and flavorful.

GOLDENSEAL

Hydrastis canadensis
hi-DRAS-tis can-ah-DEN-sis

COMMON NAMES	GOLDENSEAL, GOLDEN SEAL, ORANGE ROOT, YELLOW ROOT, GROUND RASPBERRY, INDIAN DYE, EYE BALM, INDIAN PAINT.
FAMILY	Ranunculaceae (Buttercup).
TYPE	Perennial.
LOCATION	Shade.
PLANTING	Plant seed in the spring or start in the winter indoors and set out after the last frost.
HEIGHT	12 inches.
SPREAD	8 to 12 inches.
FINAL SPACING	8 inches.
BLOOM/FRUIT	Solitary half-inch flowers are greenish white with numerous stamens; the sepals fall off when the flower opens. Fruits are clustered oblong orange-red berries with two shiny seeds.
GROWTH HABITS/CULTURE	Goldenseal is a shade-lover with erect, cylindrical, hairy stems. Grows well with ginseng—needs shade, moisture, and rich, highly organic soil. It's not an easy plant to grow.
PROBLEMS	Seed are difficult to get started in the spring.
HARVEST/STORAGE	Gather roots, dry and grind into powder. Store in glass containers in a cool dry place.
CULINARY USES	None.
MEDICINAL USES	Goldenseal is a natural anti-inflammatory and antiseptic. Take it as a tea or in capsules for skin diseases, fungal diseases, stomach ulcers, and kidney problems. It will lower blood pressure if used in large amounts. It is a good tonic for all body systems, but long-term use (two to three weeks) can destroy friendly intestinal bacteria, much like an antibiotic. Often used with ginseng.
LANDSCAPE USES	Looks good growing in a natural shady setting—if you can get it to grow.
OTHER USES	None.
INSIGHT	One of the oldest recorded medicinal herbs and one of the most widely used medicines today. Usually found growing with ginseng in the wild in forested areas. Can be toxic if used in heavy doses.

GOTU KOLA

Centella asiatica
sin-TELL-la a-she-AT-tee-ka

COMMON NAMES	GOTU KOLA.
FAMILY	Apiaceae (Umbelliferae) (Carrot or Parsley).
TYPE	Tender perennial groundcover.
LOCATION	Shade to partial shade.
PLANTING	Start seed in the early spring or fall. Set out container-grown transplants anytime during the growing season.

HEIGHT	4 to 6 inches.
SPREAD	18 to 36 inches.
FINAL SPACING	12 to 18 inches.
BLOOM/FRUIT	Tiny maroon flowers at nodes produce even tinier seed that will self-sow. You'll probably never notice the blooms.
GROWTH HABITS/CULTURE	Slow-growing groundcover that spreads like mint, but not as aggressively. Likes moist soil. Leaves are rounded and scalloped, closely resembling ground ivy or gill ivy.
PROBLEMS	Sunburn. Slugs. Will freeze in most parts of Texas.
HARVEST/STORAGE	Harvest the leaves year round; use fresh or after drying.
CULINARY USES	Use the leaves in salads and teas. Tastes somewhat like parsley.
MEDICINAL USES	Gotu kola is considered a longevity herb and brain food. It has memory-enhancing and anti-aging properties, along with high levels of vitamin B. It is diuretic, slightly laxative, tonic, sedative, and wound-healing. As a tea, it is also used topically to treat skin diseases and lesions. It can be taken in teas or eaten raw in salads. It is also used to treat liver problems and high blood pressure. According to Dr. Judy Griffin, gotu kola reduces the buildup of calcium and improves circulation. It is a mild narcotic and should not be used by pregnant women or those taking antidepressants.
LANDSCAPE USES	Temporary groundcover in shady places. Good in hanging baskets.
OTHER USES	None.
INSIGHT	Needs shade and moist, fertilized soil. Elephants love it and they have a good memory and are long-lived. Freezes in the northern half of Texas. Must be replanted each year in all but southern Texas. Some take gotu kola to try to develop spiritual powers. Large doses may cause vertigo or visions of large pink rabbits.

GOURMET PARSLEY—see **CHICORY**
GREASEWOOD—see **CREOSOTE BUSH**

Gotu kola

Hamamelis spp.—see **WITCH HAZEL**
Helichrysum italicum—see **CURRY**
HEMP TREE—see **VITEX**
HERCULES' CLUB—see **PRICKLY ASH**
Hibiscus sabdariffa—see **ROSELLE**

HOJA SANTA

Piper auritum
PIE-per aw-REE-tum

COMMON NAMES	HOJA SANTA.
FAMILY	Piperaceae (Pepper).
TYPE	Herbaceous perennial.
LOCATION	Full sun to shade—the best location is one with morning sun and afternoon shade.
PLANTING	Plant from root divisions at any time of the year (fall through spring is best). Container plants can be installed year round.
HEIGHT	8 to 10 feet.
SPREAD	6 to 8 feet.
FINAL SPACING	3 to 8 feet.
BLOOM/FRUIT	The flowers are interesting cylindrical spikes that bloom all summer.
GROWTH HABITS/CULTURE	Hoja santa is a herbaceous or semi-woody herb that sprouts from the ground with many shoots. It has large, velvety, heart-shaped leaves that are often 10 inches or more in length. It is very easy to grow in prepared soil and is perennial in an organic program. It needs moist soil.
PROBLEMS	Hail and high winds will damage the large leaves. May freeze out in the northern part of the state. Minor chewing insects are about the only pests I've ever seen on it. Completely perennial as far north as the Dallas/Fort Worth area.
HARVEST/STORAGE	Pick the large leaves as needed and use fresh, or store dry or frozen if needed for the winter

Hoja santa

Hoja santa under the author's famous gingko tree

months. Store in glass containers. Better yet, keep at least one plant in a container so you can have fresh leaves year round.

CULINARY USES   The leaves can be used to flavor dishes and to wrap various fillers of meat, fish, and vegetables. Hoja santa has a distinctive root beer taste and is a popular ingredient in Guatemalan and Mexican food. Research shows that eating large quantities of hoja santa is not healthy, so use it in moderation. Here's a good recipe for a delicious appetizer or main course. Put pieces of chicken, beef, or fish on a leaf, add some onions, garlic, peppers, and a dash of amino acids or wine (optional). Roll the leaf enchilada-style and bake for an hour at 350 degrees in a casserole dish.

MEDICINAL USES   It is said to help relieve nervous anxiety, stress, and restlessness. It can be eaten or taken as a tea. However, it is very powerful and should be used on a limited basis. Long-term use may cause liver problems.

LANDSCAPE USES   Hoja santa is useful in large pots and the perennial garden. The texture of the large leaves is distinctive, and the white flowers are interesting. Use hoja santa as a bold background planting, but give it plenty of room.

INSIGHT   *Piper methysticum* (kava-kava) is a closely related herb that is used as a calming tea. Both this plant and hoja santa should not be overused. According to the American Botanical Council, extended continuous intake can cause a temporary yellow discoloration of skin, hair, and nails. Just use common sense and don't overdo this or any other herb.

HOREHOUND

Marrubium vulgare
ma-RUE-bi-um vul-GAR-ee

COMMON NAMES	HOREHOUND, WHITE HOREHOUND, MARRUBIO, HOUNDSBANE.
FAMILY	Lamiaceae (Labiatae) (Mint).
TYPE	Perennial.
LOCATION	Full sun.
PLANTING	Set out transplants or make cuttings anytime during the growing season. Start seed in early spring.
HEIGHT	12 to 14 inches.
SPREAD	18 to 24 inches.
FINAL SPACING	12 inches.
BLOOM/FRUIT	Clusters of small white flowers followed by many small seeds that germinate freely.
GROWTH HABITS/CULTURE	Bushy and woody with fuzzy, gray-green, wrinkled, and veiny leaves. Hardy but sometimes weedy-looking. Easy to grow, even in poor soil. It tolerates drought, so it's good for arid areas.
PROBLEMS	Overwatering will kill it. Can become invasive.
HARVEST/STORAGE	Harvest and dry leaves and stems anytime, but preferably before the flowers form. Use fresh or store in glass containers in a cool dry place.
CULINARY USES	None.
MEDICINAL USES	Use the leaves and stems to make teas, syrups, and tinctures. Use dry or fresh leaves to make a tea. Drink the tea for respiratory problems. Make lozenges for coughs. Horehound is a good cough medicine and is also used as a digestive, vermifuge, and sedative as well as to treat fevers and malaria. It is said to control irregular heartbeat. It is a bitter, awful-tasting herb.
LANDSCAPE USES	Good groundcover for dry areas. Useful in landscaping as a contrast herb. Can be grown in containers.
INSIGHT	A gardening tea made from soaking the leaves in water has been used to control cankerworms and other insect pests.

Horehound

Horehound

HORSEMINT

Monarda citriodora
mo-NAR-da sit-ree-oh-DOOR-ah

COMMON NAMES	HORSEMINT, LEMON MINT, BERGAMOT.
FAMILY	Lamiaceae (Labiatae) (Mint).
TYPE	Perennial.
LOCATION	Full sun.
PLANTING	Plant seed summer through fall. Transplants can be set out in the fall.
HEIGHT	2 to 3 feet.
SPREAD	2 to 3 feet.
FINAL SPACING	10 to 18 inches.
BLOOM/FRUIT	Purple flowers in strong, upright spikes in late summer.
GROWTH HABITS/CULTURE	Upright and slow-spreading. Sturdy, tough wildflower. Easy to grow in most well-drained soils. It likes soil that is on the dry side. The leaves and foliage have a very strong lemony fragrance when bruised.
PROBLEMS	None serious.
HARVEST/STORAGE	Use fresh or store the foliage and flowers in a cool dry place or in the freezer.
CULINARY USES	Use similar to the mint species. Add to soups, stews, and meats. This is the strongest of all the monardas and not my favorite for culinary use.
MEDICINAL USES	Teas for colds, coughs, fevers, and various respiratory problems, although the other monardas are better for medicinal uses (see below). All monardas contain vitamin C.

Horsemint

Horsemint

Horseradish

LANDSCAPE USES	As a wildflower for the perennial garden.
OTHER USES	Excellent plant for attracting bees and for repelling fleas and chiggers. Fresh or dried flowers can be rubbed on pantlegs and socks to repel chiggers and other pests. Dry flowers can be crushed into powder to dust for insect control.
INSIGHT	Nothing browses any of the monardas—not even deer. The genus comprises a number of fragrant herbs with especially beautiful flowers. Most are native plants. Seeds are increasingly available from mail-order catalogs, and small plants are being seen more often in retail nurseries. This wildflower is incorrectly reported to be the source of citronella oil (the true source is a grass kin to lemongrass). *Monarda fistulosa* (wild bergamot) has pink to lavender flowers that are flat and feathery, *M. punctata* (spotted bee balm) has spotted purplish flowers, *M. alba* has feathery white flowers, and *M. didyma* has flat, feathery red flowers. See Bee Balm.

HORSERADISH

Armoracia rusticana
ar-mo-RAH-kee-ah rus-tee-KAH-nah

COMMON NAMES	HORSERADISH, DEVIL ROOT, MOUNTAIN RADISH, RED COLE.
FAMILY	Brassicaceae (Cruciferae) (Mustard).
TYPE	Hardy perennial.
LOCATION	Full sun to partial shade; morning sun, afternoon shade is best.
PLANTING	Horseradish seldom produces seeds, so you'll need to start plants from root cuttings in moist, rich soil. Cut roots into pieces 4 to 8 inches long, then plant the smaller pieces 2 to 3 inches deep, the larger pieces 2 to 4 inches deep. Space one foot apart in rows 3 to 4 feet apart. Plant in early spring or fall.
HEIGHT	28 to 39 inches.
SPREAD	12 to 18 inches.
FINAL SPACING	12 to 24 inches.
BLOOM/FRUIT	Has fragrant white flowers that bloom in summer.
GROWTH HABITS/CULTURE	Likes lots of manure or compost. In healthy soil, horseradish spreads

quickly in most soils. Plant it in an out-of-the way area where it won't matter if it spreads, or dig it completely each year from a bottomless bucket that has been sunk into the soil. Upright vigorous perennial, leafy, long leaves. Water when needed and fertilize once a year. Will grow well in any soil except light sand or very heavy clay. Horseradish roots can grow several feet deep. Good soil preparation will encourage thick, straight roots. Use lots of manure compost.

PROBLEMS
Spreads so easily it sometimes becomes a pest. If attacked by leaf-eating insects and slugs, treat with garlic-pepper tea, Fire Ant Control, and a release of decollate snails.

HARVEST/STORAGE
Pick a few spring leaves as needed for salads. Use a turning fork to dig roots in October or November, or leave in the ground and harvest roots as needed. Pick leaves as needed for salads.

CULINARY USES
Use the young leaves in salads and on sandwiches. Fresh-grated roots are used in a cream sauce as a condiment. My favorite horseradish sauce is made by adding natural vinegar and mustard.

MEDICINAL USES
Horseradish is traditionally used as an antiseptic and stimulant; it is also a laxative and strong diuretic. Cleans sinuses, treats inflamed gums, and aids digestion and respiratory problems. Roots are reported to have antibiotic properties.

LANDSCAPE USES
None.

OTHER USES
Dried leaves produce a yellow dye. Odena says that horseradish juice is used to help remove freckles and liver spots.

INSIGHT
Variegated variety available. Spikes of tiny white flowers should be removed to concentrate the plant's energy on leaf and root production. Some gardeners plant horseradish near potatoes to keep down potato diseases.

HORSETAIL REED

Equisetum hyemale or *Equisetum arvense*
eh-kwee-SEAT-um HIM-ah-lee or AR-vens

COMMON NAMES
HORSETAIL REED, HORSETAIL RUSH, SCOURING RUSH.

FAMILY
Equisetaceae (Horsetail).

TYPE
Evergreen aquatic plant.

LOCATION
Moist, wet sites—even in water. Sun and filtered light.

PLANTING
Plant division, spores, or container plants year round.

HEIGHT
2 to 4 feet.

SPREAD
Unlimited.

FINAL SPACING
18 inches.

BLOOM/FRUIT
Nonflowering spores in cone-like spikes at the end of the stems.

GROWTH HABITS/CULTURE
Slender, hollow, vertical green stems with black rings at each joint. Grows in soil or water. This is a bog or aquatic plant, so it does not need good drainage.

PROBLEMS
Invasive.

HARVEST/STORAGE
Use fresh or dried. For dried, cut into quarter-inch pieces.

CULINARY USES   None.

MEDICINAL USES   Horsetail reed has been used to strengthen fingernails and correct hair and skin problems. A good source of silica. Make a tea by covering 2 teaspoons of dried stem pieces with one cup boiling water; let steep for 15 or 20 minutes and then drink. Skeptics say the plant is a weak diuretic and little else.

LANDSCAPE USES   Bog or water-garden plant. Can be grown in containers.

OTHER USES   Florists use this plant in fresh and dried arrangements.

INSIGHT   *Equisetum arvense* has whorls of stems branching from the main shoot. It is the horsetail reed that appears in most herbals.

HOUTTUYNIA

Houttuynia cordata

who-tah-KNEE-ah core-DAH-tah

COMMON NAMES   HOUTTUYNIA, CHAMELEON PLANT, KOREAN CORIANDER.

FAMILY   Saaruraceae (Lizard's tail).

TYPE   Creeping perennial.

LOCATION   Shade in moist soil.

PLANTING   Container-grown transplants can be set out anytime. Cuttings and rhizome divisions can be made anytime during the growing season.

HEIGHT   18 inches.

Horsetail reed

Houttuynia

SPREAD	3 feet.
FINAL SPACING	12 to 18 inches.
BLOOM/FRUIT	Pretty little white flowers in summer. Extremely small seed.
GROWTH HABITS/CULTURE	Colorful low-growing groundcover that spreads aggressively. It has yellow, rosy, and red variegated foliage in full sun and small leaves resembling English ivy. Tolerates any soil condition, but does best in well-prepared, healthy soil that is wet or boggy and likes cool, moist, shaded locations.
PROBLEMS	Leaves will die back if the plant dries out. Can become very invasive.
HARVEST/STORAGE	Cut leaves in summer, preferably before the plant blooms, and dry them in sun. Best if used fresh.
CULINARY USES	In salads and as a condiment. Can be eaten raw or cooked. Used in Korean and Thai cooking. Caution: it has a very strong taste, and some people consider the fragrance unpleasant.
MEDICINAL USES	When used as a tea or eaten, it is said to help rheumatism, asthma, and colds. It also functions as a blood purifier and antibiotic. Blood purification is how most herbal antibiotics work.
LANDSCAPE USES	Attractive as a landscape groundcover plant.
INSIGHT	To control the spread, just let it dry out. Interesting plant that is worth growing. Loves wet feet—a nice surprise. Bruised foliage smells like strong citrus. This Japanese native dies completely to the ground in winter but returns aggressively each spring.

Hydrastis canadensis—see **GOLDENSEAL**

HYPERICUM—see **ST. JOHN'S WORT**

HYSSOP

Hyssopus officinalis
hi-SOAP-us oh-fis-ih-NAH-lis

COMMON NAMES	HYSSOP.
FAMILY	Lamiaceae (Labiatae) (Mint).
TYPE	Hardy perennial.
LOCATION	Sun, preferably morning sun and afternoon shade.
PLANTING	Start seed indoors in the winter. Set out transplants after the last frost. Cuttings can be taken during the growing season.
HEIGHT	24 inches.
SPREAD	18 inches.
FINAL SPACING	12 inches.
BLOOM/FRUIT	Blue, white, or pink flower spikes from summer to fall. Flowers and foliage have musky odor.
GROWTH HABITS/CULTURE	Shrubby evergreen herb with pointed, dark green leaves and small flowers that have a range of color. Slow-growing and upright. Resembles lavender. Hyssop prefers dry, slightly alkaline conditions, a light soil, and plenty of sun. Cut back to stimulate bushy growth. Can be kept clipped to 8 to 12 inches.

PROBLEMS   Few other than minor insect problems occasionally.

HARVEST/STORAGE   Store dry leaves in glass containers. Use fresh leaves for best results.

CULINARY USES   Flowers and leaves are edible and used in teas and sweet dishes.

MEDICINAL USES   Good general tonic plant. Teas made from the plant tops are good for coughs and have antiviral and digestive properties. Make a poultice for bruises and wounds. Local compresses have been used for staph infections. Should not be used during pregnancy or by anyone who has high blood pressure.

LANDSCAPE USES   Attracts beneficial insects like bees and butterflies.

OTHER USES   Primarily grown as an ornamental. Hyssop is said to deter cabbage moth and to be a good companion to cabbage and grapes.

INSIGHT   Easy to grow in dry, alkaline soil. Best to replant every four or five years. Should be grown in more gardens.

Hyssop

INDIAN LILAC—see **NEEM**
INDIAN SPICE—see **VITEX**
Inula helenium—see **ELECAMPANE**
JAMAICA—see **ROSELLE**
JASMINE SAMBAC—see **SAMBAC JASMINE**
JERUSALEM OAK—see **EPAZOTE**
Juglans nigra—see **WALNUT, BLACK**

JUJUBE

Ziziphus jujube
ZIZ-za-foos jew-JEW-bee

COMMON NAMES	JUJUBE.
FAMILY	Rhamnaceae (Buckthorn).
TYPE	Deciduous tree with edible fruit.
LOCATION	Full sun.
PLANTING	Plant seed or transplants in spring or fall. Install container plants anytime.
HEIGHT	25 to 30 feet.
SPREAD	15 to 30 feet.
FINAL SPACING	20 to 30 feet.
BLOOM/FRUIT	Clusters of small yellow flowers in early summer and shiny, date-like, red-brown fruit in the fall.
GROWTH HABITS/CULTURE	Upright-growing tree. Slow to moderate growth but will spread aggressively to become a real pest. Easy to grow in any soil.
PROBLEMS	Can spread badly by seed and root sprouts.
HARVEST/STORAGE	Harvest the fruit after it changes from red to dark brown in the late summer to fall and eat right away—unless you don't like the taste.
CULINARY USES	Edible fruit that tastes a little like dried apples.
MEDICINAL USES	Jujube is a medicinal herb used extensively in Chinese medicine. It soothes and relaxes stomach muscles and aids in absorption of nutrients. Dr. Judy Griffin uses it in her Chinese medicinals. She also cooks the leaves as well as the fruit and drinks the tea to relax. Remove the seed before cooking. For more details, see *Mother Nature's Herbal*.
LANDSCAPE USES	Good shade tree for the edible landscape.
OTHER USES	Also good for attracting birds and other wildlife.
INSIGHT	Make sure you want this unusual fruit tree before you plant it. It spreads by suckers and seed.

Jujube

JUNIPER

Juniperus spp.

joo-NIP-er-us

COMMON NAMES
ASHE JUNIPER, MOUNTAIN JUNIPER, CEDAR, NATIVE CEDAR, NATIVE JUNIPER, MOUNTAIN CEDAR, EASTERN RED CEDAR, RED JUNIPER, RED CEDAR, NATIVE JUNIPER.

FAMILY
Cupressaceae (Cypress or Redwood).

TYPE
Evergreen tree.

LOCATION
Full sun.

PLANTING
Install container plants year round. Set out transplants during the fall and winter. Plant seeds in the fall and take cuttings from late winter to fall. Collect, remove, and dry the seed from the small purple fruits in

the fall. Store over the winter at 20–40 degrees and plant in the spring. Use potting soil in containers or plant directly in the ground.

HEIGHT 18 feet, 30–40 feet.

SPREAD 12 feet, 20–30 feet.

FINAL SPACING 20 to 30 feet.

BLOOM/FRUIT Very small unimpressive flowers in the spring and small bluish purple berries or fruit in the fall on female plants. The fruits are actually miniature woody cones.

GROWTH HABITS/CULTURE Eastern red cedar (*Juniperus virginiana*) is upright, usually single-trunked, conical when young, dark green juniper-like foliage. Easy to grow in well-drained soil. In fact, these trees have become pests on poorly managed land. The Ashe or mountain cedar (*Juniperus ashei*) is more multi-trunked. Both are easy to grow in a wide range of soils.

Native Eastern red cedar

Eastern red cedar

They tolerate drought and will take over land that is mismanaged. Overgrazing or too much rest on the land can result in a proliferation of these trees.

PROBLEMS   Bagworms and spider mites when in stress. Native junipers are usually considered pests, but they are very valuable if managed properly. Cedar apple rust fungus attacks the Eastern red cedar, but it can be controlled with the Sick Tree Treatment.

HARVEST/STORAGE   Collect the fruit in the late summer and fall after it has turned a deep purple color. Try to gather the fruit and seeds from several different trees because they vary so much. Store dry in glass containers or use right away. Cut and use the wood and bark anytime.

CULINARY USES   Use the fruit in roasted meat or poultry as well as in liqueurs and vinegars. The fruits are used in wild game marinades and sauerkraut. According to Delena Tull in *Edible and Useful Plants of Texas and the Southwest*, the astringent ripe fruits of juniper trees can be used as a seasoning for meats, stews, and sauerkraut but are toxic when eaten in quantity.

MEDICINAL USES   Juniper berries are diuretic and antiseptic when taken in food or teas. They can kill fungi, reduce swollen tissue, and are good for the kidneys, urinary tract, and bladder. The fruits have been used historically to treat coughs, colds, headaches, and dysentery. Cedar oil from the wood is fragrant but very toxic. According to Mark Blumenthal of the American Botanical Council, the only species with proven medicinal benefits is the common European juniper (*Juniperus communis*).

LANDSCAPE USES   Specimen tree, border plant, or screening plant. The fruit is eaten by birds and other wildlife. Native junipers are used as shade trees but more as evergreen background plantings or screening plants. They are excellent for winter color and windbreaks.

OTHER USES   All parts of the plant make a superior mulch when shredded. It is inexpensive, smells good, repels insect pests, and is an excellent soil amendment. Wood made from the native cedars is quite resistant to decay, even when in contact with the soil. The foliage can be used in Christmas ornaments. Its fragrance is very pleasant in the house. Oils from the fruit have been used to flavor gin, perfume, soaps, and cosmetics. Bark, twigs, roots, and cones are used to make dyes. The wood is used for many purposes. Fine-textured cedar flakes make the world's best greenhouse flooring. The fragrance of cedar has insect-repelling qualities, and the resin can be used to control insect pests.

INSIGHT Eastern red cedar sometimes suffers cedar apple rust fungus whereas the mountain juniper does not. This disease is usually not a problem on any native junipers under an organic program. The allergy-causing pollen comes from the Ashe or mountain cedar in the fall. Male trees turn a golden brown when pollen production is at peak. Eastern red cedar blooms in the spring and causes few allergy problems. To get rid of unwanted cedars, spray them with strong vinegar and orange oil, then set on fire. But be careful—they burn very easily.

Juniperus—see **JUNIPER**
KNITBONE—see **COMFREY**

KUDZU

Pueraria lobata
pew-RARE-ee-ah lo-BAH-ta

COMMON NAMES	KUDZU, KUDSU, KUDZUVINE, JAPANESE ARROWROOT.
FAMILY	Fabaceae (Leguminosae) (Legume).
TYPE	Deciduous groundcover and vine.
LOCATION	Full sun.
PLANTING	Kudzu can be started from seed, cuttings, root divisions, or crowns and should be planted during the dormant season.
HEIGHT	High climber.
SPREAD	60 feet and more.
FINAL SPACING	3 to 10 feet.
BLOOM/FRUIT	Purple, pea-shaped flowers start to bloom in the late summer and fall of the third year, producing seed.
GROWTH HABITS/CULTURE	Perennial vine with high-climbing, spreading stems. Kudzu is extremely fast-growing and aggressive, spreading by underground runners. Leaves are on hard, slender, hairy stems. Each leaf has three dark green leaflets that are 3–6 inches long. Requires a normal watering and fertilizer program.
PROBLEMS	Kudzu is susceptible to root-knot nematodes and blackleg fungus in nursery soil, which can be prevented by cornmeal in the soil. Mosaic virus is also a potential problem. Not too many bugs like to eat it. The invasiveness can be easily controlled by allowing animals to graze on it or burning it in the fall. Cattle and hogs love this plant.

Kudzu

HARVEST/STORAGE	Harvest the leaves anytime. The roots should be dug in the fall and winter. The ground root should be stored in a cool dry place and in glass containers, if possible.
CULINARY USES	There is an entire book devoted to cooking with kudzu as well as its healing properties. Kudzu is used in many Japanese-style dishes, including sauces, gravies, soups, salads, vegetables, rice, desserts, and drinks. For details, see *The Book of Kudzu* by William Shurtleff and Akiko Aoyagi.
MEDICINAL USES	Kudzu has been used to treat alcohol abuse, chills, colds, coughs, asthma, nasal congestion, diarrhea, fever, sinus, and many more ailments. Be careful when buying kudzu powder—there are potato starch imitations on the market.
LANDSCAPE USES	Fast-growing groundcover for large problem areas, especially those subject to erosion. It also makes an excellent plant for trellises or other overhead structures.
OTHER USES	A terrific source of protein. Should be grown more as a crop for that purpose. Kudzu is a legume and a nitrogen fixer for the soil. It is also a superior crop for grazing animals. The honey from kudzu is excellent.
INSIGHT	Yes, I realize kudzu has done great damage to forests in the South. But that's the result of mismanagement. All that is needed to eliminate the weed aspect of the plant is to allow any kind of grazing animals into the stands. The animals love it. Seed are available from the George W. Park Seed Co., P.O. Box 31, Greenwood, SC 29647.

LADY'S LEG—see **MADRONE**
LADY'S LOVE—see **SOUTHERNWOOD**

LAMB'S EAR

Stachys byzantina
STACK-is biz-an-TEEN-ah

COMMON NAMES	LAMB'S EAR, LAMB'S EARS, WOOLLY BETONY.
FAMILY	Lamiaceae (Labiatae) (Mint).
TYPE	Evergreen perennial.
LOCATION	Full sun to light shade.
PLANTING	Plant seeds, divisions, and transplants in the spring. Seed can be started indoors in the winter.
HEIGHT	6 to 12 inches.
SPREAD	24 to 36 inches.
FINAL SPACING	12 to 18 inches.
BLOOM/FRUIT	Lavender flowers followed by many tiny seeds.
GROWTH HABITS/CULTURE	Low-growing, spreading groundcover. Drought-tolerant. Felty, light gray-green leaves. Needs excellent drainage or will die out from crown rot. Cut back in early spring.
PROBLEMS	Crown rot resulting from too much water, poorly drained soil. Hard rains beat it down and make it mushy, but it usually comes back.
HARVEST/STORAGE	Harvest the leaves anytime.

Lamb's ear

CULINARY USES None.

MEDICINAL USES The leaves of lamb's ear are antiseptic and styptic, so they are used directly on scratches, minor cuts, insect bites, and stings. My daughter, Logan, used the leaves for bandages when she was young—so did the Native Americans.

LANDSCAPE USES Good for rock gardens and sunny locations.

OTHER USES Light-colored low-growing groundcover.

INSIGHT Propagates and spreads easily by seeds and rhizomes. Cut back the flower spikes to maintain a compact appearance. Flowers are good in dried arrangements.

LAMB'S-QUARTER

Chenopodium album
chin-no-PO-dee-um AL-bum

COMMON NAMES LAMB'S-QUARTER, PIGWEED.

FAMILY Chenopodiaceae (Goosefoot or Pigweed).

TYPE Annual.

LOCATION Sun.

PLANTING Plant seeds in the spring. Set out transplants after the last frost.

HEIGHT Up to 10 feet.

SPREAD 3 feet.

FINAL SPACING 18 to 24 inches.

BLOOM/FRUIT Very small ball-shaped, greenish white flowers that product lots of seed.

GROWTH HABITS/CULTURE Lamb's-quarter is an easy-to-grow spinach-like plant that is native to Texas.

PROBLEMS Few if any; some occasional insect bites. Can spread by seed and become invasive.

HARVEST/STORAGE Pick leaves and use anytime. It does not keep well, but it grows so prolifically there's no need to store it.

Red lamb's-quarter

Lamb's-quarter

CULINARY USES   Use the leaves in salads, as a pot herb, and as edible greens. Boil leaves 10 minutes and serve with lemon or pepper sauce. Eat raw or cooked like spinach.

MEDICINAL USES   Lamb's-quarter is high in vitamin C and iron.

LANDSCAPE USES   None—it gets pretty ugly as it matures.

INSIGHT   Relative of orach. Like spinach, it contains oxalic acid. There are about 26 different *Chenopodium* species in Texas. This wild plant, commonly called pigweed, can be found all across America. Cows love to eat it. There are other plants in this family that you should *not* eat (every family has its black sheep). The dangerous ones will have a paint-like smell when the leaves are crushed, like epazote.

Larrea tridentata—see **CREOSOTE BUSH**
Laurus nobilis—see **BAY**
LAVENDER COTTON—see **SANTOLINA**

LAVENDER

Lavandula spp.
lav-VAN-dew-la

COMMON NAMES   LAVENDER.

FAMILY   Lamiaceae (Labiatae) (Mint).

TYPE   Evergreen perennial.

LOCATION   Full sun to partial shade.

PLANTING   Transplants can be set out year round. Not easy to germinate and grow. Seeds sprout best when sown on top of the ground and when the air and soil are warm.

HEIGHT   24 to 36 inches.

SPREAD   36 to 48 inches.

FINAL SPACING   18 to 24 inches.

Spanish lavender

French lavender

BLOOM/FRUIT	Spikes of fragrant lavender-blue flowers in summer.
GROWTH HABITS/CULTURE	Narrow, gray-green foliage, aromatic lavender-blue flowers on narrow stalks in spring and intermittently throughout the summer. Shrubby overall growth. English lavender is the easiest to grow. Excellent drainage is a must.
PROBLEMS	Overwatering or damp weather causes lots of trouble for lavender. Even normal rainfall can rot the roots and kill the plant unless the drainage is excellent.
HARVEST/STORAGE	Harvest leaves anytime. For the best quality, harvest flowers early— when they first come into bloom. Dry and store in glass containers.
CULINARY USES	Use in cooking as you would use rosemary. Teas should be made from the flowers and leaves. The flowers are used in spice mixes.
MEDICINAL USES	Lavender is antiseptic, sedative, and antispasmatic. It also relieves headaches. Use in capsules or tea.
LANDSCAPE USES	Perennial garden, border plants, specimen plants.
OTHER USES	Fragrance plant, used to scent linens, as a perfume, and to repel moths. Beautiful perennial for landscape.
INSIGHT	English lavender (*L. angustifolia*) has smooth-edged leaves. French lavender (*L. dentata*) has a serrated leaf. Spanish lavender (*L. stoechas*) has gray leaves and flat, purple blooms with broad, flat-topped clusters of flowers instead of a spike. The pink and white flowering varieties are not recommended.

Lavandula—see **LAVENDER**

LEEK—see **ONION**

LEMON BALM

Melissa officinalis
me-LISS-ah o-fis-ah-NALE-lis

COMMON NAMES	LEMON BALM, BALM, MELISSA, BALM MINT, BEE BALM.
FAMILY	Lamiaceae (Labiatae) (Mint).
TYPE	Perennial.
LOCATION	Likes partial shade best, preferably morning sun and afternoon shade.
PLANTING	Start seed indoors in the winter. Set out transplants in the spring. Make divisions and cuttings anytime during the growing season.
HEIGHT	20 to 24 inches.
SPREAD	24 to 48 inches.
FINAL SPACING	18 to 24 inches.
BLOOM/FRUIT	Small white flowers clustered along the stem in summer.
GROWTH HABITS/CULTURE	Bushy, spreading herb with heart-shaped, mint-like, lemon-scented leaves with scalloped edges. Likes loose, well-drained soil, little fertilizer, and occasional light feedings of compost. Overfertilization produces large leaves with little fragrance. Cut back often to maintain thick, compact plants.
PROBLEMS	Spider mites during hot and humid summers. Don't overwater; spray

Lemon balm

with a citrus-based product or Garrett Juice plus orange oil. Some infestations of worms, pill bugs, and aphids can be controlled the same way. If you let it go to seed, it will spread everywhere.

HARVEST/STORAGE Harvest the foliage anytime and use fresh if possible. Can be dried or frozen, but not without a loss in scent and flavor.

CULINARY USES Good tea plant. Odena's tri-lemon tea includes lemongrass, lemon balm, and lemon verbena. Good for flavoring desserts. Lemon balm produces high-quality honey. Use it for oils, vinegars, and liqueurs.

MEDICINAL USES Lemon balm has been used for anxiety, allergies, insomnia, nervousness, itching, shingles, and respiratory problems. It contains lots of vitamin C and is one of the longevity herbs. Good for digestion, nausea, headaches, and depression. Take as a tea.

LANDSCAPE USES Attractive in shady areas of landscape, but be careful—it will spread aggressively. Good honey plant.

INSIGHT *Melissa* is from the Greek word for "bee," indicating the plant's ability to attract these insects. Use it in potpourri and flower arrangements, too. A good garnish for dessert, fruit, and tossed salads. Variegated forms are available, but they are not as flavorful.

LEMONGRASS

Cymbopogon citratus
sim-bo-PO-gon si-TRA-tus

COMMON NAMES LEMONGRASS.

FAMILY Poaceae (Gramineae) (Grass).

TYPE Tender perennial.

LOCATION Full sun.

PLANTING Set out divisions or transplants in spring after the last frost.

HEIGHT 30 to 36 inches.

SPREAD 30 to 36 inches.

FINAL SPACING	3 feet.
BLOOM/FRUIT	Rarely if ever blooms in one season.
GROWTH HABITS/CULTURE	Aromatic clump grass with bulbous stems. Upright growth similar to pampas grass. Strongly lemon-scented foliage. Freezes easily in North Texas but can live through mild winters under heavy mulch after being cut back. Needs excellent drainage. Some gardeners cut it back in mid-season to stimulate new growth. Cut it back drastically in early winter and mulch, or lift out the clump to winter indoors in a container.
PROBLEMS	Freeze damage, rust on leaves if overwatered.
HARVEST/STORAGE	Use fresh, or store dry or frozen pieces of leaves or stalks for winter use. It's just as flavorful dried or frozen as it is fresh. Store in glass containers if possible.
CULINARY USES	Teas, stir-fry dishes. Use the stalks to make vinegar or chop the stalks for salads and Oriental and Mexican dishes. Be sure to peel first.
MEDICINAL USES	Lemongrass has antiseptic qualities and is good for colds and flu. It is high in vitamin A and is used in the compounding of vitamins.
LANDSCAPE USES	Good in pots and as a summer accent plant.
OTHER USES	Gardeners have reported that the tea makes a good mosquito repellent.
INSIGHT	Plant in a location protected from north winds in winter, or grow in containers and move to a protected location. Leaves must be broken to release the lemony fragrance. Some say that lemongrass must be boiled to yield the best tea. Others say that boiling destroys vitamins and reduces the healthful qualities of the herb. Be careful while harvesting—the leaves can cut you. The blades can be rubbed in an upward direction but never downward. Citronella essential oil is extracted from a tropical grass related to lemongrass. There are two types of citronella: the Ceylon type (*C. nardus*), grown in Sri Lanka, and the Java type (*C. winterianus*), which grows in Java, Haiti, and Guatemala. The Ceylon type is the most commonly used. The Java type is primarily used in commercial perfume because of its fine, delicate odor.

Lemongrass

Lemon verbena

LEMON MINT—see **HORSEMINT**

LEMON VERBENA

Aloysia triphylla syn. *Lippia citriodora*
a-lo-ISS-ee-a tri-FILL-la

COMMON NAMES	LEMON VERBENA.
FAMILY	Verbenaceae (Vervain).
TYPE	Tender perennial.
LOCATION	Full sun to light shade in a warm, protected place.
PLANTING	Transplants, seed, or cuttings in spring after the last frost. Softwood cuttings should be taken in late summer. The seed method is difficult.
HEIGHT	3 to 4 feet, smaller in containers.
SPREAD	3 feet.
FINAL SPACING	18 to 24 inches.
BLOOM/FRUIT	Loose clusters of fragrant, pale purple flowers that are not very spectacular. Usually blooms in late summer.
GROWTH HABITS/CULTURE	An open-growing shrub-like herb with woody stems. Leaves are narrow, pointed, rough-textured, lemon-scented, and from 1 to 3 inches long; they grow in whorls of three or four. Somewhat scraggly with long, limber branches. Freezes easily in the northern half of the state.
PROBLEMS	Spider mites, whiteflies, aphids, and worms if not grown in totally organic conditions. Under the Basic Organic Program, the plant has few problems.
HARVEST/STORAGE	Pick leaves and dry anytime during the summer. They can also be frozen, but the fresh leaves are best.
CULINARY USES	Marvelous flavor for any meat, great in teas, jellies, and sherbet. Lemon verbena is used in some cake recipes and to flavor liqueurs. It is also good for other desserts and sweet dishes.

MEDICINAL USES	Lemon verbena has lots of vitamin C and makes a very soothing and relaxing tea. It has been used for asthma, migraine headaches, vertigo, depression, nasal congestion, indigestion, and nausea.
LANDSCAPE USES	Nice in mixed plantings. Chartreuse leaves contrast with the darker greens of other plants. Very fragrant garden plant. Good container plant.
OTHER USES	Potpourri, bath and body care products. Keeps its scent for years.
INSIGHT	Try Odena's tri-lemon tea, which is made from equal parts of lemon verbena, lemongrass, and lemon balm.

Lepidium sativum—see **PEPPERGRASS**

Levisticum officinale—see **LOVAGE**

LICORICE

Glycyrrhiza glabra

gli-ser-RISE-ah GLA-bra

COMMON NAMES	LICORICE, SWEET ROOT.
FAMILY	Fabaceae (Leguminosae) (Legume).
TYPE	Herbaceous perennial.
LOCATION	Full sun.
PLANTING	Divisions, seed, and budded pieces of root can be planted in the spring. Transplants can be set out after the last frost.
HEIGHT	3 to 6 feet.
SPREAD	24 inches.
FINAL SPACING	36 inches.

Licorice plant (not the herb)

BLOOM/FRUIT	Spikes of white or pale violet-blue pea-like flowers in summer.
GROWTH HABITS/CULTURE	Photo shows licorice plant (*Helichrysum petiolatum*), a drought tolerant ornamental sold incorrectly as the herb by some nurseries. True licorice is an upright perennial with large, green, ash-like, compound leaves. Cut back foliage as it starts to die. Being a legume, licorice produces a large underground root system that has the capacity to hold nitrogen in its nodules.
PROBLEMS	It can't take wet feet. Unless it has excellent drainage, it will rot in the ground.
HARVEST/STORAGE	Dig roots and rhizomes, dry and store in the fall. Harvest the third year after planting.
CULINARY USES	Tea and candy. Some people like licorice tea, some hate it. I guess the same could be said for the candy.
MEDICINAL USES	Roots are used in cough drops and lozenges to disguise the taste of bad medicine. It has been used historically to reduce alcohol dependency and to treat respiratory, urinary, and bowel problems. High in mucilage, it is a mild laxative and has a cortisone-like effect. It is reported to help the liver detoxify drugs and is given for liver disease.
LANDSCAPE USES	Interesting plant for the perennial garden.
OTHER USES	Roots stripped of the bark are chewed like candy.
INSIGHT	The black color associated with licorice candy results from a process of crushing the roots and boiling them in water. Those with high blood pressure should avoid licorice. Consult a doctor before taking medicinally

LILAC CHASTE TREE—see VITEX

LINDEN

Tilia spp.
TILL-ee-ah

COMMON NAMES	BASSWOOD, LINDEN, CAROLINA BASSWOOD, FLORIDA BASS-WOOD, LIME BLOSSOM TREE.
FAMILY	Tiliaceae (Linden).
TYPE	Deciduous tree.
LOCATION	Sun to part shade.
PLANTING	Year round from containers. Bare-rooted in the fall. Seed or cuttings in the spring.
HEIGHT	30 to 50 feet.
SPREAD	20 to 30 feet.
FINAL SPACING	20 feet.
BLOOM/FRUIT	Small, fragrant, off-white flowers in the summer in drooping clusters attached to leaf-like bracts. The flowers make excellent honey. Fruit is a winged hard capsule with one or two seeds.
GROWTH HABITS/CULTURE	Moderate growth rate, but will grow much taller in deep, moist, healthy soils. Heart-shaped leaves are silvery on the underside. Most lindens have a neat appearance with a straight trunk and symmetrical growth.

Little leaf linden

Carolina basswood

PROBLEMS	Occasionally aphids, leaf beetles, and caterpillars. Spraying is rarely needed. Garrett Juice plus garlic tea controls minor pests.
HARVEST/STORAGE	Use the flowers and leaves fresh or dried.
CULINARY USES	The world's most valued honey is made from the flowers, which are also used in liqueurs and medicines.
MEDICINAL USES	Tea from the flowers is used as a digestive aid and a treatment for insomnia, nervous tension, and hyperactivity in children. It brings on sweating, which reduces cold and flu symptoms and headaches. Overuse can cause nausea and heart damage, so use in moderation.
LANDSCAPE USES	Shade tree and fragrant flowers.
OTHER USES	Lumber.
INSIGHT	Carolina basswood (*Tilia caroliniana*) is native to East Texas and the creeks of the Edwards Plateau in Central Texas. It grows to 90 feet in deep, rich soils. It flowers from April to June. *Tilia cordata* is the little leaf linden and is adapted for all of Texas except for white-rock soil.

Lippia citriodora—see **LEMON VERBENA**
Lippia dulcis—see **SWEET HERB**

LOVAGE

Levisticum officinale
le-VIS-ti-kum oh-fis-oh-NALE

COMMON NAMES	LOVAGE, LOVE PARSLEY, SEA PARSLEY.
FAMILY	Apiaceae (Umbelliferae) (Carrot or Parsley).
TYPE	Tender perennial.
LOCATION	Partial sun, preferably morning sun.
PLANTING	Plant from containers year round, but preferably in early spring while the weather is still cool. Seed should be started in the winter. Transplant divisions in the fall.
HEIGHT	3 to 5 feet.
SPREAD	2 feet.
FINAL SPACING	12 to 18 inches.

Lovage

Lovage seedlings

BLOOM/FRUIT	Umbels or flat clusters of small yellow-green flowers followed by many aromatic seeds.
GROWTH HABITS/CULTURE	Leaves are large, dark green, deeply cut and divided, and celery-scented with yellow stems. Easy to grow in any healthy, well-drained soil. Likes lots of manure compost and cool weather.
PROBLEMS	Cutworms, caterpillars. Hot weather and afternoon sun will burn the foliage. Not totally winter hardy.
HARVEST/STORAGE	Harvest leaves anytime. They will freeze well and can be dried. Pick leaves just before bloom. Dig roots in the fall.
CULINARY USES	Use like celery, which it resembles in appearance and taste. Use tender young leaves in soups, stews, and salads, or nibble on it fresh out of the garden. Use the seed crushed or whole. Cook with cabbage, add to soups and salads. Use the leaves fresh, but cook the stalks. Chew on the seeds when they turn brown. Seeds are used in breads and cookies. Good salt substitute.
MEDICINAL USES	Tonic and diuretic when eaten.
LANDSCAPE USES	Use at the back of a border due to its "rough" appearance. It is useful for its pleasant garden fragrance.
INSIGHT	Should be avoided by pregnant women and by those with kidney problems.

LOVER'S PLANT—see **SOUTHERNWOOD**
LUCERNE—see **ALFALFA**

MADDER

Rubia tinctoria
ROO-bee-uh tink-TORE-ee-uh

COMMON NAMES	MADDER, DYER'S MADDER.
FAMILY	Rubiaceae (Coffee or Madder).
TYPE	Herbaceous perennial.
LOCATION	Dry, sunny location.
PLANTING	Start seed indoors in the winter or directly in the garden in the spring. Cuttings can be made during the growing season.
HEIGHT	To 4 feet.
SPREAD	18 inches.
FINAL SPACING	12 to 18 inches.
BLOOM/FRUIT	Small star-shaped yellow flowers in summer followed by small purple berries.
GROWTH HABITS/CULTURE	Found in wastelands. Madder is a climbing or leaning herb with whorls of prickly and thin, pointed leaves. This hardy, sprawling perennial is easily grown from cuttings in most soils.
PROBLEMS	Few, if any.
HARVEST/STORAGE	Dry 2-year-old roots and stems and store in a cool dark place.
CULINARY USES	None.
MEDICINAL USES	Used in homeopathic medicine. The root has been used in teas or capsules to treat kidney stones. Madder has also been used to make a tonic.
LANDSCAPE USES	None—not a very good-looking plant.
OTHER USES	Madder is a fine dye source. Its colorful roots yield a beautiful red dye.
INSIGHT	*Tinctoria* means "dye plant" for shades of red, pink, purple, orange, and brown.

MADRONE

Arbutus texana
ar-BYOO-tus tex-AN-ah

COMMON NAMES	LADY'S LEG, MADRONE, NAKED INDIAN, TEXAS ARBUTUS, TEXAS MADRONE, MADROÑO.
FAMILY	Ericaceae (Heath or Blueberry).
TYPE	Evergreen tree.
LOCATION	Sun to light shade.
PLANTING	Transplant in fall and winter. Plant from containers year round. Madrone can be grown from seeds, transplants, and cuttings. Collect the seeds from November through December. Cold treatment helps

promote germination. Very difficult to root from cuttings. Try taking them in the early spring as the buds swell.

HEIGHT	20 to 30 feet.
SPREAD	20 to 30 feet.
FINAL SPACING	15 to 25 feet.
BLOOM/FRUIT	White to pale pink urn-shaped flowers in spring. Clusters of raspberry-like red to orange fruit in fall. Little bumps cover the round fruits.
GROWTH HABITS/CULTURE	Spring-blooming ornamental, usually multi-trunked, with thin, beautiful, exfoliating bark and leathery, dark green leaves. Slow growth in any well-drained soil.
PROBLEMS	Too much moisture in the soil leads to root fungi and other problems related to poor drainage. Hard to transplant. Wet soil in the winter is one of the biggest problems for this plant.
HARVEST/STORAGE	Collect and eat the berries fresh if you can get any before the birds do from September to November.

Madrone

Madrone

CULINARY USES	Delicious edible berries. Eat them fresh or in cereal.
MEDICINAL USES	None known at this time.
LANDSCAPE USES	Ornamental tree for full-sun, well-drained sites.
INSIGHT	Beautiful tree that should be used more. Much more cold-hardy than reported. You'll have to compete with the birds to get any of the berries, though.

MADROÑO—see **MADRONE**
MAIDENHAIR TREE—see **GINKGO**
MAIDEN'S RUIN—see **SOUTHERNWOOD**

MALLOW

Malva sylvestris or *moschata*
MAL-va sil-VES-tris mo-SHOT-ah

COMMON NAMES	CUTLEAF MALLOW, MALLOW, MUSK, HOLLYHOCK.
FAMILY	Malvaceae (Mallow).
TYPE	Annual, biennial, and perennial.
LOCATION	Full sun to partial shade.
PLANTING	Start seed indoors in late winter or plant directly in beds in the spring. Transplants can be set out after the last frost.
HEIGHT	Up to 3 feet.
SPREAD	24 inches.
FINAL SPACING	12 to 36 inches.
BLOOM/FRUIT	White, pink, rose, or purple flowers throughout the summer.
GROWTH HABITS/CULTURE	Musky, elegantly cut leaves on branching stems. Common mallow (*Malva sylvestris*) is a biennial normally grown as an annual. Its rosy, purple-petaled flowers, occurring in clusters of two to six, begin blooming in early spring and continue through late summer. It is easy to grow in healthy, well-drained soil. It reseeds readily.

French hollyhock

PROBLEMS	Caterpillars and other leaf-chewing insects. Spray with Garrett Juice plus garlic tea or orange oil for serious infestations.
HARVEST/STORAGE	Harvest flowers and leaves as needed.
CULINARY USES	The flowers are used in salads. Fresh, young leaves can be boiled as a vegetable.
MEDICINAL USES	Used to make other medicines more palatable. Has been used historically for bronchitis and gastrointestinal problems. Take as a tea made from the flowers.
LANDSCAPE USES	Perennial garden.
OTHER USES	Ornamental plant that provides summer color.
INSIGHT	*M. sylvestris* is the common mallow, *M. sylvestris zebrina* is the old-fashioned, easy-to-grow purple French hollyhock. *M. moschata* is the lacy-leafed mallow that has either pink or white flowers. Some of the other mallows include hibiscus, Turk's cap, and cotton.

Malva moschata—see **MALLOW**

Malva sylvestris—see **MALLOW**

Malvaviscus arboreus—see **TURK'S CAP**

MARJORAM

Origanum marjorana

o-ree-GAH-num mar-jo-RAH-na

COMMON NAMES	SWEET MARJORAM, KNOTTED MARJORAM.
FAMILY	Lamiaceae (Labiatae) (Mint).
TYPE	Perennial.
LOCATION	Full sun.
PLANTING	Start seed in the winter. Set out transplants in the early spring. Cuttings can be made during the growing season and divisions in the fall.
HEIGHT	10 to 15 inches.
SPREAD	18 to 24 inches.
FINAL SPACING	18 to 24 inches.
BLOOM/FRUIT	Tiny bud-like mauve-pink flowers, sometimes purple or white. But it's best not to let the plant bloom.
GROWTH HABITS/CULTURE	All oreganos are easy to grow in any well-drained soil. They have tough, trailing stems and require a minimum of fertilizer and care.
PROBLEMS	Few, if any.
HARVEST/STORAGE	Cut, dry, and store in a cool place.
CULINARY USES	Italian food, vegetables, salads, meats, fish, eggs, and vinaigrettes.
MEDICINAL USES	General body tonic when taken as a tea. Crushed leaves can be applied to insect stings. Use the same way as oregano.
LANDSCAPE USES	Border plant and groundcover. Greek oregano, another *Origanum* species, is especially good.
OTHER USES	Marjoram is used in potpourri, perfumes, and bath products. The seed heads make great winter feed for wild birds. The flowers attract butterflies and bees.

Marjoram

INSIGHT   The genus *Origanum* consists of about 25 species, mostly perennials. Some oreganos have green leaves, and some have hairy white leaves. Here are some of the most popular: Spanish oregano is *Origanum vulgare*. The most popular for cooking is Greek oregano (*Origanum* var. *prismaticum*). Woolly leaf oregano (*Origanum dictamnus*) is commonly called dittany of Crete. Arid conditions usually produce the best flavor from these herbs.

Marjorama spp.—see **MARJORAM**
MARRUBIO—see **HOREHOUND**
Marrubium vulgare—see **HOREHOUND**

MARSH MALLOW

Althaea officinalis
AL-thee-ah oh-fis-ih-NAL-is

COMMON NAMES	MARSH MALLOW.
FAMILY	Malvaceae (Mallow).
TYPE	Hardy herbaceous perennial.
LOCATION	Sun to partial shade.
PLANTING	Start seed indoors in the winter, set out transplants in the spring. Make root divisions in the fall. Easy to propagate from cuttings.
HEIGHT	4 to 6 feet.

SPREAD	4 to 6 feet.
FINAL SPACING	24 inches.
BLOOM/FRUIT	Pale pink, white, and purple summer flowers. Small black seeds in very interesting pods.
GROWTH HABITS/CULTURE	Upright growth, velvety gray-green leaves. Grows wild in marshes, especially near the sea. Grows best in healthy, well-drained soil, but it can also tolerate wet soils better than most herbs. Grows tall and sometimes needs staking.
PROBLEMS	Few.
HARVEST/STORAGE	Leaves, roots, and flowers are all usable. Harvest roots in fall. Harvest the young leaves right before the plant blooms. Harvest the flowers as they open.
CULINARY USES	The nutty seeds, flowers, and young leaves are used in salads. The leaves can be eaten as a vegetable.
MEDICINAL USES	Marsh mallow is soothing to the stomach and is good for ulcers. It also helps with respiratory problems and stimulates the kidneys. It is used in many medicines to make them more palatable. It contains mucilage and is used in cosmetics to soften weathered and damaged skin.
LANDSCAPE USES	Attractive summer flowers.
OTHER USES	The roots contain sugars and were used in medicinal sweets and in the original marshmallow candy.
INSIGHT	A high mucilage content gives this plant special softening and healing properties.

MAYPOP—see **PASSION FLOWER**
MEDICINAL TEA TREE—see **TEA TREE**
MELIA—see **NEEM**
MELISSA—see **LEMON BALM**
Mentha pulegium—see **PENNYROYAL**
Mentha—see **MINT**

Marsh mallow

MEXICAN MINT—see MEXICAN OREGANO
MEXICAN MINT MARIGOLD—see SWEET MARIGOLD

MEXICAN OREGANO

Poliomentha longiflora
pol-lee-oh-MINT-tha long-ee-FLOOR-ah

COMMON NAMES	MEXICAN OREGANO, MOUNTAIN MINT.
FAMILY	Lamiaceae (Labiatae) (Mint).
TYPE	Tender perennial.
LOCATION	Full sun to partial shade.
PLANTING	Spring through fall.
HEIGHT	2 to 4 feet.
SPREAD	18 to 36 inches.
FINAL SPACING	12 to 18 inches.
BLOOM/FRUIT	Flowers are tubular white to lavender-pink, 1½ inches long, and smell of oregano. It rarely sets seed in Texas. The hummingbirds love these summer blossoms.
GROWTH HABITS/CULTURE	Spreading but bushy form with strong-smelling, mint-like leaves and brittle stems. Easy to grow. Blooms over a long period—from late spring through summer. Usually not perennial in the northern half of the state.
PROBLEMS	Can freeze out in North Texas.
HARVEST/STORAGE	Use the leaves fresh from the plant or pick them when green, then dry and store in glass containers.
CULINARY USES	Good for making tea and flavoring meats, including *cabrito*. Use fresh as an oregano substitute. The flowers can be used in teas.
MEDICINAL USES	Drink the tea for respiratory problems.
LANDSCAPE USES	Use in wildflower gardens, the perennial garden, the herb garden, and in pots. Good for attracting hummingbirds.
INSIGHT	Mexican oregano is a misleading name because it doesn't resemble true oregano. But it's a good plant and should be used more.

Mexican oregano

Chocolate peppermint

MILFOIL—see YARROW

MINT

Mentha spp.

MEN-tha

COMMON NAMES	MINT.
FAMILY	Lamiaceae (Labiatae) (Mint).
TYPE	Perennial.
LOCATION	Full sun to afternoon shade.
PLANTING	Mint can be planted almost year round by root divisions or transplants. Stem cuttings are very easy to take anytime during the growing season.
HEIGHT	1 to 3 feet.
SPREAD	Unlimited.
FINAL SPACING	12 to 24 inches.
BLOOM/FRUIT	Whorls of small flowers bloom throughout summer in shades from white to lavender, followed by tiny seeds. It's best to keep the flowers cut off in order to protect the flavor of the leaves and prevent the germination of weaker plants.
GROWTH HABITS/CULTURE	Aggressively spreading plant. Highly aromatic leaves on square stems are round, oval, or slightly pointed, smooth or wrinkly, and slightly serrated on their edges. Fertilizer not recommended other than compost. Likes loose, well-drained soil. Cut back regularly to remove flowers and seed. Mints need frequent and consistent moisture.

Apple mint

Doublemint

PROBLEMS Some chewing insects but none serious. Whiteflies and aphids occasionally. Susceptible to rust when kept too damp. Mints are very invasive and will take over your garden. Be careful where you plant them. Planting mints by plunging bottomless pots into the garden soil is one way to keep them from spreading so much. Use a cold chisel to remove the bottom from old clay pots, then plunge the pots into the garden soil. Plastic pots and flue tiles will also work. This technique can also be used for plants that need to be brought indoors in the winter.

HARVEST/STORAGE Cut and use fresh, dry and store in glass containers, or freeze and store in plastic. It's always best to use mints fresh.

CULINARY USES Used to flavor all kinds of foods, especially green peas, salads, desserts, and drinks. Add to beef or lamb for a special flavor in both Greek and Italian cuisine. Spearmint with cucumbers makes a delicious salad. Sprinkle chopped mint over thick slices of tomato and drizzle with extra-virgin olive oil. Peppermint is good on ice cream and for peppermint candy. Mint is also good with avocado.

MEDICINAL USES Mints are used to flavor medicines and for coughs, colds, respiratory problems, and sinus headaches. They produce a mild sedative effect. The most common is peppermint, which is a stimulant and an excellent digestive aid, a pain reliever, and a caffeine substitute. Spearmint is cooling and reduces fever. Mints are best taken in teas.

LANDSCAPE USES Groundcover in areas of wet soil. Also good in pots.

OTHER USES Mints are used to flavor toothpastes, mouthwashes, and other dental products. Mint can be used in stored grain and seeds to ward off insect pests. Peppermint is reported to repel insects and mice.

INSIGHT Mints are broadly divided into two groups according to fragrance: the spearmints (*M. spicata*) and the peppermints (*M. piperita*). The chief constituent of peppermint oil is menthol, while that of spearmint oil is primarily carvone. Apple mint (*M. suaveolens* 'Variegata') has cream-edged leaves. Black peppermint (*M. piperita* 'Vulgaris') has forest-green leaves with deep purple veins and stems. Watermint (*M. aquatica*) has reddish-purple stems and round lilac flowers. Spearmint is best for children because of its milder flavor.

Monarda fistulosa—see **HORSEMINT**
Monarda citriodora—see **HORSEMINT**
Monarda didyma—see **BEE BALM**
MOSS ROSE—see **PURSLANE**
MOTHER ELDER—see **ELDERBERRY**
MOUNTAIN MINT—see **MEXICAN OREGANO**

MUGWORT

Artemisia vulgaris
ar-tay-MEEZ-ee-ah vul-GAR-iss

COMMON NAMES   MUGWORT, SAILOR'S TOBACCO, SMOTHERWOOD.
FAMILY   Asteraceae (Compositae) (Sunflower or Daisy).
TYPE   Herbaceous perennial.
LOCATION   Full sun.

Mugwort

PLANTING	Plant seeds or cuttings anytime during the growing season. Set out transplants in the spring after the last frost.
HEIGHT	Up to 8 feet.
FINAL SPACING	2 to 3 feet.
BLOOM/FRUIT	Small creamy white flowers that are sometimes darker.
GROWTH HABITS/CULTURE	Very easy to grow. Bushy, aromatic, sprawling herb, not too attractive. Gray-green foliage with downy underside. Shear to maintain a more compact appearance. May need root pruning every few years.
PROBLEMS	Invasive, grows very large.
HARVEST/STORAGE	Cut, dry, and store foliage anytime.
CULINARY USES	Used in making Italian and German sausage. Also used in making beers, ales, and a bitter tea. Used to flavor rice cakes and stuffing.
MEDICINAL USES	Mugwort is reported to aid digestion and regulate menstruation. It has also been used in cancer treatments. Drink sparingly as a tea: it is one of the most toxic of all the artemesias.
LANDSCAPE USES	Limited—can be pruned into a decent-looking plant.
OTHER USES	Insect repellent, remedy for skin problems.

MULBERRY

Morus spp.
MOR-us

COMMON NAMES	MULBERRY.
FAMILY	Moraceae (Mulberry).
TYPE	Deciduous tree with edible fruit.
LOCATION	Full sun to fairly heavy shade.
PLANTING	Mulberry can be planted spring through fall, but fall is the ideal time. Can be grown from seed or transplants. Seed can be planted outdoors immediately after harvest in the fall or in the spring after being stored in the refrigerator all winter. Can also be propagated from semi-hardwood cuttings taken in late winter.

Mulberry

HEIGHT	30 to 50 feet.
SPREAD	40 to 60 feet.
FINAL SPACING	20 to 30 feet.
BLOOM/FRUIT	Male and female flowers in drooping catkins, followed by fruit that resembles blackberries.
GROWTH HABITS/CULTURE	Handsome tree with large, glossy leaves and an abundance of delicious blackberry-like fruit. Red fruit is the most common, but a white variety exists that tastes even better. Very easy to grow in almost any soil. Requires moderate water and fertility.
PROBLEMS	Birds eat the fruit and make a mess on pavement and cars. Plant trees away from the house. Webworms are controlled by trichogramma wasps released in the early spring.
HARVEST/STORAGE	Collect the blackberry-like fruit when it is ripe and eat fresh or freeze for later use. Mulberries are almost black when ripe—unless they are the white variety.
CULINARY USES	Edible fruit. It can be eaten fresh off the tree or made into jellies, jams, syrups, and wine.
MEDICINAL USES	Leaves, roots, and bark are diuretic and said to lower blood pressure. Mulberry is reported to be effective for coughs, colds, asthma, bronchitis, constipation, and premature graying of hair.
LANDSCAPE USES	Specimen shade tree. But be careful about the planting location. The tree is pretty and the fruit is delicious, but the fruits are very messy, especially after they have gone through the birds.
OTHER USES	Natural food for birds and other wildlife. The wood is used in the manufacture of bats and other sports equipment. Leaves of the white mulberry (*M. alba*) are fed to silkworms.
INSIGHT	The fruitless mulberry is a worthless big weed and should not be planted.

MULLEIN

Verbascum thapsus
ver-BAS-kum THAP-sus

COMMON NAMES	MULLEIN, FLANNEL LEAF, OLD MAN'S FLANNEL, VELVET DOCK.
FAMILY	Scrophulariaceae (Foxglove, Figwort, or Snapdragon).
TYPE	Hardy biennial.
LOCATION	Full sun.
PLANTING	Plant the seeds year round; the best time is fall or early spring.
HEIGHT	6 to 7 feet.
SPREAD	12 to 18 inches.
FINAL SPACING	One here and one there or about 3 feet apart.
BLOOM/FRUIT	Yellow, white, or purple flowers on tall spikes that form the second year. There is only a rosette of low leaves the first year.
GROWTH HABITS/CULTURE	Large, fuzzy gray leaves, upright growth, yellow, white, or purple flowers. Treat like a wildflower—this native plant is very easy to grow in most any soil.

Mullein

PROBLEMS	Leaf-chewing insects create cosmetic damage only.
HARVEST/STORAGE	Harvest leaves anytime, harvest flowers when they first open.
CULINARY USES	Tea ingredient. Flowers are sweet, leaves are bitter, but both are aromatic.
MEDICINAL USES	Coughs, asthma, allergies, and respiratory diseases are helped by drinking mullein tea. Oil made from the flowers is supposed to be good for earaches. Leaves are used as bandages.
LANDSCAPE USES	Ornamental specimen plants. Use in the wildflower garden or as a dramatic background plant.
INSIGHT	Plant in a well-drained area in full sun and forget it. You will pretty much have it from now on. Don't harvest this or any other herb from the roadside because of environmental pollution. Mullein rhymes with "sullen."

MUSK—see **MALLOW**

MUSTARD

Brassica spp.
BRA-si-ka

COMMON NAMES	MUSTARD.
FAMILY	Brassicaceae (Cruciferae) (Mustard).
TYPE	Annual.
LOCATION	Full sun.
PLANTING	Direct seed in late summer.
HEIGHT	3 feet and taller.
SPREAD	6 inches.
FINAL SPACING	6 to 9 inches.
BLOOM/FRUIT	Small edible yellow flowers followed by long slender pods containing small brown or black seeds.
GROWTH HABITS/CULTURE	Leafy salad herb. Mustard likes cool weather and is cold-hardy down

to about 20 degrees. Planting for maturity in the fall will yield the best results. Improve beds with compost, lava sand, Texas greensand, and soft rock phosphate.

PROBLEMS
Grasshoppers, cabbage loopers, green worms. Spray regularly with Garrett Juice and add orange oil for heavy infestations.

HARVEST/STORAGE
Harvest the seed when the pods are beginning to turn brown. Wait too late and the seeds scatter.

CULINARY USES
Leaves can be boiled to make a delicious food. Young seed pods are excellent to eat—just like radishes. Seeds are used as a condiment. Sprouts are also good to eat. Use the flowers in salads. There are several types: black mustard (*B. nigra*), white mustard (*B. hirta*), and brown mustard (*B. juncea*). Black mustard seed is the spiciest and hottest.

MEDICINAL USES
A poultice for the skin is made from the crushed seeds diluted in olive oil. Be careful—it can burn the skin. Seeds can be eaten to stimulate circulation and reduce inflammation; a local application can be applied to ease joint pain. Good for coughs, colds, and other respiratory problems.

LANDSCAPE USES
Dramatic tall spikes of edible yellow flowers for the garden.

OTHER USES
Good crop for the vegetable garden.

Mustard

Myrtle

Myrrhis odorata—see **CICELY**
MYRRH—see **CICELY**

MYRTLE

Myrtus communis
MUR-tus kom-EW-nis

COMMON NAMES	MYRTLE, SWEET MYRTLE, TRUE MYRTLE.
FAMILY	Myrtaceae (Myrtle or Eucalyptus).
TYPE	Hardy evergreen shrub.
LOCATION	Full sun to partial shade.
PLANTING	Start from cuttings between spring and fall. Very easy to propagate. Set out container-grown transplants year round.
HEIGHT	Up to 15 feet.
SPREAD	6 to 8 feet.
FINAL SPACING	12 inches.
BLOOM/FRUIT	Compact, attractive, 1-inch white flowers in early summer. Sometimes followed by blue-black berries.
GROWTH HABITS/CULTURE	Small, aromatic, glossy dark green foliage. Bushy and slow-growing. Beautiful when in bloom. Sweet-scented leaves and flowers.
PROBLEMS	Few if any; can freeze in the northern part of the state.
HARVEST/STORAGE	Pick flowers while in full bloom and store in glass containers with tight-fitting lids in a dark place. Will last in these conditions for three years.
CULINARY USES	Flower buds and berries can be used in sweet dishes, the leaves in meat dishes.
MEDICINAL USES	The leaves are antiseptic and astringent and are used on bruises, acne, and hemorrhoids. According to the book *Herbs* by Lesley Bremness, it is used as a poultice, tea, or tincture.
LANDSCAPE USES	Attractive in containers. Can be pruned into topiaries. Good edging plant in the landscape and in knot gardens.
OTHER USES	The flowers are used to make toilet water, the dried leaves for herb pillows and potpourri. Plays a role in weddings as a symbol of chastity and beauty.
INSIGHT	Good little plant that should be used more.

Myrtle

Myrtus communis—see
MYRTLE

NAKED INDIAN—see MADRONE

NASTURTIUM

Tropaeolum majus
tro-PIE-oh-lum MAY-jus

COMMON NAMES	NASTURTIUM, INDIAN CRESS.
FAMILY	Tropaeolaceae (Nasturtium).
TYPE	Annual.
LOCATION	Full sun or partial shade.
PLANTING	Plant the large, easy-to-sprout seeds in late winter for spring bloom, in mid-summer for fall bloom. Set out transplants in early spring and again in late summer for fall bloom.
HEIGHT	18 inches to 6 feet.
SPREAD	24 inches to 6 feet.
FINAL SPACING	6 to 12 inches.
BLOOM/FRUIT	Blooms best in poor to average soil. Flowers range from reds to oranges to bright yellows.
GROWTH HABITS/CULTURE	Dwarf bushy and trailing forms available. Round flowers and leaves. Easy to grow and a favorite with children. Don't overdo the mulch or watering. Soil that is too good will produce mostly leaves and few flowers.
PROBLEMS	Doesn't like heat, prefers the cool parts of the season. Few if any insects and diseases.

Nasturtium

Neem

Nasturtium

HARVEST/STORAGE	Harvest the leaves, buds, and flowers anytime and use fresh.
CULINARY USES	All parts of the plant are edible, even the tender stems. Excellent in salads. Seed pods are delicious and have a peppery taste similar to watercress. Flowers and leaves are good on sandwiches.
MEDICINAL USES	Nasturtium is a good source of vitamin C and has been used to promote appetite. The seeds have been used historically as an antibiotic and for respiratory and urinary tract problems. The seeds can have a toxic effect on some people.
LANDSCAPE USES	Good in hanging baskets and pots.
OTHER USES	The flowers make an excellent garnish. Use the leaves and flowers in vinegars. The seeds can be pickled in vinegar and used like capers.

Nasturtium officinale—see **WATERCRESS**

NEEM

Azadirachta indica
ah-ZAD-eh-rack-tah IN-di-ka

COMMON NAMES	NEEM, INDIAN LILAC, NIM, MARGOSA, AZADARACH, BEAD TREE, PRIDE OF CHINA, HOLY TREE.
FAMILY	Meliaceae (Neem).
TYPE	Broadleafed tropical evergreen tree.
LOCATION	Full sun in containers.
PLANTING	Container plant. The tree is easily propagated by seed, seedlings, saplings, root suckers, or tissue culture. However, it is normally grown from small transplants or seed planted directly on-site.
HEIGHT	40 to 60 feet in the tropics, much smaller here in pots.
SPREAD	30 feet in the tropics.
FINAL SPACING	One tree is enough. It will have to be grown in a container or in the very southern tip of Texas to survive the winter freeze.

BLOOM/FRUIT Small white bisexual flowers in clusters in the spring. They have a honey-like scent and attract bees. The clustered olive-like fruit is a smooth, elliptical drupe about 1 inch long; it is yellow to greenish yellow and has a sweet pulp. Animals like the outer part, but the seed in the center is the source of the active ingredient. The seed is composed of a shell and a kernel. It is the kernel that is most effective for pest control. Neem trees normally begin fruiting after 3 to 5 years and become fully productive in about 10 years. They can produce up to 100 pounds of kernels annually and live for as long as 200 years.

GROWTH HABITS/CULTURE Neem is very easy to grow and can stand severe pruning. It is a tropical tree but will grow in any soil in almost any condition. It is fast-growing and has very few pests, if any.

PROBLEMS Occasionally scale insects, leaf-cutting ants, and some larvae of moths. Root rot will attack trees that are overwatered, and canker and other diseases will attack plants in stress. Neem trees cannot stand fire, high winds, or shade. Rats and other gnawing pests will sometimes kill young seedlings. But these are problems only if you live in the tropics where neem can be grown year round. You should not have trouble with goats and camels if you grow it in pots at your house. There is evidence that neem can damage aquatic life such as tadpoles and mosquito-eating gambia fish. Neem seed falling into ponds in the tropics have killed tilapia fish. There is some evidence that neem can hurt beneficials, such as ladybugs and the larvae of hoverflies. Bees and butterflies drinking nectar from neem-treated plants might pick up traces of neem, leading to reduced reproduction.

HARVEST/STORAGE It's best to use commercial products and enjoy the novelty of growing neem in a container.

CULINARY USES None.

MEDICINAL USES Many. Neem has been used to treat dental problems, Chagas disease, and malaria. For more details, read *Neem: A Tree for Solving Global Problems* from the National Academy Press in Washington, D.C.

LANDSCAPE USES Container plant.

OTHER USES Neem honey is tasty and popular and reported to contain no trace of the herbal ingredient in neem. The seeds are mostly used for pest control; the leaves also contain the pesticidal ingredients but are less effective than the seed. Neem can be used to control a very wide range of insects and soil nematodes. Some reports say that neem extract kills snails and slugs as well as fungi, aflatoxin, and other disease organisms. Trials in some countries have indicated that neem oil significantly reduces viruses, which could become its most primary use. Neem does not seem to have a negative effect on earthworms. Neem wood is used in construction and carpentry because of its resistance to termites. The seed oil is used in lubricants, oil-burning lamps, and soap-making.

INSIGHT *Melia* is the previous name. Neem seems strangely benign to spiders, butterflies, and pollinating insects, although some research suggests that it is detrimental to ladybugs. The seed of the neem tree has attracted the most scientific attention in recent years as being the most powerful part of the tree.

Nepeta cataria—see **CATNIP**
Nepeta musimi—see **CATNIP**
Ocimum basilicum—see **BASIL**
Oenothera—see **EVENING PRIMROSE**
OLD MAN SOUTHERNWOOD—see **SOUTHERNWOOD**
OLD MAN'S FLANNEL—see **MULLEIN**

ONION

Allium cepa
A-lee-um SEE-pa

COMMON NAMES	ONION, LEEK.
FAMILY	Liliaceae (Lily).
TYPE	Perennial bulbs.
LOCATION	Sun or dappled shade.
PLANTING	Start seeds in the fall. Sets and bulblets are planted in late winter.
HEIGHT	8 to 30 inches.
SPREAD	8 to 12 inches.
FINAL SPACING	4 to 8 inches.
BLOOM/FRUIT	Round clusters of small flowers on hard stems.
GROWTH HABITS/CULTURE	Strap-like leaves, underground bulbs. Bulb size is determined by the size of the green top.
PROBLEMS	Cutworms, nematodes, thrips, and various soil diseases. None is serious in an organic program.
HARVEST/STORAGE	Harvest the onion greens (tops) anytime. Bulbs are best gathered and eaten after the tops have turned brown. Unlike garlic, onions can be

Elephant garlic or leek

Onion and garlic heads

left in the ground for some time without losing any food or medicinal value.

CULINARY USES Excellent flavoring agent for vegetables, meats, sauces, gravies, soups, and just about anything else. Great salad and pizza ingredient. One of the most health-giving foods on earth.

MEDICINAL USES Eating onions helps to prevent and relieve colds and arthritis and to regulate blood pressure. The high sulfur content is too strong for tender tummies and can cause allergic reactions, according to Dr. Judy Griffin. Externally used for insect bites, light wounds and burns, warts, and bruises.

LANDSCAPE USES Decorative ornamental plant.

INSIGHT Wild garlic or wild onion is *Allium canadense* var. *canadense*. It blooms mostly in the spring, forming white, yellow, pink, red, and purple umbels atop slender stalks. The seeds are black and white and wrinkled. *Nothoscordum bivalve*, crow poison, is the dangerous look-alike and has white or cream-colored flowers with a dark stripe on the outside. Crow poison blooms in the spring and sporadically year round. Pedicals of each flower are longer than the wild onion's. The presence of either of these plants in the lawn means that the soil has a chemical imbalance, low humus, and a predominance of anaerobic microbes. Giant or elephant garlic (*Allium scorodoprasum*) is a leek that has a milder flavor than true garlic and produces a fist-size bulb that sometimes fails to produce individual cloves. Its culture is the same as for common garlic.

ONION CHIVES—see **CHIVES**

ORACH

Atriplex hortensis
AH-tri-plex hor-TEN-sis

COMMON NAMES ORACH, PURPLE ORACH.
FAMILY Chenopodiaceae (Goosefoot or Pigweed).
TYPE Annual.
LOCATION Full sun to partial shade.
PLANTING Start seed indoors in the winter and set out transplants in the spring.
HEIGHT Up to 8 feet.
SPREAD 3 feet.
FINAL SPACING 3 to 4 feet.
BLOOM/FRUIT Uninteresting flowers with small seeds.
GROWTH HABITS/CULTURE Easy-care plant with arrowhead-shaped leaves and spikes of insignificant flowers. Orach will grow in normal garden conditions or in soil that is on the moist side.
PROBLEMS Few pest problems.
HARVEST/STORAGE Pick leaves fresh as needed. Freeze if necessary.

Orach

CULINARY USES	Leaves and young shoots are used in salads and soups and cooked as spinach. Stems can be stir-fried, and the seeds can be ground into flour.
MEDICINAL USES	Eat the leaves for sore throat, jaundice, and gout. Orach has medicinal value fresh or cooked.
LANDSCAPE USES	As a colorful hedge, *A. hortensis rubra* can be spectacular.
INSIGHT	A seldom-cultivated pot herb deserving of wider usage.

OREGANO

Origanum vulgare
o-ree-GAH-num vul-GAR-ee

COMMON NAMES	OREGANO, WILD MARJORAM.
FAMILY	Lamiaceae (Labiatae) (Mint).
TYPE	Perennial, evergreen in most of the state.
LOCATION	Full sun to partial shade.
PLANTING	Start from seed in the winter, set out transplants in early spring. Cuttings root easily anytime during the growing season.
HEIGHT	8 to 30 inches.
SPREAD	15 to 30 inches.
FINAL SPACING	18 inches.
BLOOM/FRUIT	White to purple summer flowers followed by tiny seed.
GROWTH HABITS/CULTURE	Very winter-hardy and drought-resistant. Sprawling, low-growing plant. Slightly woody stems. Leaves are oval to elliptical in shape and generally slightly hairy underneath with an aromatic scent.
PROBLEMS	Very few.
HARVEST/STORAGE	Harvest the leaves anytime. Stores well and is easy to dry. Best to use the leaves fresh from the garden.

CULINARY USES   Used in Greek and Italian food and especially in dishes with tomatoes, chili powder, and many other foods. Known as the pizza herb. Excellent herb tea ingredient. Chopped oregano is also good in scrambled eggs.

MEDICINAL USES   Tea made from *Origanum* has been used traditionally to treat coughs, muscle spasms, headaches, menstrual pain, and sore joints. Essential oil of oregano has also been used as a skin antiseptic and to relieve pain, sprains, and swellings.

LANDSCAPE USES   Greek oregano makes a good evergreen groundcover. The flowers of all oreganos are interesting. See Dittany of Crete for an excellent container plant.

OTHER USES   Oregano seems to help deter insect pests.

INSIGHT   When taking the tea, inhale the vapors while drinking. Oregano has a stronger taste and aroma than marjoram.

Origanum—see **OREGANO**
Origanum dictamnus—see **DITTANY OF CRETE**
Origanum marjorana—see **MARJORAM**
Origanum vulgare—see **OREGANO**

Greek oregano

P

PAINTED DAISY—see **PYRETHRUM**

Panax quinquefolius—see **GINSENG**

PARSLEY

Petroselinum crispum

pet-ro-see-LEEN-um KRIS-pum

COMMON NAMES	PARSLEY.
FAMILY	Apiaceae (Umbelliferae) (Carrot or Parsley).
TYPE	Biennial.
LOCATION	Full morning sun with afternoon shade is best.
PLANTING	Plant seed or transplants in early spring or late summer for fall garden plants. It's best to plant two crops a year.
HEIGHT	12 inches.
SPREAD	8 to 12 inches.
FINAL SPACING	12 inches.
BLOOM/FRUIT	Umbels of white flowers followed by aromatic seeds.
GROWTH HABITS/CULTURE	Slow to germinate from seed. Easy culture from transplants. Likes cool weather and moist, well-drained soil. Feed with occasional light applications of organic fertilizer. Cut seed heads off to maintain compact growth. Italian parsley (*P. crispum* var. *neapolitanum*) has flat, glossy, dark green leaves resembling those of celery and grows to 1½ feet. Curly parsley (*P. crispum*) grows to 10 inches in height.
PROBLEMS	Parsleyworm, which becomes the beautiful swallowtail butterfly. Spider mites and aphids can be controlled with the Basic Organic Program.
HARVEST/STORAGE	Harvest whenever the foliage is present. Store by freezing if necessary. Parsley can be cut like a cut flower and stored in water in the refrigerator for a time; however, it grows well almost year round here in Texas.
CULINARY USES	Italian parsley has a better flavor for cooking, especially when fresh. Use in salads, vegetables, soups, and garnishes. Add the leaves to potatoes, salmon, trout, poultry, and pasta, the seeds to bread. Hamburg-type parsley root can be cooked as a vegetable. Chop just before using and add to food at the last minute to preserve vitamins and minerals. Don't cook parsley—it destroys the vitamins and much of the food value. Avoid dry products from the grocery store.
MEDICINAL USES	Parsley is a free-radical scavenger. It is high in vitamins C and A, is a natural source of potassium and magnesium, and reportedly helps fight cancer. It deodorizes the breath, especially after eating garlic or onions;

Italian parsley

Curly parsley

it is also good for the liver, kidneys, and bladder, and aids digestion when eaten. It is mildly diuretic and is reported to stop lactation. One of the best foods to help prevent osteoporosis and relieve arthritis symptoms.

LANDSCAPE USES Curly parsley makes an excellent border plant.

OTHER USES Traditionally grown near roses to empower the fragrance of roses. Parsley can also be used in herb teas. Mix parsley seed with radishes as a marker in the garden. Radishes will be ready to be thinned or harvested when the parsley germinates—in about three weeks.

INSIGHT There are two main kinds of parsley: the curly French parsley, which is sold in grocery stores for garnish, and the Italian flat-leaf (var. *neapolitanum*) or plain parsley, which gourmet cooks insist has superior flavor. A third type, the Hamburg variety, is cultivated as a root crop.

Passion flower

Passion flower fruit

PASSION FLOWER

Passiflora incarnata
pass-sih-FLO-ruh in-kar-NAY-tuh

COMMON NAMES	MAYPOP, PASSION FLOWER, PASSION VINE.
FAMILY	Passifloraceae (Passion Flower).
TYPE	Perennial vine.
LOCATION	Sun or light shade.
PLANTING	Install year round from containers. Cuttings and transplants are easy anytime.
HEIGHT	High-climbing.
SPREAD	Unlimited.
FINAL SPACING	3 to 6 feet.
BLOOM/FRUIT	Gorgeous, intricately detailed summer flowers in many colors, usually whites, pinks, and purples, although red, yellows, and oranges are available. The edible fruit, which comes in many sizes and colors, is reported to have aphrodisiac qualities. In most species the fruit is ripe when it turns to a yellow-orange color. Some species have fruit that are yellow, red, or purple.
GROWTH HABITS/CULTURE	Large, deeply cut leaves. Climbs quickly by tendrils. Blooms almost all summer with spectacular flowers. Easy to grow in any soil, drought-tolerant. Dies to the ground each winter but returns in spring.
PROBLEMS	Butterfly caterpillars. The Gulf fritillary loves this plant. Hand-pick them if there are too many but don't kill them all.
HARVEST/STORAGE	Harvest the leaves, flowers, and fruit and use fresh.
CULINARY USES	The juicy oval fruit has fragrant and delicious pulp that can be used in drinks and ice cream or cooked into jellies and jams.
MEDICINAL USES	The leaves have been used in teas to calm nerves, treat headaches, and relieve nervous hypertension. Passion flower may be hallucinogenic for some individuals. It's best to make a weak tea or cold-water infusion of the flower.

LANDSCAPE USES	Beautiful decorative vine for beds or pots.
OTHER USES	Good in pots.
INSIGHT	Passion flower is a nursery plant for the beautiful Gulf fritillary butterfly. The name passion flower comes from the flower parts, which are said to symbolize the crucifixion. There are over 430 species of passion flower.

PASSION VINE—see PASSION FLOWER

PATCHOULI

Pogostemon cablin
po-GOS-tah-mon CAB-lin

COMMON NAMES	PATCHOULI, PUTCHA-PAT, PATCHOULY.
FAMILY	Lamiaceae (Labiatae) (Mint).
TYPE	Tender perennial.
LOCATION	Partial to heavy shade. A location with morning sun and afternoon shade is best.
PLANTING	Install transplants after the last frost.
HEIGHT	3 to 4 feet.
SPREAD	2 to 3 feet.
FINAL SPACING	24 inches.
BLOOM/FRUIT	White flowers on spikes, but don't let the plant bloom. The leaves are the main feature of the herb.
GROWTH HABITS/CULTURE	Upright, shrubby. Easy to grow. Needs hot weather and likes sun as well as shade. Roots easily from semi-woody cuttings taken in fall or winter. Plant in well-prepared soil and apply water and fertilizer in moderation.
PROBLEMS	Slugs like this plant. Spray garlic-pepper tea and treat the mulch under the plants with a mixture of natural diatomaceous earth, hot pepper, and cedar flakes.

Patchouli

Pennyroyal

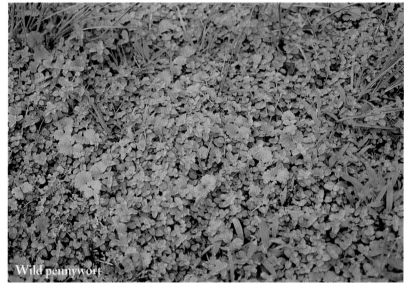

Wild pennywort

HARVEST/STORAGE	Harvest leaves anytime, dry and store in glass containers. Use the leaves fresh if possible.
CULINARY USES	None.
MEDICINAL USES	A tea containing essential oil from the leaves has been used as an antidepressant or antiseptic. The oil can also be used on insect bites.
LANDSCAPE USES	Makes a pleasant planting for partially shaded areas. The foliage has an interesting texture.
OTHER USES	Fragrance in the garden. Cosmetics and other fragrances. Used extensively in aromatherapy.
INSIGHT	Needs ample water, partial shade, and no hot afternoon sun. Normally doesn't live through our Texas winters in the northern half of the state.

Pelargonium spp.—see **SCENTED GERANIUM**

PENNYROYAL

Mentha pulegium
MEN-tha poo-LEG-ee-um

COMMON NAMES	PENNYROYAL, RUN BY THE GROUND, MOSQUITO PLANT.
FAMILY	Lamiaceae (Labiatae) (Mint).
TYPE	Tender perennial.
LOCATION	Partial to full shade.
PLANTING	Plant sprigs or transplants in the spring after the last frost.
HEIGHT	2 to 6 inches maximum.
SPREAD	3 to 4 feet.
FINAL SPACING	12 to 18 inches.
BLOOM/FRUIT	Small lavender flowers in tight whorls.
GROWTH HABITS/CULTURE	Low-growing, creeping, matted, small-leafed mint with very strong fragrance. One of the smaller mints, it creeps along the ground rarely

more than a few inches high and forms a fragrant mat of green. Likes moist soil and moderate fertilization.

PROBLEMS	Spider mites occasionally, rust. Adjust the watering schedule and these problems usually go away. Use the Basic Organic Program.
HARVEST/STORAGE	Dry and store in a cool dry place.
CULINARY USES	Some people recommend using pennyroyal as a tea, but I strongly advise against it. It especially shouldn't be used by children, pregnant animals, pregnant women, or cats.
MEDICINAL USES	Abortifacient. Pregnant women should definitely avoid ingesting it.
LANDSCAPE USES	An excellent groundcover between stepping stones and in other small spaces. Don't plant too much of it because it can freeze out in the northern half of the state.
OTHER USES	Flea, fly, and tick repellent. A strong infusion (tea) of its leaves has been used as an insect spray.
INSIGHT	Pennyroyal is a known abortifacient (causes miscarriages).

PEPPER

Capsicum spp.
CAP-see-cum

COMMON NAMES	CAPSICUM, PEPPER, RED PEPPER.
FAMILY	Solanaceae (Nightshade or Potato).
TYPE	Tender perennial.
LOCATION	Full sun to moderate shade. Peppers will produce very well with morning sun and afternoon shade.
PLANTING	Seeds can be started indoors in the winter or directly in beds. Set out transplants in spring after the weather turns warm. The timing is usually two weeks after the tomatoes have been planted. Cuttings can be taken anytime.
HEIGHT	12 inches to 5 feet tall.
SPREAD	18 inches to 6 feet.
FINAL SPACING	12 to 18 inches.
BLOOM/FRUIT	Small white flowers produce fruit of varying sizes, shapes, and colors. Peppers are beautiful and should be grown more for their color.

Habanero peppers

Dried habanero peppers

Peppers

GROWTH HABITS/CULTURE   These nightshades vary greatly in size and heat. The fruit comes in all sizes, shapes, and colors—shades of purple, red, green, yellow, and orange. Easy to grow in almost any soil. Add compost, lava sand, Texas greensand, and soft rock phosphate. Spray often with Garrett Juice. Use small amounts of fertilizer at bloom time.

PROBLEMS   Cold sensitive. Minor insect problems, cutworms when young. Treat soil with citrus oil or ground-up peelings to cure nematode problems.

HARVEST/STORAGE   Pick green or when fully ripe and store in a cool dry place. Harvest green for pickling. Don't break the peppers from the plant. Cut the stems to prevent damage to the plant.

CULINARY USES	Eat peppers whole, put them in salads raw, cook them with all kinds of foods. Don't eat the hot ones if you have stomach or digestion problems.
MEDICINAL USES	Eat peppers to aid circulation, reduce fever, and promote digestion. Peppers keep you warm in winter, and direct application of a lotion or oil can stop bleeding.
LANDSCAPE USES	Peppers make beautiful landscape and pot plants. The smaller fruiting varieties are the best from a purely decorative standpoint.
OTHER USES	Use in garlic-pepper tea to repel insects, animal pests, slugs, snails, and pill bugs. The tea also works very well on mice, rats, raccoons, and sometimes dogs.
INSIGHT	Wait to plant outdoors until the soil temperature is 75 degrees. Plant them two weeks after you set out tomatoes. Peppers like warm soil and warm weather. People with osteoarthritis should avoid eating them, but a topical application of lotion or an over-the-counter product will relieve pain.

PEPPER, BLACK

Piper nigrum
PIE-per NI-grum

COMMON NAMES	BLACK PEPPER.
FAMILY	Piperaceae (Pepper).
TYPE	Tropical vine.
LOCATION	Rich healthy soil in a shady location.
PLANTING	Install transplants in the spring after the last frost. Start seed indoors in the winter.
HEIGHT	Vine to 15 feet.
SPREAD	24 inches.
FINAL SPACING	3 feet, or plant individually.

Malabar black pepper

BLOOM/FRUIT	White flowers followed by berries that yield commercial pepper.
GROWTH HABITS/CULTURE	Common black pepper is the dried, unripened fruit of this tropical semi-woody vine. White pepper is exactly the same fruit with the pericarp, or outer black covering, removed. Needs rich, moist, shaded soil. Best grown in containers and protected in winter. It can be trained around a plant totem. It has large, shiny, dark green leaves and interesting blossoms. It is easy to grow in healthy soil with good drainage and a little feeding now and again. Use the Basic Organic Program.
PROBLEMS	Freezes. Must be container-grown in most of Texas.
HARVEST/STORAGE	Gather mature seeds and store in a cool dry place.
CULINARY USES	Seasoning for all kinds of foods.
MEDICINAL USES	Black pepper has been used to treat flatulence and colds. It is a mild diuretic, a stimulant, an appetite inducer; it aids digestion and helps prevent constipation. Avoid black pepper if you are allergic or suffer from gastrointestinal distress.
LANDSCAPE USES	Makes an attractive annual vine or a unique groundcover or greenhouse plant.
OTHER USES	Some perfumes and massage oils are made from black pepper.
INSIGHT	Green dried fruits make black pepper. Mature berries yield white pepper. Used worldwide.

PEPPERGRASS

Lepidium sativum
le-PID-ee-um sa-TEE-vum

COMMON NAMES	PEPPERGRASS, CRESS, SHEPHERD'S PURSE.
FAMILY	Brassicaceae (Cruciferae) (Mustard).
TYPE	Annual.
LOCATION	Sun.

Peppergrass

PLANTING	Plant seed in spring, summer, and fall or start indoors in the winter. Set out transplants anytime after the last frost.
HEIGHT	18 to 24 inches.
SPREAD	18 inches.
FINAL SPACING	12 to 18 inches.
BLOOM/FRUIT	Small yellow flowers, followed by flat, heart-shaped seed capsules that are edible.
GROWTH HABITS/CULTURE	Rounded plant with woody stems and very small leaves that have a peppery taste. Matures quickly. Will grow in cold weather.
PROBLEMS	Few if any.
HARVEST/STORAGE	Harvest green leaves and eat fresh. Seeds can be collected green or dry. Both can be stored dry in glass containers in a cool place.
CULINARY USES	Peppergrass is good in salads and on sandwiches, especially with cream cheese. The seeds function as a pepper substitute. Use the leaves on sandwiches as a lettuce substitute or cook them as greens.
MEDICINAL USES	Leaves and seed are high in Vitamin C and iron. Remember that iron is not absorbed unless combined with animal protein. Milk doesn't count.
LANDSCAPE USES	Seeded-out plants are very decorative. Peppergrass is especially good in the wildflower or perennial garden.
OTHER USES	The dried seed heads work well for dried arrangements indoors.
INSIGHT	Unfortunately considered a weed by most people.

PEPPERMINT—see **MINT**

PERILLA

Perilla frutescens
pa-RIL-ah fru-TESS-enz

COMMON NAMES	BEEFSTEAK PLANT, SHISHO PLANT, PERILLA.
FAMILY	Lamiaceae (Labiatae) (Mint).
TYPE	Annual.
LOCATION	Full sun.
PLANTING	Start seed indoors in the winter or directly in beds in the spring after the last frost. Set out transplants in the spring.
HEIGHT	3 feet.
SPREAD	3 feet.
FINAL SPACING	6 to 12 inches.
BLOOM/FRUIT	Purplish flowers, purple or green leaves. Small black seeds on decorative seed pods.
GROWTH HABITS/CULTURE	A vigorous, easy-to-grow annual, with dark burgundy or purple leaves and a growth habit similar to that of coleus and basil. In fact, it is often mistakenly called opal basil and black coleus. There is also a green-leaf variety. Perilla needs only a moderate amount of fertilizer and water.

Perilla

Shisho

Perilla

PROBLEMS	Will reseed and spread to become a problem. The plant hybridizes, so do not plant green and purple types near each other. Many of the available plants have already been crossed, however.
HARVEST/STORAGE	Harvest and use the leaves anytime during the growing season. The leaves can also be dried and stored in glass containers.
CULINARY USES	The leaves are used as an ingredient in salads and a flavoring for beefsteak (some like it, some don't) and vinegars.
MEDICINAL USES	Perilla is said to be an antibiotic when eaten fresh; it is used in sushi to help control bacteria. The Japanese use it to detoxify raw fish. The dried leaves are used in teas for coughs, colds, flu, and nausea.
LANDSCAPE USES	The purple variety is especially attractive in the border or color garden. Looks good with gray plants like wormwood or Texas sage.

OTHER USES Makes a pretty, wine-red vinegar that is excellent in salad dressings and in oriental dishes.

INSIGHT Perilla is a pass-along plant to anyone who will take it. Odena doesn't like this plant, but I do. It is similar to mint. If you let it go to seed and shatter, all your neighbors on the downhill side will have perilla next season. A thick layer of mulch keeps it from reseeding.

Perilla frutescens—see **PERILLA**
Petroselinum crispum—see **PARSLEY**
PIGWEED—see **LAMB'S-QUARTER**
Pimenta dioica—see **ALLSPICE**
Pimpinella anisum—see **ANISE**

PINEAPPLE

Ananas comosus
A-na-nas ko-MO-sus

COMMON NAMES PINEAPPLE.
FAMILY Bromeliacae.
TYPE Tropical herbaceous perennial.
LOCATION Full sun.
PLANTING The easiest way for the homeowner to grow pineapples at home is to buy organic fruit from the grocery store. Enjoy the delicious fruit but save the top foliage and a tiny slice of the yellow fruit. Let it dry and harden off in a cool spot and then plant by plunging into organic potting soil. This is best done in the fall in pots indoors. The location needs to resemble that of a very bright greenhouse. Keep watered and a new pineapple plant will soon take root and grow. Move the pots outdoors into full sun in the spring after the last frost.

Pineapple

HEIGHT	30 to 36 inches.
SPREAD	30 to 36 inches.
FINAL SPACING	24 to 30 inches.
BLOOM/FRUIT	Spikes of reddish purple flowers with yellow bracts. The sweet fleshy seedless fruit is comprised of many small fruitlets.
GROWTH HABITS/CULTURE	Pineapple is a bromeliad that grows in the ground instead of in trees. It produces a dense mass of channeled leaves. It is drought tolerant but tropical and will freeze easily. So it must be grown in containers and moved indoors for the winter. It's best to start propagation of the tops in the fall or winter in greenhouse conditions and then move out to full sun when the weather warms in the spring.
PROBLEMS	Freeze damage, root rot from overwatering.
HARVEST/STORAGE	Harvest and eat the pineapples when they are ripe. The fruit can also be stored in the refrigerator for short periods of time.
CULINARY USES	The pineapple meat can be eaten raw or cooked. It can also be jellied, candied, or juiced. An alcoholic drink made from pineapples is called vin d'ananas.
MEDICINAL USES	Pineapple is loaded with vitamins and enzymes. It has been shown to aid digestion. Bromelain is the chemical in pineapple that helps prevent inflammation. Trainers recommend it to athletes for preventing and treating injuries. James A. Duke in *The Green Pharmacy* recommends pineapple for treating injuries and helping the immune system. Lesley Bremness, in her book *Herbs,* says that the fruit is sometimes eaten by smokers to clear the lungs and that it can aggravate the skin rashes of some people.
LANDSCAPE USES	Beautiful container plant.
OTHER USES	Tea made from the foliage is used to treat spider bites.

PINEAPPLE SAGE

Salvia elegans
SAL-vee-ah EL-ee-ganz

COMMON NAMES	PINEAPPLE SAGE.
FAMILY	Lamiaceae (Labiatae) (Mint).
TYPE	Tender perennial.
LOCATION	Partial shade. Morning sun and afternoon shade is the best location.
PLANTING	Start seed indoors in the winter, set out transplants in late spring. Container-grown plants can be installed anytime after the last freeze.
HEIGHT	4 feet.
SPREAD	4 feet.
FINAL SPACING	3 feet.
BLOOM/FRUIT	Bright red flowers that attract hummingbirds and butterflies. The flowers are edible and very fragrant.
GROWTH HABITS/CULTURE	Easy culture—likes warmth and lots of water. Pineapple sage needs healthy, well-drained soil and moderate fertilization. Use the Basic Organic Program.

Pineapple sage

Prickly ash

PROBLEMS	Few.
HARVEST/STORAGE	Dry the leaves and flowers. They dry well and hold their color.
CULINARY USES	The flowers make a beautiful garnish. They are edible and good in salads. The flowers and leaves are good for flavoring cold drinks and teas.
MEDICINAL USES	None known at this time.
LANDSCAPE USES	Great color in the landscape in partially shaded locations.
OTHER USES	Pineapple sage is a good room deodorizer. Use it in potpourri. Excellent plant for attracting hummingbirds, butterflies, and other beneficial insects to the garden.

Piper auritum—see **HOJA SANTA**

Piper nigrum—see **PEPPER, BLACK**

PLEURISY ROOT—see **BUTTERFLY WEED**

POET'S JASMINE—see **SAMBAC JASMINE**

Pogostemon cablin—see **PATCHOULI**

Poliomentha longiflora—see **MEXICAN OREGANO**

Polygonatum—see **GOLDENSEAL**

Portulaca oleracea—see **PURSLANE**

POT HERB—see **CALENDULA**

POT MARIGOLD—see **CALENDULA**

Poterium sanquisorba—see **SALAD BURNET**

PRICKLY ASH

Zanthoxylum clava-herculis
zanth-OX-i-lum CLA-va-her-QUE-lis

COMMON NAMES	PRICKLY ASH, HERCULES' CLUB, TOOTHACHE TREE, TICKLETONGUE TREE, YELLOW WOOD, SUTERBERRY.
FAMILY	Rutaceae (Citrus or Rue).
TYPE	Small deciduous tree.
LOCATION	Sun.
PLANTING	Transplants can be installed year round. Easy to grow from seed collected in the fall and kept in the refrigerator over the winter, then planted in the spring. It can also be propagated from root cuttings gathered in the winter.
HEIGHT	15 to 30 feet.
SPREAD	15 to 30 feet.
FINAL SPACING	15 to 20 feet.
BLOOM/FRUIT	Small yellowish green flower clusters in spring. The brown fruit contains a single seed that ripens from mid- to late summer.
GROWTH HABITS/CULTURE	Native to East Texas and the blackland prairie. Often found in fence rows. Will grow well in most any soil. Compound leaves with 5–15 leaflets. Large, nasty spines on the trunk and limbs.
PROBLEMS	Caterpillars eat the foliage, but these are the larvae of the beautiful swallowtail butterfly, so don't kill them.
HARVEST/STORAGE	Cut and use the bark anytime. Harvest the berries after they have matured.
CULINARY USES	Use the seeds like pepper. In Japan the leaves are used as a garnish called *sansho*.
MEDICINAL USES	Native Americans chewed the bark for toothaches and drank tea made from the berries for sore throats. The bark and berries are stimulants and have been used historically to treat digestive problems, rheumatism, skin diseases, nervous headaches, varicose veins, and congestion.
LANDSCAPE USES	Seldom cultivated, should be planted more often. Prickly ash is an attractive small tree.
OTHER USES	Thorns provide cover for wildlife and help create biodiversity. Kids trick their friends by getting them to chew a piece of the bark, which makes the mouth feel fuzzy and deadened.

PURPLE CONEFLOWER—see ECHINACEA

PURSLANE

Portulaca oleracea
por-chew-LAC-ah o-le-RAH-kee-a

COMMON NAMES	PURSLANE, ROSE MOSS, PORTULACA.
FAMILY	Portulacaceae (Purslane).
TYPE	Annual.
LOCATION	Full sun or at least a half day of morning sun.

PLANTING   Easily transplanted or set out from containers anytime in the growing season.

HEIGHT   6 inches.

SPREAD   12 inches.

FINAL SPACING   12 inches.

BLOOM/FRUIT   Numerous rose-like blooms followed by small capsules containing many small black seeds. The wild plant, considered by many to be a weed, has yellow flowers. The hybrid plants are available in several colors.

GROWTH HABITS/CULTURE   Low-growing and flat to the ground. Good groundcover. Good plant for containers and hanging baskets. Drought resistant and heat loving. Purslane will grow in any soil unless kept too moist. It has low fertilizer needs.

PROBLEMS   Snails, slugs, and cutworms. The flowers close in the afternoon heat. None of these are serious problems.

Hybrid purslane

Wild purslane

Upright purslane (supposedly most powerful herbal qualities)

HARVEST/STORAGE	Leaves and stems can be used fresh or pickled. Pick flowers fresh and use as a garnish.
CULINARY USES	Purslane is great in salads or eaten fresh out of the garden. It is also used as a pot herb. The fleshy leaves have a vinegary taste and are excellent in soups. The British use the leaves in sandwiches with cream cheese. Leaves can be pickled and are good in soups.
MEDICINAL USES	Soothing to the stomach. High in iron and vitamin C, Omega 3 fatty acids, beta-carotene, and many trace minerals. Purslane has historically been used to soothe the stomach. The upright form is the most powerful.
LANDSCAPE USES	Groundcover for sunny areas. Another ornamental hybrid is *Portulaca grandiflora*. Good in pots and hanging baskets. Low-maintenance summer color.
OTHER USES	Excellent plant for attracting honeybees and other pollinators.
INSIGHT	Many people waste time and money spraying wild purslane with weed-killers. Although the hybrid is edible, it may not have the same high food value. Furthermore, hybrids are grown primarily by greenhouse operations that still foolishly use synthetic fertilizers and toxic pesticides. It's hard to know how long those toxins remain in a plant and when it is safe to eat.

PYRETHRUM

Chrysanthemum cinerariifolium
kris-ANTH-ee-mum sin-er-rare-eye-FOLL-ee-um
Listed in some books as *Tanacetum cinerariifolium*

COMMON NAMES	DALMATION DAISY, PAINTED DAISY, PYRETHRUM.
FAMILY	Asteraceae (Compositae) (Sunflower or Daisy).
TYPE	Perennial.
LOCATION	Full sun.

Pyrethrum

PLANTING	Plant seed or transplants in the spring after the last frost.
HEIGHT	To 24 inches.
SPREAD	15 to 18 inches.
FINAL SPACING	9 to 12 inches.
BLOOM/FRUIT	Beautiful white, daisy-like flowers in the summer.
GROWTH HABITS/CULTURE	Foliage is finely textured, pungent, and gray-green. A different species (*Tanacetum coccineum*) has flowers in varying shades of red and pink as well as white. Both bloom all summer. Easy to grow with moderate fertilizer and water. Likes a hot spot with rocky, well-drained, alkaline soil. Easy to grow from seed or transplants.
PROBLEMS	Pyrethrum insecticide will kill bees and other beneficial insects. Bees and other pollinators like hoverflies will avoid flowers sprayed with pyrethrum. The live plants are not toxic to insects. The active ingredients in the flower centers become toxic only after being extracted and concentrated.
HARVEST/STORAGE	Harvest the flowers just when they open, then dry and grind into powder. The insecticide is made from the powdered dried leaves, stems, and flowers, but the most powerful part is the flower center.
CULINARY USES	None.
MEDICINAL USES	Pyrethrum is reported to be a bitter herb that can reduce fever, vertigo, headaches, and arthritic pain. It is a toxic material, however, and I do not recommend taking it internally for any reason.
LANDSCAPE USES	Perennial garden or border.
OTHER USES	Beautiful cut flowers. Natural insecticide. Dust or spray late in the day to minimize harm to beneficials. Use only as a last resort.
INSIGHT	Skin contact can cause dermatitis. Although organic, this plant makes a very powerful and toxic insecticide. It should be used with great care. Never use any pyrethrum products that contain PBO (piperonyl butoxide), a synthetic chemical that affects liver function. I'm no longer comfortable using pyrethrum.

R

RASPBERRY—see **BLACKBERRY**
RED CLOVER—see **CLOVER**
RIVER LOCUST—see **FALSE INDIGO**
ROQUETTE—see **ARUGULA**

ROSE

Rosa spp.
RO-sa

COMMON NAMES	ROSE.
FAMILY	Rosaceae (Rose).
TYPE	Perennial with edible flowers and fruit, or hips.
LOCATION	Full sun is best. Morning sun is critical.
PLANTING	Roses can be installed year round if container grown. Bare-rooted plants should be installed in fall and winter. Cuttings can be taken from early summer through fall.
HEIGHT	1 to 10 feet.
SPREAD	3 to 10 feet.
FINAL SPACING	3 to 5 feet.
BLOOM/FRUIT	Flowers of many colors are followed by the hips, which contain the seed. The hips are ripe and ready to use when they change from orange to red.

Rugosa rose and hip

Native wild rose

GROWTH HABITS/CULTURE   Most roses are thorny and either bushy or climbing. They all like well-drained soil in sunny locations. Growth varieties include low-spreading to tall bushes. The old roses, or heirlooms, are much better-looking plants than the hybrids, and the flowers and hips are better for eating and making teas. Roses need extra amendments in the bed preparation. Beds should contain more compost, volcanic rock material, cornmeal, rock phosphate, alfalfa meal, and other organic amendments than most other plants. The beds should be raised or mounded and the bare soil should be mulched year round. The best mulch for roses is 1 inch of compost or earthworm castings followed by 3 to 4 inches of shredded native cedar. Foliar feed three times a season and spray Garrett Juice weekly. Add garlic tea to the spray for minor insect and disease infestations.

PROBLEMS | Black spot and other fungus problems are controlled by applying cornmeal to the soil and spraying the soil with Garrett Juice plus garlic tea. Add potassium bicarbonate for severe disease infestations. Thrips are controlled with the same tools plus neem. Orange oil products can also be used. Follow the Organic Rose Program (see Appendix).

HARVEST/STORAGE | Dry petals and hips can be stored in a cool dark place. Use the petals and ripe hips when they are fresh.

CULINARY USES | The hips are used in teas, sorbets, cakes, syrups, soups, jams and jellies, rosewater, and wine, the petals in salads, jams and jellies, teas, and desserts. Petals are best when the flowers first open.

MEDICINAL USES | A distillation of rose petals is used for eye baths and as a sedative. The hips contain lots of vitamin C and work as a diuretic, blood purifier, and infection fighter. Rose hips were used by the ancients to build blood and stamina. Take as a tea. To make rose-hip tea, boil about 2 tablespoons of ripe rose hips in a pint of water for about 10 minutes. Add honey, mint, or other herbs for taste and enjoy a delicious, healthy hot tea.

LANDSCAPE USES | Great plant for the landscape and perennial garden.

OTHER USES | Floral arrangements, potpourri, and perfumes. Oil is distilled from flowers or extracted with hexane.

INSIGHT | Antique roses yield the largest hips. There are countless varieties of roses. The best choices for usable hips include 'Old Blush,' *Rogosa* spp., 'Duchesse de Brabant,' 'Souvenir de la Malmaison,' 'Mutabilis,' 'Katy Road Pink,' 'Dortmund,' 'LaMarne,' and 'Belinda's Dream.' *Rosa rugosa* 'Hansa' and *Rosa cania* (dog rose) are especially good.

ROSE MOSS—see **PURSLANE**

ROSELLE

Hibiscus sabdariffa
hi-BIS-kus sab-da-RIFF-ah

COMMON NAMES | ROSELLE, JAMAICA SORREL, FLORIDA CRANBERRY.

FAMILY | Malvaceae (Mallow).

TYPE | Annual shrub.

LOCATION | Full sun.

PLANTING | Start seed indoors in the winter and set out transplants in the spring.

HEIGHT | 4 to 12 feet.

SPREAD | 4 to 8 feet.

FINAL SPACING | 24 to 36 inches.

BLOOM/FRUIT | Yellow and maroon hibiscus-like flowers in October or later. Flowers are dried and used for teas and flavoring. Red pods are used to color punches and teas, to make jellies, and to substitute for cranberries.

GROWTH HABITS/CULTURE | Roselle is an annual shrub that resembles okra and has yellow-petaled flowers that drop off, leaving protective sepals that swell into a succulent fruit. Easy to grow in healthy soil. Use ample soil amendments, including orange peeling and pulp to control nematodes.

PROBLEMS
The plant dies after pods are produced. Subject to nematodes and poor drainage.

HARVEST/STORAGE
Cut flowers throughout the blooming period, dry, and store in glass containers in a cool place.

CULINARY USES
The flowers make a delicious ruby-red tea with a tart, lemony taste. The young leaves can be cooked or eaten raw.

MEDICINAL USES
Roselle is a diuretic when taken as a tea. The swollen red sepals can be added to herb teas to treat coughs.

LANDSCAPE USES
Use it in the landscape and in pots just like any other hibiscus.

OTHER USES
All parts of the plant are used medicinally in Asia.

INSIGHT
Take root cuttings in August for attractive Christmas plants. Roselle has a short-day requirement, so don't let light hit the plant in the fall when it is trying to set its flowers. *Hibiscus acetosella* is a short-lived perennial called false roselle. It looks like a red maple seedling with maroon, maple-shaped leaves. It blooms from November to May. The flower petals are used fresh for teas, and the leaves are added to stir-fry dishes for a sorrel taste. All the *Hibiscus* species have edible flowers.

Roselle

Hibiscus

ROSEMARY

Rosmarinus officinalis
roz-mah-RINE-us o-fish-ih-NALE-lis

COMMON NAMES	ROSEMARY, POLAR PLANT, COMPASS-WEED, COMPASS PLANT.
FAMILY	Lamiaceae (Labiatae) (Mint).
TYPE	Evergreen.
LOCATION	Partial shade to full sun.
PLANTING	Buy organically grown and maintained container plants from organic nurseries. Rosemary can also be grown from stem cuttings, but it is difficult to grow from seed.
HEIGHT	1 to 5 feet.
SPREAD	4 feet.
FINAL SPACING	12 to 18 inches.
BLOOM/FRUIT	Blue or white flowers bloom intermittently throughout the year. Sometimes the plants are very showy.
GROWTH HABITS/CULTURE	Rosemary is an upright-growing shrub, but creeping varieties are also available. The edible leaves resemble short, thick pine needles. The light blue, white, or pink flowers are very fragrant and often bloom all winter long. The foliage is velvety and resinous to the touch. Likes alkaline soil but will grow in any soil. While full sun is ideal, rosemaries will tolerate a considerable amount of shade under tall trees. Provide excellent drainage and avoid overwatering and underwatering.

Rosemary

Creeping rosemary

PROBLEMS Freeze damage, spider mites, wet feet. Good drainage is a must. Many people regard the upright form as more cold-hardy than the spreading form, but experience shows that the spreading form is just as tough. Rosemary has many tiny, hairlike roots and wilts quickly if it lacks water. Water lightly but often and mulch heavily. Rainy seasons cause adventitious roots to form along the stem of the plant. Rosemary can also be killed by overwatering. Applying cornmeal to the soil can save plants that are being weakened by root diseases.

HARVEST/STORAGE Harvest the foliage and flowers anytime, dry and store in airtight containers. Use fresh green cuttings if possible.

CULINARY USES Indispensable in cooking beef, wild game, and meats of all kinds. Delicious in breads, vinegars, butters, and teas.

MEDICINAL USES Rosemary is used as an antiseptic, a memory stimulator, a digestive, and a longevity herb. It is a bath herb and improves hair condition. Compresses are used to relieve headaches.

LANDSCAPE USES Good as a groundcover and in pots and hanging baskets.

OTHER USES Rub on your dog's fur after baths to help repel fleas. Rosemary flowers attract birds and bees and other beneficial insects. Burning rosemary in sick chambers together with juniper berries to deodorize and kill bacteria is an old practice. Rosemary tea has a red color and can be used to spray or splash on the skin of dogs to repel insects. Some people use the tea to rinse dark hair. Tie together a small bundle of the branches and use as a brush for the barbecue.

INSIGHT 'Arp' has a reputation for tolerating frost, but it seems to be somewhat overblown. All forms seem to be cold tolerant in most of Texas—if grown under an organic program.

Rosmarinus officinalis—see **ROSEMARY**
Rubia tinctoria—see **MADDER**

RUE

Ruta graveolens
ROO-ta gra-VEE-o-lenz

COMMON NAMES RUE, HERB OF GRACE, HERBYGRASS.
FAMILY Rutaceae (Citrus or Rue).
TYPE Evergreen perennial.
LOCATION Full sun.

Rue

PLANTING	Rue can be grown from stem cuttings and from seed, but it's best to buy a small plant from an organic nursery and plant it in the spring after the last frost.
HEIGHT	24 to 36 inches.
SPREAD	36 inches.
FINAL SPACING	12 to 18 inches.
BLOOM/FRUIT	Small yellow flowers followed by seed.
GROWTH HABITS/CULTURE	Sprawling growth habit. Will sometimes fall over. Lacy, blue-green foliage. Good winter plant. Prune to control its spread.
PROBLEMS	Handling it, especially in the summer, will cause a skin rash in many people that can be severe.
HARVEST/STORAGE	Harvest seed pods for dried arrangements.
CULINARY USES	Not recommended as a cooking herb, mainly because it's a toxic plant.
MEDICINAL USES	Reportedly an abortifacient, not recommended for medicinal use at all. It is used to repel fleas and flies and also as a germicide.
LANDSCAPE USES	Beautiful in the landscape, especially in the winter.
OTHER USES	Its strong musty odor makes it a pretty good insect and rodent repellent. Some gardeners use it to repel cats. Rue can also be used to raise certain butterflies. Giant swallowtails lay multitudes of eggs in the spring and summer, the larvae of which are large yellow, green, and black caterpillars. The rue usually gets eaten down but springs back between broods, getting bigger with each successive invasion. It's almost as if it depends on the butterflies.
INSIGHT	The leaves of the plant can cause serious dermatitis in sensitive individuals, so be sure to wear gloves and use care when handling or working around rue.

Rumex acetosa—see **SORREL**
Ruta graveolens—see **RUE**

SABAL—see SAW PALMETTO

SAFFLOWER

Carthamus tinctorius
CAR-tha-mus tink-TOE-ree-us

COMMON NAMES	SAFFLOWER, FALSE SAFFRON, BASTARD SAFFRON, ZAFFER.
FAMILY	Asteraceae (Compositae) (Sunflower or Daisy).
TYPE	Some are annual, others are biennial.
LOCATION	Full sun.
PLANTING	Plant seed in beds in the early spring. Plants can be started from seed indoors during the winter.
HEIGHT	Up to 36 inches.
SPREAD	12 inches.
FINAL SPACING	12 inches.
BLOOM/FRUIT	Flowers are orange-yellow and contain two coloring properties: red and yellow. The yellow is used for coloring foods, the red to dye silks or tint cosmetics.
GROWTH HABITS/CULTURE	Erect and rough-leaved, grows to 2 or 3 feet in full sun, sprouting easily from white, shell-shaped seeds. Upright growth, prickly leaves.
PROBLEMS	Few if any.
HARVEST/STORAGE	Harvest flowers anytime and dry the petals. Harvest seeds anytime after they mature.

Safflower

CULINARY USES	The tender shoots are edible. The flower petals can be used in rice to produce a yellow color. This plant has no taste of saffron, as some suggest. Hopi Indians use the petals to color bread. Seeds produce a cooking oil that has become controversial. Sally Fallon's *Nourishing Traditions* rails at it as one of the "bad oils."
MEDICINAL USES	A tea made from the seeds and flower petals is used as a laxative.
LANDSCAPE USES	A beautiful annual landscape plant in the background. Very nice-looking ornamental. The flowers attract beneficial insects.
OTHER USES	Seeds for parrots, yellow dye plant.
INSIGHT	Safflower can become a weed by falling from the bird feeder. It has been reported that seeds were found in the tomb of Tutankhamen.

SAFFRON

Crocus sativus
CROW-kus sa-TEE-vus

COMMON NAMES	SAFFRON, SAFFRON CROCUS.
FAMILY	Iridaceae (Iris).
TYPE	Perennial corm.
LOCATION	Full sun.
PLANTING	Plant between spring and fall before the rain starts.
HEIGHT	4 to 6 inches.
SPREAD	6 inches.
FINAL SPACING	6 inches.
BLOOM/FRUIT	Lavender flowers with brick-red stigmas, which produce the spice of commerce.
GROWTH HABITS/CULTURE	Saffron is grown from a corm and has grass-like foliage. It looks like a typical crocus. Flowers emerge ahead of the foliage in late October to early November. Fairly easy to grow in loose organic soil.
PROBLEMS	Squirrels, rabbits, and gophers are the most serious problems because they dig up and eat the bulbs. Rabbits also eat the foliage. Repel them with hot pepper, castor oil, and fast dogs.
HARVEST/STORAGE	It takes two years for saffron to mature. Harvest around Thanksgiving. About 5,000 stigmas (1,700 flowers) yield one ounce of spice. Harvest the dark red stigmas on the first day of bloom, then dry and store in a cool, dark place. Shelf life is about 10 years.
CULINARY USES	Flavoring for many foods, including rice, meats, soups, and vegetables. Dark red in its dried state, saffron imparts a rich, golden yellow color to cooked food. It is popular in rice dishes and soups. Saffron is an expensive spice, costing more than fifty dollars per ounce.
MEDICINAL USES	According to Odena, a tea or tincture is good for lightheadedness. Saffron is considered an aphrodisiac, but too much may produce a narcotic effect.
LANDSCAPE USES	Beautiful bulb for fall flower color.
OTHER USES	Cosmetics, dyes, and perfumes.
INSIGHT	Plant and leave alone for three years. Then dig, divide, and set out the

Saffron

divisions or give some to friends. When buying this herb ready to use, get the threads instead of powder, which is more likely to be adulterated. For more details, read Odena's *Saffron—King of Spice*. Safflower stigmas are sold as "false saffron," "Turkish saffron," "American saffron," and "Mexican saffron." They color the food but have no taste. Too much saffron can turn a dish bitter. Cooking at high temperatures or for too long can kill the flavor. The flavor sometimes gets better with age.

SAGE

Salvia officinalis
SAL-vee-ah o-fis-ih-NALE-lis

COMMON NAMES	COMMON GARDEN SAGE, EDIBLE SAGE, GARDEN SAGE, SAGE.
FAMILY	Lamiaceae (Labiatae) (Mint).
TYPE	Hardy perennial.
LOCATION	Sun to partial shade.
PLANTING	Start from container-grown transplants anytime from spring through fall. Start seed indoors in late winter. Take cuttings anytime during the growing season.
HEIGHT	24 inches.
SPREAD	18 inches.
FINAL SPACING	18 to 24 inches.

Variegated garden sage

'Indigo spires'

Russian sage

Garden sage

Gregg salvia

BLOOM/FRUIT	Purple spikes followed by small round seeds.
GROWTH HABITS/CULTURE	Upright to sprawling character. Grows to 24 inches or taller with rough gray leaves. Beautiful purple flowers, but it's best to keep them from blooming. Cut established plants back severely in the early spring. This helps to prevent crown rot disease and die-back. The cuttings can be rooted. Sage is easy to grow from seed.
PROBLEMS	Too much water will knock it out from crown rot.
HARVEST/STORAGE	Harvest anytime but try to avoid heavy harvesting during the first year. Store dry in a tightly sealed glass jar.
CULINARY USES	Cook with beans, potatoes, breads, vegetables, meats, dressings, gravies, eggs, potatoes, and beans. Also used in beer, wine, and vinegars.
MEDICINAL USES	Said to be good for memory and the digestive system. Some people eat a leaf raw each day. It's excellent in teas and can be crushed and

ground and added to toothpaste to serve as an antiseptic and to help remove plaque. Sage is also used as a gargle to treat tonsillitis. It has been reported that a sage-leaf bath can help stimulate blood circulation and even help with serious degenerative disorders.

LANDSCAPE USES	Makes a decent container plant.
OTHER USES	Use the leaves to line the bottom of a bowl or basket for storing tomatoes and other vegetables. Make a sage pillow from dry leaves for a relaxing sleep.
INSIGHT	One of the longevity herbs. For the most flavorful leaves, don't let it bloom. The dried leaves can become carcinogenic due to the high levels of volatile oils, so use fresh or within six months after drying. All salvia leaves and flowers lose their flavor when heated.

SAGE TREE—see VITEX

SALAD BURNET

Sanguisorba minor
sang-gwi-SOR-ba MY-nor

COMMON NAMES	SALAD BURNET.
FAMILY	Rosaceae (Rose).
TYPE	Short-lived perennial.
LOCATION	Full sun.
PLANTING	Plant from containers in the spring after the last frost. Or start seed indoors in the winter and set out transplants in the spring.
HEIGHT	12 inches.
SPREAD	12 inches.
FINAL SPACING	12 to 18 inches.
BLOOM/FRUIT	Grows in a rosette clump with arching stems and small, round, ugly, reddish flowers. Small, round, toothed, blue-green leaves with a cucumber taste.

Salad burnet

GROWTH HABITS/CULTURE	Easy to grow, likes cool weather. Evergreen unless the winter is severe. Undemanding when grown in healthy soil with organic techniques.
PROBLEMS	Occasional pill bugs. Doesn't do well in the severe summer heat.
HARVEST/STORAGE	Harvest and use fresh or dry. For the best flavor, gather before flowers form.
CULINARY USES	Salad burnet provides cucumber flavor for salads, vinegars, butters, asparagus, celery, beans, mushrooms, potato salad, and other dishes.
MEDICINAL USES	Considered a diuretic. Best when eaten fresh in salads.
LANDSCAPE USES	Low border plant.
OTHER USES	Good plant for containers.
INSIGHT	Likes cooler weather, makes a good plant for the winter.

SAILOR'S TOBACCO—see MUGWORT

Salvia elegans—see PINEAPPLE SAGE

Salvia officinalis—see SAGE

SAMBAC JASMINE

Jasminum sambac

yas-MEE-num SAM-bac

COMMON NAMES	SAMBAC JASMINE, JASMINE SAMBAC, POET'S JASMINE.
FAMILY	Oleaceae (Olive).
TYPE	Tender perennial.
LOCATION	Full sun to partial shade, preferably a location with morning sun and afternoon shade.
PLANTING	Plant from containers in the spring after the last frost.
HEIGHT	Climbs to 6 feet.
SPREAD	3 to 6 feet.
FINAL SPACING	3 to 4 feet.
BLOOM/FRUIT	Continuous show of fragrant white flowers that last only one day.

Sambac jasmine

GROWTH HABITS/CULTURE	Vining growth, white fragrant flowers all summer. Prune tips of the shoots to keep the plant compact and bushy. Needs healthy, well-drained, rich organic soil. Use lots of compost and earthworm castings.
PROBLEMS	Freeze damage in the northern two-thirds of the state.
HARVEST/STORAGE	Harvest flowers while in full bloom. They can be dried for later use or used fresh.
CULINARY USES	The flowers make a delicious tea. Also used steeped in coffee, to sweeten desserts, and to give fragrance to beverages.
MEDICINAL USES	The tea is reported to reduce fever and enlarged lymph nodes. Tea from the flowers is used as an eyewash, the roots are used for fever and burns.
LANDSCAPE USES	Summer annual.
OTHER USES	Potpourri. Good container plant.
INSIGHT	The flowers and all other parts of the so-called Carolina jasmine (actually jessamine), *Gelsemium* spp., are highly toxic. It is not a true jasmine.

Sambucus canadensis—see **ELDERBERRY**

SANTOLINA

Santolina chamaecyparissus
san-toe-LEEN-ah kam-ah-sip-eh-RIS-us

COMMON NAMES	SANTOLINA, LAVENDER COTTON.
FAMILY	Asteraceae (Compositae) (Sunflower or Daisy).
TYPE	Evergreen perennial.
LOCATION	Full sun.
PLANTING	Plant one-gallon containers year round. You can also grow the plant from stem cuttings.
HEIGHT	12 to 18 inches.
SPREAD	24 inches.

Santolina

FINAL SPACING	18 to 24 inches.
BLOOM/FRUIT	Small, yellow, button-like flowers on slender stems. Tiny seed.
GROWTH HABITS/CULTURE	Low-growing, spreading, drought-tolerant. Gray and green forms available. The green form (*Santolina virens*) is more difficult to grow and thus less desirable.
PROBLEMS	Poor drainage, overwatering, and spider mites, but these problems can be prevented with the Basic Organic Program.
HARVEST/STORAGE	Harvest the foliage anytime.
CULINARY USES	None.
MEDICINAL USES	Historically used as a tea to treat internal parasites, jaundice, kidney problems, and skin diseases.
LANDSCAPE USES	Landscape plant for borders, rock gardens, and hot, dry places.
OTHER USES	Insect repellent that is especially good for moths. The flowers can be used in dried arrangements and potpourris.
INSIGHT	Gray santolina contrasts well with chrysanthemums.

Santolina chamaecyparissus—see **SANTOLINA**
Saponaria officinalis—see **BOUNCING BET**

SASSAFRAS

Sassafras albidum
SASS-ah-frass al-BEE-dum

COMMON NAMES	SASSAFRAS, AGUE TREE, CINNAMON WOOD, SAXIFRAX.
FAMILY	Lauraceae (Laurel).
TYPE	Deciduous tree.
LOCATION	Full sun.
PLANTING	Plant seed, container-grown plants, or root cuttings.
HEIGHT	20 to 40 feet.
SPREAD	20 to 25 feet.
FINAL SPACING	15 to 20 feet.
BLOOM/FRUIT	Chartreuse yellow flowers in clusters, followed by green berries that turn black as they mature.
GROWTH HABITS/CULTURE	Soft-looking tree with mitten-shaped leaves. Ideal conditions include sandy, acid soil, but the tree will occasionally adapt to other soils.
PROBLEMS	It will not grow in alkaline soil.
HARVEST/STORAGE	Harvest the leaves green and dry to make filé. Harvest roots in the fall, dry and store. Harvest berries when ripe.
CULINARY USES	The leaves are dried and ground into a filé for soups and cajun food. Root bark can be used as a substitute for cinnamon bark, such as in cakes, cookies, desserts, and puddings. A good tea herb is made from the roots.
MEDICINAL USES	Chewing the bark helps to break the tobacco habit. Sassafras is a diuretic and is used in cough medicines. Drink a tea made from the roots. Historically it was used as a blood purifier for syphilis—but it didn't work, according to Dr. Judy Griffin.

Sassafras

LANDSCAPE USES   Birds love the seeds that mature in the fall. It provides beautiful fall color—green, orange, red, and yellow at the same time. Should be used more on sandy soil sites.

INSIGHT   Saffrol, a concentrated extract of sassafras oil, is said to be carcinogenic and cause liver damage. However, some books report that it is not nearly as carcinogenic as the ethanol in beer. I hate to hear that about the beer.

Sassafras albidum—see **SASSAFRAS**
Satureja hortensis—see **SAVORY**
Satureja montana—see **SAVORY**

SAVORY

Satureja hortensis—SUMMER SAVORY
sat-ew-RAY-ah hor-TEN-sis
Satureja montana—WINTER SAVORY

COMMON NAMES   SAVORY, SUMMER SAVORY, WINTER SAVORY, BEAN HERB.

Winter savory

Summer savory

Creeping savory

FAMILY	Lamiaceae (Labiatae) (Mint).
TYPE	Annual (summer savory), perennial (winter savory).
LOCATION	Full sun.
PLANTING	Start seed in the winter, set out transplants in the spring.
HEIGHT	8 to 12 inches or somewhat taller.
SPREAD	20 inches.
FINAL SPACING	12 inches.
BLOOM/FRUIT	Blooms are small, white-to-lilac whorls of small star-shaped flowers.
GROWTH HABITS/CULTURE	Compact, low and spreading. Summer savory is more upright with small, aromatic, dark green leaves and grows a little taller. Winter savory is stiffer, woody, and evergreen. Savory needs healthy, fertile soil. Use the Basic Organic Program for maintenance.
PROBLEMS	Spider mites, especially on summer savory. Watch the watering and spray with Garrett Juice to solve the problem.
HARVEST/STORAGE	Harvest the foliage anytime during the growing season. Since winter savory is an evergreen, it can be snipped anytime. Summer savory dies out during hot summers and should be harvested in early summer.
CULINARY USES	Savory is one of the best seasonings for beans—especially green beans. Also good with other vegetables and poultry.
MEDICINAL USES	Savory is a diuretic and said to be good for respiratory problems. Chew the leaves or just add to foods as a seasoning.
LANDSCAPE USES	Makes a good border plant, widely used in knot gardens.
OTHER USES	Bees and other beneficial insects love this herb when it is in flower.
INSIGHT	Winter savory is a better choice for the Texas climate.

SAW PALMETTO

Serenoa repens
ser-ah-NOAH RAY-penz

COMMON NAMES	SAW PALMETTO, SABAL.
FAMILY	Aracaceae (Palmae) (Palm).
TYPE	Fan palm tree.
LOCATION	Full sun.
PLANTING	Plant anytime from containers.
HEIGHT	To 3 to 7 feet usually, sometimes up to 25 feet.
SPREAD	6 to 8 feet.
FINAL SPACING	8 to 10 feet.
BLOOM/FRUIT	Dusky 1-inch red to brownish black berries follow early summer flowers that are branched, white, and very fragrant.
GROWTH HABITS/CULTURE	Small fan palm with blue-gray-green leaves that are about 2 feet wide. Each blade ends in two sharp points. Likes sandy soil the best. Hardy to about 10 degrees. Tough, drought- and salt-tolerant palm. Difficult to transplant but very easy to grow after establishment.
PROBLEMS	Freeze damage in the northern part of the state. Palmetto weevils can be controlled with Garrett Juice plus garlic tea.

Saw palmetto

Saw palmetto

HARVEST/STORAGE	Benefit comes only from professionally prepared extractions, so the experts say. Why can't you just eat the fruit?
CULINARY USES	The flowers are a significant source of honey.
MEDICINAL USES	Traditionally used as a diuretic and a treatment for chronic cystitis and enlarged prostate. Extracts from the dry berries are now used as an antiandrogenic (a type of sex hormone) and for treatment of noncancerous enlargement of the prostate gland. Not effective when taken as a tea. Preparations must contain the fat-soluble components of the herb.
LANDSCAPE USES	Excellent small palm tree for the garden.
OTHER USES	The leaves are used primarily in the north for Christmas decorations. The stems are a source of tannic acid extract.
INSIGHT	According to Dr. James Duke in his book *The Green Pharmacy*, saw palmetto helps prevent male baldness, and may help breast enlargement and loss of libido. Even the American Medical Association now confirms that saw palmetto improves urinary tract symptoms and flow measures in men with prostate problems and that the extract from the plant has fewer adverse effects, and costs less, than the synthetic alternatives.

SEA PARSLEY—see **LOVAGE**

SCENTED GERANIUM

Pelargonium spp.
pell-ar-GO-nee-um

COMMON NAMES	SCENTED GERANIUM.
FAMILY	Geraniaceae (Geranium).
TYPE	Tender perennial.
LOCATION	Full sun to moderate shade.

PLANTING	Start seeds indoors in the winter. Set out plants in the spring after the last freeze.
HEIGHT	18 to 36 inches.
SPREAD	12 to 18 inches.
FINAL SPACING	12 to 18 inches.
BLOOM/FRUIT	Small, fragrant flowers followed by black seeds.
GROWTH HABITS/CULTURE	Tender perennial that has interesting leaves with various shapes and textures. They are all rose-scented, but the fragrances vary. More than seventy different varieties. Easy to grow in most well-prepared garden soils or potting soils. Overfertilization ruins the strong fragrances.
PROBLEMS	None usually. Mealy bugs if the plant undergoes stress.
HARVEST/STORAGE	Gather leaves when green, dry in the shade. Use dried leaves for teas, fresh green leaves for everything else. Fresh leaves can also be used for teas.
CULINARY USES	Rose geranium is especially good for herb teas, sherbets, and cakes. *Pelargonium crispum* has small variegated leaves that don't go limp in hot tea.
MEDICINAL USES	Scented geraniums have been used historically for respiratory problems. Currently the essential oil is used as an antifungal, antidepressant, and antiseptic. Take as a tea for the taste, but use the steam-distilled essential oil to get the medicinal benefits.
LANDSCAPE USES	Good addition to the landscape for fragrance. Best in containers. Rose geranium makes a good border plant.
OTHER USES	Potpourris and perfumes. Lemon geranium is reported to be a mosquito repellent. Coconut geranium, a good basket plant, has lots of small white flowers.
INSIGHT	Scented geraniums are grown for their fragrant foliage. To preserve fragrance, use a diluted mix of Garrett Juice in the soil rather than the stronger dry fertilizers. Here are the dominant fragrances of the most common types: *Pelargonium crispum* (lemon), *P. denticulatum* (pine), *P. fragrans* (nutmeg), *P. graveolens* (rose), *P. nervosum* (lime), *P. odoratissimum* (apple), *P. scabrum* (apricot), *P. tomentosum* (peppermint).

Scented geranium

Lemon scented geranium

Serenoa repens—see **SAW PALMETTO**
SHEPHERD'S PURSE—see **PEPPERGRASS**
SHISHO PLANT—see **PERILLA**
SMOTHERWOOD—see **MUGWORT**
SOAPWORT—see **BOUNCING BET**

SOCIETY GARLIC

Tulbaghia violacea
tull-BAG-ee-ah vy-oh-LACE-ee-ah

COMMON NAMES	SOCIETY GARLIC.
FAMILY	Liliaceae (Amaryllidaceae) (Lily).
TYPE	Perennial corm.
LOCATION	Full sun to partial shade.
PLANTING	Plant divisions anytime from spring through fall. Set out container plants or transplants in the spring.
HEIGHT	12 to 18 inches.
SPREAD	18 to 24 inches.
FINAL SPACING	12 inches.
BLOOM/FRUIT	Lavender to purple flower clusters on long stems.
GROWTH HABITS/CULTURE	Flowers through the summer. One variety has attractive white stripes on its narrow, strap-like leaves.
PROBLEMS	Few if any. Slugs and snails occasionally.
HARVEST/STORAGE	Harvest the flowers and foliage as needed.
CULINARY USES	The foliage of society garlic may be used in the same manner as garlic chives.
MEDICINAL USES	According to Dr. Judy Griffin, the leaves are somewhat medicinal—similar to garlic at a lesser dose. Add toward the end of the cooking time.

Society garlic

Sorrel

| LANDSCAPE USES | One of the herbs that bloom through the heat of our summer. Should be used more. |
| INSIGHT | A continuous bloomer. |

Solidago virgaurea—see **GOLDENROD**

SORREL

Rumex acetosa
ROO-mex ass-ah-TOE-sa

COMMON NAMES	SORREL, FRENCH SORREL, GARDEN SORREL, SOUR DOCK.
FAMILY	Polygonaceae (Knotwood).
TYPE	Hardy perennial.
LOCATION	Full sun or partial shade. The best location is one with morning sun and afternoon shade.
PLANTING	Start seed in the winter, set out transplants in the early spring. It can be divided in the fall or early spring.
HEIGHT	12 to 24 inches.
SPREAD	24 inches.
FINAL SPACING	12 inches.
BLOOM/FRUIT	The tall bloom stalk should be cut away.
GROWTH HABITS/CULTURE	Very easy to grow, considered a weed by many. Deep-rooted perennial with leafy, fountain-like growth. Grows in clumps like lettuce or spinach. Blooming stalks will grow to 18 inches. A good cool weather plant.
PROBLEMS	Seedlings are a nuisance if you let it go to seed. Watch for slugs, snails, and caterpillars. These are usually not serious problems.
HARVEST/STORAGE	Gather and use the fresh leaves anytime as needed. Leaves can also be frozen for later use. Best when used fresh.
CULINARY USES	Can be cooked or used fresh like lettuce. Makes a good soup, adds zip to salads, great on roast beef sandwiches. Consuming large amounts may upset the stomach or even damage the kidneys. Due to its high oxalic acid content, sorrel is not recommended for those with kidney disease, kidney stones, or Crohn's disease. Some cooks wrap sorrel around tough meat as a tenderizing agent.
MEDICINAL USES	Sorrel is an astringent and diuretic that is rich in vitamins A, B, and C. It has been used as a tea to treat wounds topically as well as kidney and liver ailments. The leaves have been used to soothe nettle stings.
LANDSCAPE USES	Sometimes planted to stop erosion.
OTHER USES	The flower stalks can be used in dried arrangements, and the leaves can be used to remove rust, mold, and ink stains. The active ingredient is oxalic acid.
INSIGHT	Oxalic acid makes iron unavailable in the human body and reduces calcium absorption. Eat iron foods at another meal. *Rumex crispus* or *Rumex hymenosepalus* is curly dock or sour dock, the common roadside weed. Both are used as an astringent.

SOUR DOCK—see **SORREL**

SOUTHERNWOOD

Artemisia abrotanum

ar-tay-MEEZ-ee-ah a-BROT-an-um

COMMON NAMES	LAD'S LOVE, LOVER'S PLANT, MAIDEN'S RUIN, OLD MAN, SOUTHERNWOOD.
FAMILY	Asteraceae (Compositae) (Sunflower or Daisy).
TYPE	Hardy perennial.
LOCATION	Full sun.
PLANTING	Plant cuttings, layers, or transplants anytime from spring through fall.
HEIGHT	3 to 4 feet.
SPREAD	4 to 5 feet.
FINAL SPACING	24 to 36 inches.
BLOOM/FRUIT	Small yellow flowers in late summer.
GROWTH HABITS/CULTURE	Shrubby evergreen with thread-like foliage. Soft, feathery, gray-green foliage that is silky to the touch. Very fragrant, smells much like a tangerine. Cut back in the spring to encourage new compact growth.
PROBLEMS	Gets leggy unless pruned back annually.
HARVEST/STORAGE	Cut the foliage and dry anytime during the summer.
CULINARY USES	Most herbalists don't recommend any culinary uses.
MEDICINAL USES	Used to treat insomnia and skin diseases. A tea made from the leaves is used as a tonic and vermifuge.
LANDSCAPE USES	A tall groundcover in the landscape. Also a good companion plant for roses. Grows well in containers.
OTHER USES	Place among clothes to repel moths. Makes a good vinegar. Rub on skin to repel flies. The leaves are sometimes put in pillows to ease insomnia.
INSIGHT	Good for the fragrance garden.

Southernwood

SPEARMINT—see **MINT**
SPINACH TREE—see **CHAYA**
Stachys byzantina—see **LAMB'S EAR**

ST. JOHN'S WORT

Hypericum perforatum
hi-PEER-eh-cum pur-fo-RAH-tum

COMMON NAMES	HYPERICUM, ST. JOHN'S WORT, HARDHAY, AMBER, GOATWEED.
FAMILY	Clusuaceae (Guttiferae) (St. John's Wort or Garcinia).
TYPE	Perennial.
LOCATION	Full sun to partial shade.
PLANTING	Set out transplants year round. Take stem cuttings during the growing season or in late winter as the buds start to swell.
HEIGHT	2 to 3 feet.
SPREAD	3 to 4 feet.
FINAL SPACING	18 to 24 inches.
BLOOM/FRUIT	Attractive, 2- to 3-inch yellow flowers with five petals. Blooms from late spring through summer.
GROWTH HABITS/CULTURE	Low-growing and bushy with beautiful yellow flowers in summer. Can be pruned to control. Cut back after a major bloom to maintain compact form and force additional blooms.
PROBLEMS	Few if any.
HARVEST/STORAGE	Harvest the flowers during the growing season and put them in oil for two weeks or more.
CULINARY USES	The leaves are sometimes used as an ingredient in salads and a flavoring in liqueurs.
MEDICINAL USES	The flowers and leaves are used for skin diseases and wounds. Oil or extract from the flowers is used as an antiviral, astringent, and sedative. It has become a popular substitute for Prozac.

St. John's wort

LANDSCAPE USES	Mass, accent, summer color. Interesting landscape plant. Several good varieties are available for landscape use, such as *H. patulum henryi* and *H. beanii*.
OTHER USES	Yellow and red dyes are made from the flowers.
INSIGHT	The herb is not good for everyone. Some people are very allergic to it and have had some rather severe reactions.

STEVIA

Stevia rebaudiana
STEE-vee-ah re-BAH-dee-an-ah

COMMON NAMES	STEVIA, SWEET HERB, SWEET LEAF OF PARAGUAY.
FAMILY	Asteraceae (Compositae) (Sunflower or Daisy).
TYPE	Tropical annual.
LOCATION	Full sun to partial shade. A location with morning sun and afternoon shade is best.
PLANTING	Stevia has very small flowers, and I don't know how to grow it from seed. Even if seed can be found, the plant is difficult to grow from seed and will not necessarily come true. Use transplants from the garden center or take stem cuttings. Stevia is very easy to grow from stem cuttings.
HEIGHT	24 to 36 inches.
SPREAD	24 to 36 inches.
FINAL SPACING	15 to 18 inches.
BLOOM/FRUIT	Very small white flowers in the summer.
GROWTH HABITS/CULTURE	Stevia grows wild in Central and South America but should be treated as an annual in Texas. Fairly easy to grow here unless you overwater it or forget to water it at all. When it gets floppy, cut back by about 50 percent. It will become more compact and you'll still have plenty to use.
PROBLEMS	Rots if overwatered or grown without excellent drainage.
HARVEST/STORAGE	Collect and use the leaves fresh as needed. The leaves and stems can also be dried, ground into a powder, and stored in glass containers.
CULINARY USES	A herbal substitute for sugar. Stevia is used to sweeten soy sauce, pickles, and soft drinks—mostly in Japan. The other sweet herb is *Lippia dulcis*. People tend to prefer one or the other. Stevia has been used for centuries by the Guarani Indians of Paraguay to sweeten their tea. Use it to sweeten teas and various dishes.
MEDICINAL USES	Stevia has historically been used in foods and teas to treat hearing problems, obesity, hypertension, heartburn, and hypoglycemia. It is also antifungal, a diuretic, and a tonic for those with diabetes and high blood pressure.
LANDSCAPE USES	Stevia is a homely plant. It gets floppy if not cut back regularly.
OTHER USES	Stevia is a sensible replacement for Aspartame and saccharin.
INSIGHT	Steviocide is the active ingredient offering the sweet taste. It seems that the national sweetener giants are trying to keeping the lid on

Stevia

Sweet Annie

these natural sweeteners. Are they afraid that they will replace their patented, synthetic, and more expensive sweetener products? For additional information, read *Sugar-Free Cooking with Stevia* by James and Tanya Kirkland.

STRAWBERRY—see **BLACKBERRY**

SWEET ANNIE

Artemisia annua
ar-tay-MEEZ-ee-ah AN-you-ah

COMMON NAMES	SWEET ANNIE, SWEET WORMWOOD.
FAMILY	Asteraceae (Compositae) (Sunflower or Daisy).
TYPE	Annual.
LOCATION	Sun.
PLANTING	Start seed indoors in winter, set out transplants in the spring after last frost or later during the growing season.
HEIGHT	Up to 8 feet.
SPREAD	4 feet.
FINAL SPACING	3 feet apart or more.

BLOOM/FRUIT
: Tiny ball-shaped, yellow-green flowers that produce lots of seed.

GROWTH HABITS/CULTURE
: A tall-growing annual with feathery, very fragrant foliage. Easy to grow. Can be used as a background plant. The green stems are sometimes red in the fall. Although an annual, the plant seeds out in the fall and returns the next spring unless heavy mulch is used around the plant.

PROBLEMS
: Can spread invasively from seed. Mulching the soil usually stops the problem.

HARVEST/STORAGE
: Use the stems in wreaths, dried arrangements, and potpourri.

CULINARY USES
: None.

MEDICINAL USES
: Historically used as a tea to treat fevers, colds, jaundice, dysentery, malaria, and skin disorders. Very toxic, so use only topically.

LANDSCAPE USES
: Background plant worth growing for fragrance.

OTHER USES
: Dried arrangements and potpourri.

INSIGHT
: Will grow even in the cracks of driveways.

SWEET BASIL—see **BASIL**

SWEET BAY—see **BAY**

SWEET CHERVIL—see **CICELY**

SWEET CICELY—see **CICELY**

SWEET FENNEL—see **FENNEL**

SWEET HERB

Lippia dulcis
LIP-ee-ah DOOL-sis

COMMON NAMES
: SWEET HERB.

FAMILY
: Verbenaceae (Vervain).

TYPE
: Tender perennial herb.

LOCATION
: Sun to partial shade.

Lippia dulcis—the other sweet herb

PLANTING	Can be grown from stem cuttings taken during the growing season. Seed can be started indoors in the winter. Transplants can be set out in the spring after the last frost.
HEIGHT	3 to 6 inches.
SPREAD	12 to 18 inches.
FINAL SPACING	12 inches.
BLOOM/FRUIT	Sweet herb has small, white, cylindrical summer flowers.
GROWTH HABITS/CULTURE	Very easy to grow in various soils and will perennialize in the southern half of the state. It has normal fertilizer and water requirements. Don't overdo either or the sweetness will be diminished.
PROBLEMS	Sometimes develops chlorosis, a trace mineral deficiency, but can be treated with earthworm castings and Texas greensand. A mix of rock powders, including volcanic material, will also help the condition.
HARVEST/STORAGE	Harvest the leaves and use anytime. They can also be frozen or dried and stored in glass containers.
CULINARY USES	The leaves are used as a sugar substitute in foods and drinks. Pound for pound, this plant is considerably sweeter than sugar.
MEDICINAL USES	An alternative to refined sugar.
LANDSCAPE USES	Makes an interesting low border plant or groundcover. Also good in pots and hanging baskets.
INSIGHT	*Lippia* is a better looking plant, but stevia is the better sugar substitute.

SWEET LEAF OF PARAGUAY—see **STEVIA**

SWEET MARIGOLD

Tagetes lucida syn. *Tagetes florida*
ta-JET-teez LOO-see-da

COMMON NAMES	SWEET MARIGOLD, ANISE MARIGOLD, MEXICAN MINT MARIGOLD.
FAMILY	Asteraceae (Compositae) (Sunflower or Daisy).
TYPE	Perennial to evergreen in the southern half of the state.
LOCATION	Full sun to partial shade.
PLANTING	Sweet marigold can be grown from seeds, cuttings, root divisions, or transplants. It will also root in water. It reseeds readily in the late fall. Seed can be started indoors in the winter. They germinate in a few days. Start approximately six weeks before planting time. Set plants outdoors in the early spring.
HEIGHT	18 to 24 inches.
SPREAD	24 to 36 inches.
FINAL SPACING	12 to 18 inches.
BLOOM/FRUIT	Yellow or golden marigold-like flowers, followed by black seeds.
GROWTH HABITS/CULTURE	Upright, clumping. Flowers in late summer to early fall. Strong anise scent. Likes loose, well-drained soil. Best in morning sun and afternoon shade. Very easy to grow from seed. Glossy lance-shaped leaves.

Sweet marigold

Cut back to maintain compact look. Needs plenty of water and moderate fertilization.

PROBLEMS   Mealy bugs and spittlebugs, which may burrow in emerging leaves during high humidity. Some spider mite damage possible during hot months. These and other minor pests can be controlled by spraying Garrett Juice plus garlic tea.

HARVEST/STORAGE   Harvest the foliage anytime to use fresh or to dry and store in glass containers. It's best to use fresh green foliage during the growing season.

CULINARY USES   Use the flowers in salads and as a garnish. Use the foliage to season any kind of meat, poultry, fish, and eggs. Use fresh—it loses its flavor when dried. You don't need much—this herb is very strong.

MEDICINAL USES   Sweet marigold is made into an essential oil for skin cancer patients.

LANDSCAPE USES   Makes an attractive low planting for the border. Blooms profusely in late summer or fall. Very fragrant. Good for the perennial garden.

OTHER USES   Potpourri and dried arrangements.

INSIGHT   Mexican mint marigold is a terrible name. I don't know how it got started, but this plant has no relation to mint. Sweet marigold is probably the best name. Texas marigold is good, too. Legend has it that when it blooms, cold weather follows within a few weeks. Tea of sweet marigold is very strong. According to Dr. Judy Griffin, the foliage was used by the Aztecs to dull the senses of sacrificial victims.

SWEET MAUDELINE—see **COSTMARY**

SWEET WOODRUFF

Galium odoratum, also known as *Asperula odorata*
ga-LEE-um o-doe-RAH-tum

COMMON NAMES	SWEET WOODRUFF.
FAMILY	Rubiaceae (Coffee or Madder).
TYPE	Perennial.
LOCATION	Shade or partial shade.
PLANTING	Start seed in the winter, set out plants in the spring. Transplants can be installed anytime during the growing season.
HEIGHT	6 to 12 inches.
SPREAD	12 inches.
FINAL SPACING	12 to 15 inches.
BLOOM/FRUIT	Clusters of tiny white spring flowers.
GROWTH HABITS/CULTURE	Spreading, low-growing whorls of pointed leaves on square stems. Spreads by stolons. Divide plants in the spring. Cover with thick mulch (4 to 6 inches) in winter. Needs abundant moisture and well-drained, healthy soil with plenty of organic matter.
PROBLEMS	Heat leads to stress and pest problems. Healthy soil with lots of compost and rock powders are very important.
HARVEST/STORAGE	Harvest foliage anytime during the growing season. Leaves contain the blood thinner coumadin.
CULINARY USES	None. Do not eat.
MEDICINAL USES	Sweet woodruff's medicinal values are limited. It is an antispasmodic and relaxant but it can be toxic to the liver. Do not use internally. Use bruised (crushed) fresh leaves topically on wounds as an anticoagulant.
LANDSCAPE USES	A shade-loving groundcover. Plant beneath a magnolia tree where the grass will not grow.
OTHER USES	Potpourri, fragrance for the garden, insect repellent. Its scent gets stronger as the leaves dry. Pick several hours prior to use.
INSIGHT	Plant in shade, mulch heavily.

SWEET WORMWOOD—see **SWEET ANNIE**
Symphytum officinale—see **COMFREY**

Sweet woodruff

Tagetes lucida—see **SWEET MARIGOLD**
Tanacetum vulgare—see **TANSY**

TANSY

Tanacetum vulgare
tan-ah-SEE-tum vul-GAR-ree

COMMON NAMES	TANSY.
FAMILY	Asteraceae (Compositae) (Sunflower or Daisy).
TYPE	Perennial.
LOCATION	Sun to partial shade.
PLANTING	Can be started from seed in the winter for transplanting in the spring or grown from stem cuttings.
HEIGHT	3 to 4 feet.
SPREAD	3 to 6 feet.
FINAL SPACING	18 to 24 inches.
BLOOM/FRUIT	Yellow button-like flowers in late summer. Long-lasting on the plant and after drying, tansy flowers are popular in arrangements and wreaths.
GROWTH HABITS/CULTURE	Can become invasive, very sprawling if not kept trimmed. Opens up in the shade. Drought-tolerant. Evergreen foliage has a camphor fragrance.
PROBLEMS	Can be as aggressively invasive as mint and allelopathic to other plants.

Tansy

HARVEST/STORAGE	Harvest the leaves anytime, the flowers when in full bloom.
CULINARY USES	None.
MEDICINAL USES	Native Americans crushed the leaves and rubbed on the skin to prevent insect bites.
LANDSCAPE USES	Use around doorways to repel flies.
OTHER USES	Yellow dye from the yellow flowers, green dye from the rhizomes. Excellent ant, flea, and fly repellent. The dried root is more powerful than the foliage, but you must kill the plant to use it. Sprinkle chopped, crushed foliage on ants. The dried flowers are pretty in wreaths.
INSIGHT	Tansy likes healthy soil and plenty of room. Dwarf forms are available as well as a gray form.

Taraxacum officinale—see **DANDELION**

TARRAGON

Artemisia dracunculus

ar-tay-MEEZ-ee-ah dra-KUN-kew-lus

COMMON NAMES	FRENCH TARRAGON, TARRAGON.
FAMILY	Asteraceae (Compositae) (Sunflower or Daisy).
TYPE	Hardy perennial.
LOCATION	Full sun to partial shade.
PLANTING	Tarragon is grown only from root divisions and cuttings during the growing season.
HEIGHT	2 feet.
SPREAD	18 inches.
FINAL SPACING	15 inches.
BLOOM/FRUIT	Tarragon has rare and insignificant yellowish flowers that rarely open fully. Seed are even rarer.
GROWTH HABITS/CULTURE	A wild-looking, many-branched perennial that tends to have a sprawling nature. It has narrow, dark green leaves and is very cold tolerant. When it becomes woody, cut it back to the ground.
PROBLEMS	Too much water will kill it. Heavy feeder. Winter-hardy if kept somewhat dry. Rats seem to enjoy eating it.
HARVEST/STORAGE	Pick foliage fresh and use immediately or cut the stems and hang in a cool dry place. When the leaves are dry, store in glass containers.
CULINARY USES	Leaves have a peppery, anise, or licorice taste and are used to season all kinds of foods: fish, chicken, butter, and breads. Tarragon is used to make oils, great vinegars, and a delicate béarnaise sauce. Use in salads and casseroles. A tea made from the leaves stimulates the appetite. To preserve the freshness, aroma, and nutritional value of tarragon, wait until the last 15 minutes of cooking time before adding it to food.
MEDICINAL USES	Tarragon is a digestive aid and diuretic. Used as a tea or condiment, it will relieve gas and stimulate the appetite. The roots have been used to relieve toothache. The leaves contain iodine. Chewing the leaves

Tarragon

numbs the taste buds prior to taking bitter medicine, according to Lesley Bremness in her book *Herbs*.

LANDSCAPE USES   None. Tarragon is a really ugly plant.

OTHER USES   For convenience, plant in pots, baskets, or other containers near the kitchen.

INSIGHT   Appears to be in a permanent state of wilt. An easy-to-grow substitute is sweet marigold (*Tagetes lucidum*). Neither can stand wet feet. Russian tarragon (*Artemisia dracunculoides*) is a weed with little taste, so it is not a culinary herb. Its leaves are larger and coarser, but it tastes worse than it looks.

TEA TREE

Melaleuca alternifolia
mel-ah-LOO-kah al-ter-na-FO-lee-ah

COMMON NAMES   TEA TREE, MEDICINAL TEA TREE.

FAMILY   Myrtaceae (Myrtle).

TYPE   Tropical tree.

LOCATION   Full sun.

PLANTING   Can be grown in Texas only in containers because it freezes with the first frost; can be overwintered in greenhouses. For medicinal uses, it is best to buy commercial products from health food stores.

HEIGHT   15 to 20 feet.

SPREAD   10 to 12 feet.

FINAL SPACING   Planting one tree for education and interest is enough.

BLOOM/FRUIT   Slender creamy white flower spikes and very small seed.

GROWTH HABITS/CULTURE   Hardy to about 32 degrees. A tropical shrub or small tree with papery bark and narrow, pointed leaves.

PROBLEMS   Freeze damage in Texas.

HARVEST/STORAGE   It is best to use commercially produced products. Enjoy the living plant as a container plant and a novelty.

CULINARY USES   None.

MEDICINAL USES   Tea tree is a powerful antiseptic, parasiticide, and insecticide. It also improves skin cells. It is more effective against certain bacteria than many of the antiseptic soaps. It is an ingredient in deodorants and soaps, mouthwashes, and toilet waters. Tea tree has been used in various products to treat denture sores, gum infections, gingivitis, and bad breath. Several different species are used medicinally. Tea tree was used medicinally by Australian forces during World War II as a wound dressing. It stimulates the immune system and is antibacterial and antifungal. It has been used for thrush, vaginal infections, acne,

Tea tree

Tea tree

athlete's foot, warts, insect bites, cold sores, and head lice. There are several commercial products on the market. The best way to use tea tree for head lice is to buy commercial shampoos containing the herb. The oil itself can be added for very severe problems. A formula that is often recommended is 5 drops of tea tree oil to 1 teaspoon of neutral shampoo. Mix in very well and leave on the hair for 5 minutes before rinsing. Wash all combs and brushes in hot water with tea tree oil added. Always avoid the eyes because tea tree can be irritating. Repeat the treatment every 5 days for three applications.

LANDSCAPE USES Interesting container plant.

OTHER USES Tea tree oil can be used as a deodorizer and is also found in cleaning products. It can be used to control dust mites, fleas, and other pests. When applied to the skin, it repels mosquitoes.

INSIGHT Keep tea tree oils and all essential oils out of the reach of children. Tea tree oil is a solvent—it may damage plastics and the finish on wood furniture.

Teucrium spp.—see **GERMANDER**
Teucrium marum—see **CAT THYME**
TEXAS ARBUTUS—see **MADRONE**
TEXAS MADRONE—see **MADRONE**

THYME

Thymus spp.
TIME-us

COMMON NAMES THYME.
FAMILY Lamiaceae (Labiatae) (Mint).
TYPE Perennial.
LOCATION Full sun.

PLANTING	Can be started from seed, cuttings, layers, or root divisions. It is easy to start from stem cuttings. Transplants can be set out anytime during the growing season, but spring is best.
HEIGHT	3 to 12 inches (creeping thyme), 15 to 18 inches (common thyme).
SPREAD	18 to 36 inches (creeping thyme), 15 to 18 inches (common thyme).
FINAL SPACING	12 to 24 inches.
BLOOM/FRUIT	Tiny star-like flowers bloom throughout the spring and summer in shades from crimson to pink or white.
GROWTH HABITS/CULTURE	Small, slightly pointed leaves, ⅛ to ¼ inch in length, highly aromatic, ranging from glossy dark green to woolly silver or variegated green and gold. Woody stems. Upright and prostrate varieties are available. Hardy to below zero degrees. Like well-drained soils and full sun. If not kept pruned, branches become very woody and are easily split by wind or animals.
PROBLEMS	Susceptible to root rot, crown rot, and fungal disease when grown in unhealthy soil, especially if poorly drained, too heavy, or watered too much.
HARVEST/STORAGE	Harvest anytime during the growing season just before the plant blooms. Cut off entire stems and store dried or frozen.
CULINARY USES	Use fresh for the best flavor. Thyme is used to flavor many foods and teas. The flavor is best in teas if the leaves are boiled for a few minutes instead of simmered; to maintain vitamins and nutrients, steep 5 to 10 minutes in hot water, covered. Thyme infused in oil makes a good salad oil and is also good in vinegar.

Creeping thyme

MEDICINAL USES   Thyme has been used to relieve colds, flus, bronchial congestion, and other respiratory problems as well as stomachaches. The tea can be gargled for a sore throat and as an antiseptic mouthwash.

LANDSCAPE USES   Good border plant and low-growing groundcover for the landscape. Stepping on the edges of the plant along garden paths produces a wonderful fragrance. Avoid stepping on the crown, though—it will damage the plant.

OTHER USES   Thymes are good for bonsai planting.

INSIGHT   Thymes are notorious cross pollinators, like the mints, and new hybrids pop up every year. Thymes fall into three broad groups: upright subshrubs (12 to 18 inches tall), creeping herbs (up to 6 inches tall), and very flat creepers (only 1 to 2 inches tall). The culinary thymes are primarily in the upright subshrub category, and nearly all are cultivars of common thyme (*Thymus vulgaris*), creeping mother of thyme. Thymes are among the easiest herbs to propagate. Semi-woody cuttings taken in fall, winter, or early spring will root quickly in potting soil. Because of their branching habits, thymes are well adapted to layering. Peg down a branch with soil or a rock, and roots will form quickly. The new plant can be cut away and carefully transplanted. The seed are tiny—there are about 170,000 seed per ounce. Seeds stay viable for three to four years.

Upright thyme

Caraway thyme—a creeping thyme

Turk's cap

Thymus spp.—see **THYME**
Tilia spp.—see **LINDEN**
TICKLETONGUE TREE—see **PRICKLY ASH**
TOOTHACHE TREE—see **PRICKLY ASH**
Trigonella foenum-graecum—see **FENUGREEK**
Tropaeolum majus—see **NASTURTIUM**
Tulbaghia violacea—see **SOCIETY GARLIC**

TURK'S CAP

Malvaviscus arboreus
mal-vah-VISS-kus ar-BOR-ee-us

COMMON NAMES	TURK'S CAP.
FAMILY	Malvaceae (Mallow).
TYPE	Deciduous perennial shrub.
LOCATION	Shade or filtered light to full sun. A location with morning sun and afternoon shade is best.
PLANTING	Turk's cap can be grown easily from seed, which can be started indoors in the winter or outdoors after the last frost. No treatment is needed. It is also easy to grow from softwood cuttings during the growing season or from root divisions in the fall or early spring.
HEIGHT	5 to 8 feet.
SPREAD	5 to 8 feet.
FINAL SPACING	3 to 5 feet.
BLOOM/FRUIT	Red, fez-like flowers in summer. Red fruit resembling rose hips in the late summer.
GROWTH HABITS/CULTURE	Bushy, shrublike growth with many stems from the ground. The flowers are excellent for attracting hummingbirds and butterflies. Likes moist soil and partial shade.
PROBLEMS	Various leaf-chewing insects like caterpillars and grasshoppers but none serious if the plant is in healthy soil.
HARVEST/STORAGE	Dry and store flowers and fruit for year-round use.
CULINARY USES	Flowers and fruit make a good herb tea. Young leaves, fruit, and flowers are edible raw or cooked. The fruit is full of pulp and seed; cooked down, it produces a good jelly or syrup. The flavor of the raw fruit resembles that of watermelon or apple.
MEDICINAL USES	Historically the fruit and flowers have been used to treat diarrhea.
LANDSCAPE USES	Provides perennial color and attracts hummingbirds and beneficial insects.
OTHER USES	For use all over Texas. One of the best flowering plants for shady areas. Some people consider it a perennial, but it looks more like a shrub. Used to produce red dye.
INSIGHT	This native Texas plant attracts pollinators like bumblebees and hummingbirds.

TURMERIC

Curcuma domestica
KUR-kew-ma doe-MESS-tee-ka

COMMON NAMES	TURMERIC.
FAMILY	Zingiberaceae (Ginger).
TYPE	Tender perennial.
LOCATION	Full sun.
PLANTING	Grow from rhizomes and set out in the spring.
HEIGHT	24 to 30 inches.
SPREAD	18 to 24 inches.
FINAL SPACING	24 inches.
BLOOM/FRUIT	Interesting yellow flowers with pink bracts in summer.
GROWTH HABITS/CULTURE	A tropical herb that looks like ginger or a small banana plant and has exotic yellow and purple flowers. Leaves are large, 6 to 8 inches wide, with maroon band on both sides of the mid-rib. Aromatic rhizomes. Grows in clumps and tends to spread.
PROBLEMS	Freezes if not protected. Few if any insect problems.
HARVEST/STORAGE	Dig and store the bright orange roots in late summer or fall.
CULINARY USES	Flavors pickles, rice, and soups. Gives yellow color to curry powder, rice, and other foods.
MEDICINAL USES	Anti-inflammatory. Tea from the roots is used to treat cancer and arthritis. Inhibits blood clotting and metabolizes fats, according to Dr. Judy Griffin in *Mother Nature's Herbal.*
LANDSCAPE USES	Use as an annual for interesting texture and dramatic flowers.
OTHER USES	Ornamental potted plant, yellow dye plant.
INSIGHT	Turmeric is a tender ginger. The powdered root is sometimes sold as fake saffron for a much lesser price.

VALERIAN

Valeriana officinalis
va-le-ree-AH-na oh-fis-ih-NALE-is

COMMON NAMES	VALERIAN, CAT'S VALERIAN, COMMON VALERIAN, GARDEN HELIOTROPE.
FAMILY	Valerianaceae (Valerian).
TYPE	Perennial.
LOCATION	Sun to partial shade. Morning sun and afternoon shade is the best location.
PLANTING	Grow seeds indoors in the winter. Make root divisions in early spring or fall. Set out transplants in spring after the last frost.
HEIGHT	3 to 4 feet.
SPREAD	18 to 24 inches.
FINAL SPACING	12 to 18 inches.
BLOOM/FRUIT	Flowers are rounded white to dark pink on hollow hairy stems.
GROWTH HABITS/CULTURE	Hardy perennial with heart-shaped serrated leaves. Needs moist, well-drained soil. Divide plants every three or four years.
PROBLEMS	Valerian is easy to grow in healthy soil with morning sun. Afternoon shade is helpful. Use Garrett Juice plus garlic tea for minor insect problems.

Valerian

HARVEST/STORAGE	Dig the carrot-shaped root in the fall, then dry and store.
CULINARY USES	None.
MEDICINAL USES	Valerian is called nature's tranquilizer and is used in sleep-inducing teas. It doesn't taste or smell good—something like dirty socks. Only the white variety is used medicinally. Valerian can cause drowsiness or can even become addictive. It is not recommended for people taking antidepressants or for menopausal women.
LANDSCAPE USES	Good perennial ornamental, backdrop for herb borders. Very fragrant flowers that have a smelly undertone.
OTHER USES	Attractive to cats and rats (said to be what the Pied Piper used to lure the rats). Makes excellent cut flowers.
INSIGHT	The roots of valerian have a strong odor when freshly dug; they spread and can sometimes become invasive in areas where they adapt. Red valerian (*Centranthus ruber*) is not related to true valerian. It has attractive flowers but is known as an invasive perennial.

Valeriana officinalis—see **VALERIAN**
Verbascum thapsus—see **MULLEIN**

VERVAIN

Verbena officinalis
ver-BEAN-ah oh-fis-ih-NALE-is

COMMON NAMES	VERVAIN.
FAMILY	Verbenaceae (Vervain or Verbena).
TYPE	Hardy perennial.
LOCATION	Full sun.
PLANTING	Start seed indoors in the winter, transplant outdoors in the spring.
HEIGHT	18 inches.
SPREAD	12 inches.
FINAL SPACING	12 inches.
BLOOM/FRUIT	Small white or purple mid-summer flowers, small seed.
GROWTH HABITS/CULTURE	A herbaceous perennial weed with deeply cut leaves. Not very showy. It grows wild.
PROBLEMS	None.
HARVEST/STORAGE	Harvest leaves in the spring or summer, dry in the shade and store in a dry place.
CULINARY USES	None.
MEDICINAL USES	The leaves and flowering tops have been used historically to treat all kinds of problems, including coughs, colds, fever, dysentery, eye problems, liver disorders, insomnia, menstrual cramps, stomach problems, urinary problems, skin problems, and even cancer. The only problem is that vervain makes a bad-tasting tea.
LANDSCAPE USES	None.
INSIGHT	Vervain is a common wild plant in dry grasslands and along roadsides.

Vervain

Vetiver

VETIVER

Vetiveria zizanioides
vet-ah-VER-ee-ah ziz-an-ee-OID-eez

COMMON NAMES	VETIVER.
FAMILY	Poaceae (Gramineae) (Grass).
TYPE	Perennial.
LOCATION	Sun.
PLANTING	Can be grown from division or from seed planted indoors in the winter. Transplants can be set out anytime during the growing season.
HEIGHT	5 to 6 feet.
SPREAD	2 to 3 feet.
FINAL SPACING	2 to 3 feet.
BLOOM/FRUIT	We've never seen any flowers, but it supposedly has plumes.
GROWTH HABITS/CULTURE	Decorative grass with plumes similar to those of a small pampas grass. Fragrant plant with a deep, tenacious root system.
PROBLEMS	None serious.
HARVEST/STORAGE	Harvest the roots in the fall.
CULINARY USES	The distilled oil is used to flavor sweet dishes.
MEDICINAL USES	An essential oil from the root is used to treat rheumatism.
LANDSCAPE USES	Vetiver makes a fine accent plant in the landscape and can help control soil erosion.
OTHER USES	Fragrance plant. Roots are very fragrant and used in potpourri. The powdered root is said to repel clothes moths. Vetiver is used as a fixative in men's perfumes. Yuck! I don't recommend perfume for women, much less men!
INSIGHT	Vetiver needs plenty of sun and moist, rich soil. It is a cousin of the familiar pampas grass but not as showy. The top growth may freeze back in a severe winter, but it is root-hardy. Cut the top back in the spring so the fresh young leaves have a clear path.

VIOLET

Viola odorata

vy-OH-la o-do-RAH-ta

COMMON NAMES   VIOLET, GARDEN VIOLET.

FAMILY   Violaceae (Violet).

TYPE   Perennial.

LOCATION   Shade to partial shade.

PLANTING   Can be grown from seed, but it's easier to set out transplants or divisions in the spring.

HEIGHT   6 inches.

SPREAD   8 to 12 inches.

FINAL SPACING   12 inches.

BLOOM/FRUIT   Purple, rose, yellow, and white flowers. Heart-shaped leaves. Forms mound about 6 inches high. Makes lots of tiny seed.

GROWTH HABITS/CULTURE   Low-growing, spreading, and aggressive. A very easy to grow plant for the naturalized garden. Grows best in well-prepared soils with plenty of organic matter and moisture.

PROBLEMS   Aggressive, invasive.

HARVEST/STORAGE   Harvest the leaves when they are young and the flowers anytime during the growing season.

CULINARY USES   Purple syrup can be made from the blossoms. The leaves and flowers are edible and can be used for salads.

MEDICINAL USES   Contains lots of vitamins, especially A and C. Eat the flowers and leaves. Due to their antiseptic properties, the leaves are used for bruises, skin ulcers, and other wounds. Martha Washington used the syrup to treat coughs and bronchitis in children, according to Dr. Judy Griffin in *Mother Nature's Herbal*. Here's the recipe: Boil 3 pounds of sugar in 2 cups of water for 10 minutes. Remove any scum. Crush 1 pound of violet flowers in a mortar, add to syrup, and cook until it loses color. Strain and bottle in glass when cool.

LANDSCAPE USES   Low border plant. Adds fragrance to the garden. Good perennial border in shady or partly shady locations.

Johnny-jump-ups

Wild violets

OTHER USES	The violet oil used in perfume is a synthetic chemical—another reason I don't like perfume. True violet oil is distilled from the leaves; it's very expensive and has little scent.
INSIGHT	Johnny-jump-ups and pansies, members of the violet family, also have edible flowers.

Viola odorata—see **VIOLET**

VITEX

Vitex agnus-castus
VY-teks AG-nus CAST-us

COMMON NAMES	VITEX, LILAC CHASTE TREE, INDIAN SPICE, HEMP-TREE, WILD PEPPER, SAGE TREE.
FAMILY	Verbenaceae (Vervain).
TYPE	Deciduous tree.
LOCATION	Sun.
PLANTING	Can be grown from seed planted in the spring or from container transplants set out anytime of the year.
HEIGHT	20 feet.
SPREAD	25 feet.
FINAL SPACING	15 to 20 feet.
BLOOM/FRUIT	Purple or white flowers in early summer.
GROWTH HABITS/CULTURE	Vitex is a spreading tree, usually multi-stemmed, has brittle wood, and is not long-lived. Nicely textured foliage, easy to grow in most soil, drought-tolerant.

PROBLEMS Generally short-lived. Freeze damage is possible in the northern part of the state.

HARVEST/STORAGE Harvest and dry the leaves and roots. Collect and store the seeds when mature and dry.

CULINARY USES Use seeds as you would pepper and as a condiment.

MEDICINAL USES The dried fruits of vitex contain hormone-like substances that is said to reduce sexual desire in men. A tincture of the dried berries is said to help regulate the menses and treat symptoms of premenstrual syndrome. The leaves, fruit, and root have been used historically to treat malaria, coughs, and bacterial dysentery.

LANDSCAPE USES A secondary or ornamental tree for special interest.

OTHER USES The flowers make good cut flowers.

INSIGHT Incorrectly called a Texas native. It is a native of Europe and Asia that has become naturalized here.

Vitex

W-Y-Z

WALL GERMANDER—see GERMANDER

WALNUT, BLACK

Juglans nigra
JEW-gluns NI-gra

COMMON NAMES	BLACK WALNUT.
FAMILY	Juglandaceae (Walnut).
TYPE	Deciduous shade tree.
LOCATION	Sun.
PLANTING	Plant seed in the fall. Install container plants year round.
HEIGHT	50 feet.
SPREAD	50 feet.
FINAL SPACING	20 to 50 feet.
BLOOM/FRUIT	Male flowers are slender, green, drooping catkins. Female flowers occur in short terminal spikes. The fruit is the walnut.
GROWTH HABITS/CULTURE	Open, branching character. Yellow fall color and dark bark. Large, distinctive leaves of uniform size, evenly arranged on each side of stem. Moderate to slow growth. Likes deep soil and good drainage. Likes a neutral soil but will tolerate alkaline soil.
PROBLEMS	Roots and leaves give off a toxin (juglon) harmful to some other plants. The nut is delicious, but it is almost all structure (very little meat) and extremely hard to shell.
HARVEST/STORAGE	Store the nuts in a cool dry place.

Walnut

CULINARY USES   Delicious and nutritious nuts.

MEDICINAL USES   Walnut consumption is said to reduce the bad form of cholesterol. Tincture of walnut bark cleanses the body of parasites such as tapeworms and amoebas and is also good for the skin. It should be used internally with caution and only for a short time (one to two weeks). Black walnut bark is very laxative.

LANDSCAPE USES   Shade tree.

OTHER USES   Beautiful lumber from the trunks.

INSIGHT   Don't plant walnut trees near your vegetable garden. The leaves, flowers, and roots will severely retard growth of certain plants, especially the nightshades like tomatoes, peppers, potatoes, and flowering tobacco. *Juglans regia* is the English walnut.

WATERCRESS

Nasturtium officinale

nas-TUR-she-um o-fish-oh-NALE

COMMON NAMES   WATERCRESS, INDIAN CRESS.

FAMILY   Brassicaceae (Cruciferae) (Mustard).

TYPE   Hardy perennial.

LOCATION   Full sun to partial shade.

PLANTING   Plant seeds or divisions anytime during the growing season.

HEIGHT   2 to 24 inches.

SPREAD   Creeper.

FINAL SPACING   12 inches.

BLOOM/FRUIT   Tiny white insignificant flowers.

GROWTH HABITS/CULTURE   Grows easily, roots form at every joint. Plant seed in moist soil or let divisions root in water. For best results, cover sprouts until root system is established.

PROBLEMS   Needs lots of water.

HARVEST/STORAGE   Harvest and use fresh.

Watercress

CULINARY USES	Watercress is used in salads, soups, and sandwiches. It's delicious raw.
MEDICINAL USES	Containing lots of minerals, watercress is a diuretic, expectorant, blood cleanser, tonic for anemia, and appetite and digestive aid. It is good for gall bladder ailments and helps prevent scurvy. Eat it fresh.
LANDSCAPE USES	Bog plant.
OTHER USES	Can be grown in containers.
INSIGHT	Watercress is not related to the common nasturtium (*Tropaeolum majus*).

WAX BEGONIA—see **BEGONIA**
WILD ANISE—see **FENNEL**
WILD HOLLYHOCK—see **MALLOW**
WILD MARJORAM—see **OREGANO**
WILD PEPPER—see **VITEX**
WINTER SAVORY—see **SAVORY**

WITCH HAZEL

Hamamelis spp.
ham-ah-MAY-liss

COMMON NAMES	WITCH HAZEL, HAZELNUT, SNAPPING HAZEL, WINTER BLOOM.
FAMILY	Hamamelidaceae (Witch Hazel).
TYPE	Deciduous ornamental tree.
LOCATION	Full sun to partial shade.
PLANTING	Plant from containers year round. Take cuttings in late winter. Can be grown from seed, but the seed takes two years to germinate.
HEIGHT	10 to 15 feet.
SPREAD	8 to 10 feet.
FINAL SPACING	8 to 10 feet.
BLOOM/FRUIT	Golden yellow flowers in the fall and winter after the leaves have fallen. The flowers of some species have a red or purple cast near the base. Seeds form inside woody capsules. Fruit and flowers form simultaneously. The seed are ejected from the capsules when ripe.
GROWTH HABITS/CULTURE	Witch hazel is a large shrub or small tree with fragrant yellowish flowers in the fall. It likes moist soil and seems to be happy in a wide range of soils.
PROBLEMS	Few if any, none serious.
HARVEST/STORAGE	The foliage can be harvested anytime, but the new young leaves are the best for teas. Collect the seed after they mature in the fall.
CULINARY USES	The seeds are edible, and the leaves are used in herb teas.
MEDICINAL USES	Extracts, lotions, and salves are made from the bark, stems, and leaves by a distillation process. Witch hazel has been used for its disinfectant and astringent properties to treat skin problems. *Hamamelis virginiana* is a good skin tonic when taken as a tea. It has also been used as a gargle for sore throats.
LANDSCAPE USES	Witch hazel is an attractive small tree and should be used more in the landscape.

Witch hazel

OTHER USES	The tree is commonly used to make divining rods to find water and mineral deposits. The seeds are excellent bird food.
INSIGHT	Vernal witch hazel (*H. vernalis*) is more shrubby and blooms in the winter or early spring. A distillate of witch hazel was once used by barbers on nicks and cuts.

WOOLLY BETONY—see **LAMB'S EAR**

WORMWOOD

Artemisia absinthium
ar-tay-MEEZ-ee-ah ab-SINTH-ee-um

COMMON NAMES	WORMWOOD.
FAMILY	Asteraceae (Compositae) (Sunflower or Daisy).
TYPE	Perennial subshrub.
LOCATION	Full sun or partial shade.

PLANTING	Plant year round from seed, divisions, or transplants.
HEIGHT	3 to 4 feet.
SPREAD	2 to 3 feet.
FINAL SPACING	18 to 24 inches.
BLOOM/FRUIT	Yellowish green flowers in mid-summer.
GROWTH HABITS/CULTURE	Fast-growing, very pungent, upright to sprawling, extremely aromatic foliage. Leaf color is silvery when young but darkens to pale green with age. Can be invasive. Cut back in the fall or early spring to prevent a leggy look.
PROBLEMS	Leggy and untidy if not kept trimmed.
HARVEST/STORAGE	Cut the foliage anytime and use fresh or hang upside down to dry. Store in a cool place.
CULINARY USES	A bitter herb used to flavor campari vermouth and absinthe.
MEDICINAL USES	Historically wormwood was used to make a bitter tea taken as a vermifuge. It was also used to aid digestion and to treat liver and gallbladder problems, fever, and gout. However, it is very toxic and should not be ingested.
LANDSCAPE USES	Makes a good border plant and provides color contrast in the garden.
OTHER USES	Used as an insect repellent for fleas, ticks, and moths. Good in wreaths.
INSIGHT	Wormwood is a good insect repellent and attractive in the landscape. The essential oil of wormwood is very dangerous. The toxic substance absinthin will leach out of the leaves of wormwood and will inhibit the growth of nearby plants.

Wormwood

YARROW

Achillea millefolium
ah-KILL-ee-ah meel-lee-FOE-lee-um

COMMON NAMES	YARROW, MILFOIL, CARPENTER'S WEED, DEVIL'S NETTLE, BLOODWORT, THOUSAND WEED, STAUNCHWEED.
FAMILY	Asteraceae (Compositae) (Sunflower or Daisy).
TYPE	Perennial.
LOCATION	Sun or partial shade.
PLANTING	Start from cuttings or divisions in the spring or fall, plant anytime from containers. Start seed indoors in winter, set out transplants in the spring.
HEIGHT	24 to 36 inches.
SPREAD	1 to 2 feet.
FINAL SPACING	1 to 2 feet.
BLOOM/FRUIT	Flat-topped umbels produce seed.
GROWTH HABITS/CULTURE	Feathery foliage produces a pleasant fragrance when crushed. Flat-topped clusters of flowers in white, rose, pink, yellow, and red. Very

Yarrow

easy to establish and grow in well-drained soil. Can become invasive.

PROBLEMS   Some varieties grow tall and need to be staked. Can spread and become a pest in refined gardens.

HARVEST/STORAGE   Harvest flowers at the peak of bloom, gather the foliage anytime.

CULINARY USES   The flowers are chopped fine and used in soups, cheese, and salads. They are also used to flavor liqueurs and in herb teas. The leaves are toxic.

MEDICINAL USES   Taken as a tea, yarrow flowers are good for colds and the flu. As a blood-clotting agent, yarrow also reduces blood pressure; as an antiseptic, it fights yeast infections. Avoid using during pregnancy. Otherwise take only in small doses. Overuse can make the skin sensitive to sunlight. The leaves will help stop bleeding when applied topically.

LANDSCAPE USES   Beautiful in the landscape but can be invasive. *A. millefolium* is a white-flowering native plant.

INSIGHT   An excellent choice for a splash of color in the herb garden. Requires little maintenance. The tall, showy flower heads are popular and long-lasting in dried arrangements.

Zingiber officinale—see **GINGER**
Ziziphus jujube—see **JUJUBE**

RECOMMENDED READING

Several periodicals that will help you with herb choices are *The Herb Companion* (201 East Fourth Street, Loveland, CO 80537-9977), *The Herb Quarterly* (P.O. Box 689, San Anselmo, CA 94979-0689), *HerbalGram* (American Botanical Council, P.O. Box 144345, Austin, TX 78714-4345), and *The Dirt Doctor's Dirt* (groundcrew@yahoo.com). Some good books for herb gardeners are listed below.

Beck, C. Malcolm, and John Howard Garrett. *Texas Bug Book.* Austin: University of Texas Press, 1999.

Blumenthal, Mark, Werner Busse, et al. *The Complete German Commission E Monographs.* Austin, Tx.: American Botanical Council, 1998.

Board on Science and Technology for International Development. *Neem: A Tree for Solving Global Problems.* Washington, D.C.: National Academy Press, 1992.

Brannam, Odena. *Saffron—Spice of Kings.* Dallas: Old Bell Farm Publishers, 1990.

Bremness, Lesley. *Herbs.* Eye Witness Handbooks. London: Dorling Kindersley, 1994.

Diggs, George M., Jr., Barney L. Lipscomb, and Robert J. O'Kennon. *Shiner's and Mahler's Illustrated Flora of North Central Texas.* Fort Worth: Austin College Center for Environmental Studies and Botanical Research Institute of Texas, 1999.

Duke, James A. *The Green Pharmacy.* Emmaus, Pa.: Rodale Press, 1997.

Griffin, Judy. *Mother Nature's Herbal.* St. Paul, Minn.: Llewellyn Publications, 1997.

Gruenwald, Joerg, Thomas Brendler, and Christof Jaenicke. *PDR for Herbal Medicines.* Montvale, N.J.: Medical Economics Company, 1998.

Hill, Madalene, and Gwen Barclay. *Southern Herb Growing.* Fredericksburg, Tex.: Shearer Publishing, 1987.

Hutson, Lucinda. *The Herb Garden Cookbook.* Houston: Gulf Publishing Co., 1998.

Kirkland, James, and Tanya Kirkland. *Sugar-Free Cooking with Stevia.* Available from www.steviapetition.org or 817-557-5309.

Marcin, Marietta Marshall. *The Herbal Tea Gardens.* Pownel, Vt.: Story Books, 1999.

Shurtleff, William, and Akiko Aoyagi. *The Book of Kudzu: A Culinary and Healing Guide.* Brookline, Mass.: Autumn Press, 1977.

Tull, Delena. *Edible and Useful Plants of Texas and the Southwest: A Practical Guide.* Austin: University of Texas Press, 1999.

Tyler, Varro E. *The Honest Herbal.* 3d ed. Binghamton, N.Y.: Haworth Press, 1993.

HOME RECIPES

COMPOST TEA

Here's how to make compost tea at home. Any type of container will work, but a 5- to 15-gallon plastic bucket is easy for the homeowner. Fill the bucket half full of compost, then finish filling with water. Let the mixture sit for 10 to 14 days. Strain out the solids with old pantyhose, cheesecloth, or row cover material. Dilute the dark mixture and spray on the foliage of plants. Manure or manure-based compost is not essential, but it makes the tea more powerful and effective.

How much to dilute the compost tea before using it depends on the compost used. A rule of thumb is to dilute the leachate down to one part compost liquid to four to ten parts water. It should look like iced tea. Add 2 tablespoons of molasses to each gallon of spray for more power. Add citrus oil for even greater pest-killing power.

Full-strength compost tea makes an excellent fire ant mound drench when mixed with molasses and citrus oil. If the ant mound is adjacent to a herb, however, the full-strength mix can kill the plant. Apply only enough diluted drench to cause the ants to relocate; then you can kill them with a stronger mix.

FIRE ANT CONTROL DRENCH

Mix equal parts molasses, compost tea, and orange oil. Use 4 to 6 ounces per gallon of water and pour into the center of the ant mounds. Then splash the mixture on the rest of the mound and on the ants that are trying to run away or up your leg. Commercial products that contain citrus include Citrex Garden-Ville Fire Ant Control and GreenSense Soil Drench.

GARLIC-PEPPER TEA

2 bulbs garlic
2 hot peppers (cayenne, habanero, or any other type of hot pepper)

Liquefy the garlic and hot peppers in a blender that is half to a third full of water. Strain out the solids, then add enough water to the garlic-pepper juice to make one gallon of concentrate. Use ¼ cup of concentrate per gallon of spray. Some gardeners prefer to cook the oils out of the garlic and peppers.

To make straight garlic tea, simply omit the pepper and add another bulb of garlic. There are now commercial products such as Maestro-Gro Garli-Pepper Tea on the market if you don't like making your own brews.

GARLIC-PEPPER-SEAWEED TEA

Add 1 tablespoon of liquid seaweed to each gallon of ready-to-use garlic-pepper tea.

GARRETT JUICE

My basic organic foliar spray is available commercially, or you can make your own. Mix the following ingredients and you'll have a solution that's ready to spray.

1 cup concentrated manure compost tea (see recipe above)
1 ounce molasses
1 ounce natural apple cider vinegar
1 ounce liquid seaweed
1 gallon water

For additional disease and insect control, add one of the following:

¼ cup garlic tea (see recipe above) *or*
¼ cup garlic-pepper tea (see recipe above) *or*
2 ounces orange oil

For a homemade fire ant killer, add 2 ounces citrus oil. Make sure the ready-to-use solutions never contain more than 2 ounces of orange oil per gallon.

HERB TEA FOR FOLIAR FEEDING

Add a handful of the following herbs to 5 gallons of water. Let the mixture sit for about 3 to 7 days. Then mix 1 cup per gallon of water. Use by itself or mix with other natural sprays.

epazote (*Chenopodium* spp.)
mint (*Menta* spp.)
comfrey (*Symphytum officinale*)
dandelion (*Taraxacum* spp.)
purple coneflower (*Echinacea* spp.)
sage (*Salvia officinalis*)
garlic (*Allium sativum*)
ginkgo (*Ginkgo biloba*)

ORGANIC HERBICIDE

Mix 2–4 ounces of orange oil with a gallon of full-strength, 100-grain (10 percent) vinegar. Do not add any water. Spray weeds on a sunny day. This spray is nonselective, so be careful to avoid any desirable plants. An even stronger (20 percent) vinegar is also available. It is very powerful and should be used with care.

TREE TRUNK GOOP
Combine equal parts of the following and mix together in water:

soft rock phosphate *or* fireplace ashes
natural diatomaceous earth
manure compost

Slop the mixture on any physical injuries to tree trunks. Reapply if rain or irrigation washes it off. For disease control spray hydrogen peroxide on the wounds before treating with Tree Trunk Goop.

ORGANIC ROSE PROGRAM

Roses should be grown only organically since they are one of the best medicinal and culinary herbs in the world. If they're loaded with toxic pesticides and other chemicals, you'll miss many of the added benefits of growing roses. Drinking rose hip tea after spraying the plants with synthetic poisons is a really bad idea. For best results with roses, follow this program:

SELECTION
Choose adapted roses such as antiques, Austins, and well-proven hybrids. The old roses will have the largest hips and the ones containing the most vitamins. *Rugosa* roses have the most vitamin C.

PLANTING
Prepare beds by mixing the following into existing soil (per 1,000 sq. ft.) to form a raised bed:

6 inches compost
½ to 1 inch lava sand
20 pounds alfalfa meal
20 pounds cottonseed meal
40 pounds Texas greensand
20 pounds Alliance wheat bran, cornmeal, molasses soil amendment

Soak the the plant's bare roots or root ball in water with 1 tablespoon of seaweed per gallon and 1 tablespoon of natural apple cider vinegar, Garrett Juice, or commercial biostimulant such as Medina, Agrispon, or Vitazyne. Settle soil around plants with water, not tamping.

MULCHING
After planting, cover all the soil in the beds with 1 inch of compost or earthworm castings followed by 2–3 inches of shredded native tree trimmings or shredded hardwood bark. Native cedar is the best choice. Do not pile the mulch up on the stems of the roses.

WATERING

If possible, save and use rainwater. If not available, add 1 tablespoon of natural apple cider vinegar per gallon of water to regular tap water, but don't overwater. Avoid salty wellwater or treat with liquid humate.

FERTILIZING PROGRAM

The following applications are based on 1,000 sq. ft.

ROUND 1 (FEBRUARY 1–15)

20 pounds organic fertilizer (i.e., Garden-Ville, GreenSense, Bradfield, Maestro-Gro, Bioform Dry, Sustane, or Alliance Soil Amendment)
80 pounds lava sand
2–5 pounds sugar

ROUND 2 (JUNE 1–15)

20 pounds organic fertilizer
80 pounds Texas greensand (or 30 pounds soft rock phosphate in sandy acid soils)

ROUND 3 (SEPTEMBER 15–30)

20 pounds organic fertilizer
20 pounds sul-po-mag (or 30 pounds soft rock phosphate in sandy acid soils)

FOLIAR FEEDING

Apply the first spraying at pink bud in the spring, with additional sprayings as necessary. For best results, spray every two weeks but at least once a month. The first two sprayings of the season should include Garrett Juice and garlic tea. When the soil is healthy, nothing but Garrett Juice is needed in the spray.

PEST CONTROL

For minor diseases or insect infestations, add the following to each gallon of Garrett Juice (see recipe above):

¼ cup garlic tea or commercial garlic spray (follow label directions)
citrus oil, orange oil, or d-limonene (1 ounce as a spray, 2 ounces as a drench)
1 rounded tablespoon baking soda (potassium bicarbonate is a superior substitute)
liquid biostimulants such as Agrispon, AgriGro, Medina, Vitazyne, Bio-Innoculant, or similar product (follow label directions)
neem (follow label directions)
1–2 ounces fish emulsion for additional nutrients (may not be needed when using compost tea)
Apply beneficial nematodes to soil prior to bud break in early spring.

ORGANIC NUT AND FRUIT TREE PROGRAM

Pecans and walnuts can be grown organically. No, you don't have to spray with toxic pesticides. Plant adapted varieties. Very little pruning is needed or recommended. Maintain cover crops and natural mulch under the trees year round. Never cultivate the soil under nut and fruit trees.

PLANTING

Plant the trees in wide, ugly holes (not small round holes). Then replace the soil (no amendments), settle the soil with water (no tamping), add a 1-inch layer of lava sand and compost mix, and finish with a 3- to 5-inch layer of coarse-textured mulch. Don't stake the tree, wrap the trunk, or cut back the top. Mechanical aeration of the root zone of existing trees is beneficial, but tilling, disking, or plowing destroys feeder roots and should never be done. Trees should never have bare soil. The root zone should always be covered with mulches or native grasses and legumes.

FERTILIZING

The following applications are based on 1,000 sq. ft.

ROUND 1 (FEBRUARY 1–15)
20 pounds organic fertilizer (i.e., Garden-Ville, GreenSense, Bradfield, Bioform Dry, Maestro-Gro, Sustane, or Alliance Soil Amendment)
80 pounds lava sand
2–5 pounds dry molasses

ROUND 2 (JUNE 1–15)
10 pounds organic fertilizer
40–80 pounds Texas greensand (or soft rock phosphate in acid soils)

ROUND 3 (SEPTEMBER 15–30)
10 pounds organic fertilizer
20 pounds sul-po-mag

Note: Once soil health has been achieved, the schedule can probably be cut to one application a year. Large-scale orchards can use livestock manure or compost at 1–2 tons per acre per year along with green manure cover crops. Lava sand and other rock powders can be applied any time of the year.

FOLIAR FEEDING

Apply Garrett Juice (see recipe above) monthly or more often. Add garlic tea to the first spraying of the year just prior to bud break.

PEST CONTROL

Add the following to each gallon of Garrett Juice (see recipe above) for additional control:

¼ cup garlic tea or commercial garlic product (follow label directions)
citrus oil, orange oil, or d-limonene (1 ounce as a spray, 2 ounces as a drench)
1 rounded tablespoon baking soda (potassium bicarbonate is a superior substitute)
liquid biostimulants such as Agrispon, AgriGro, Medina, Bio-Innoculant, or Vitazyne (follow label directions)
neem (follow label directions)
1–2 ounces fish emulsion for additional nutrients (may not be needed when using compost tea)

INSECT RELEASE

Trichogramma Wasps—weekly releases of 10,000–20,000 eggs per acre or residential lot starting at bud break for three weeks

Green Lacewings—weekly release of 4,000 eggs per acre or residential lot for one month

Ladybugs—release 1,500–2,000 adult beetles per 1,000 sq. ft. at the first sign of shiny honeydew on foliage

SICK TREE TREATMENT

To treat any tree in stress for any reason, other than choice of an ill-adapted plant, use the following program:

1. Aerate the root zone heavily. Start between the dripline and the trunk and go far out beyond the dripline. A 7- to 12-inch depth for the aeration holes is ideal, but any depth is beneficial. An alternative is to spray the root zone with a product containing living organisms (such as Bio-Innoculant or AgriGro) or a biological stimulant (such as Agrispon, Medina, or Vitazyne).
2. Apply the following (per 1,000 sq. ft.): 40–80 lbs. Texas greensand, 40–80 lbs. lava sand, 10–20 lbs. cornmeal, 5 lbs. sugar or dry molasses. Cornmeal is a natural disease fighter and sugar is a carbon source that feeds the microbes in the soil.
3. Apply a 1-inch layer of compost, followed by a 3- to 5-inch layer of shredded native tree trimmings. Native cedar is the very best source for mulch.
4. Spray the foliage and soil monthly or more often if possible with Garrett Juice (see recipe above). For large-scale farms and ranches, a one-time application of the spray is beneficial if the

budget doesn't allow ongoing sprayings. Adding garlic tea to the spray is also beneficial while the tree is in trouble.

5. Stop using high-nitrogen fertilizers and toxic chemical pesticides. The pesticides kill the beneficial microorganisms and insects. The fake fertilizers are destructive to the important mycorrhizal fungi on the roots.

Note: Premixes of some of these materials are now available from organic suppliers.

DIRT DOCTOR'S POTTING SOIL

The following mix is for outdoor plants in pots, hanging baskets, and other containers. It is very powerful and needs little if any additional fertilizer. This mix is usually too strong for indoor plants.

10 parts compost
8 parts lava sand or granite sand
6 parts peat moss
4 parts cedar flakes
2 parts earthworm castings
1 part Texas greensand
1 part bran/cornmeal amendment
½ part sul-po-mag
½ part dry molasses

Index